STONE'S COMPANION GUIDE

STONE'S COMPANION GUIDE TO ENFORCEMENT

4TH EDITION

ANNE ROBINSON

with

DEBORAH FOX

SWEET & MAXWELL

Published in 2010 by
Thomson Reuters (Legal) Limited
(Registered in England & Wales, Company No 1679046. Registered Office and
address for service: 100 Avenue Road, London, NW3 3PF) trading as
Sweet & Maxwell

For further information on our products and services, visit
www.sweetandmaxwell.co.uk

Typeset by EMS Print Design
Printed and bound in Great Britain by CPI Antony Rowe,
Chippenham and Eastbourne

No natural forests were destroyed to make this product; only farmed timber
was used and re-planted.

A CIP catalogue record for this book is available from the British Library.

ISBN 978-0-414-04491-3

Crown copyright material is reproduced with the permission of the Controller
of HMSO and the Queen's Printer for Scotland.

CONTENTS

FOREWORD

In the 1999 edition of the *Companion Guide to Enforcement*, Nigel Stone discussed early resistance by probation practitioners and academics to National Standards and the more rigorous enforcement of court orders. He took issue with some of these criticisms, as outlined in Drakeford's diatribe, *The Probation Service, Breach and the Criminal Justice Act 1991* (Drakeford, 1993). Instead he argued that for the probation service:

"The challenge is to develop a distinctive and creative approach to enforcement, informed by values and principles, not the squeamish and unfair rigidity feared by Drakeford"

(Stone, 1999: 1)

That challenge still remains for the service and for the now more varied mix of professionals involved in offender management. Chapter 1 of this guide attempts to grapple with developments since 1999, which have brought enforcement of orders even more centre stage, but mingled with sometimes competing concerns about offender engagement and compliance and about the human rights agenda. There are tensions within this but also opportunities for practitioners who are confident about working within the legal frameworks around enforcement and with the ethical, practical and other dilemmas that are thrown up in the course of managing orders. This book intends to make some contribution—however modest—towards building such confidence and equipping practitioners with the requisite knowledge and expertise.

Engaging with debates around enforcement necessarily involves discussion of the shifting priorities and imperatives of criminal justice agencies and, most particularly, the probation service. Indeed, it could be said that:

"Few areas of probation practice illustrate the changes in function, culture and activity that have taken place in the probation service as emblematically as enforcement"

(Nicholls, 2007: 120)

The service has experienced significant changes since the Criminal Justice Act 1991 came into force and the publication of the first version of National Standards. As part of a wider programme of modernisation and reform, the service has become a national organisation, rather than the 54 individual services that existed before 2001. It is now more closely aligned with the prison service within the National Offender Management Service (NOMS) and local areas have formed into Trusts contracted with NOMS to deliver probation services. Alongside this structural change, the service has focused on public protection and management of risk, adopting a more consistent and stringent approach to ensuring that offenders comply with their court orders and are held to account where they do not. This re-orientation towards enforcement is summed up by Mair and Canton (2007) when they say that:

"The overwhelming importance of enforcement to the probation service is signalled by the fact that it is the first of the three official aims of the service: enforcement, rehabilitation and public protection. This contrasts sharply with the situation ten years ago, when enforcement of community penalties tended to be seen as one of the more distasteful tasks of a probation officer and to be avoided if at all possible. Lax and inconsistent practice with regard to enforcement is indefensible and the introduction of National Standards began the process of tightening up the enforcement of community penalties.

No matter how onerous the requirements of a community sentence, it comes to little if it is not enforced...... a passive or recalcitrant prisoner is still being punished; an unenforced community penalty, by contrast, is indistinguishable from impunity"

(Mair and Canton, 2007: 270)

The probation service and other agencies involved in offender management recognise the importance of enforcement in terms of credibility with the public, with sentencers and with the politicians who hold critical purse strings. However, over and above this, there are issues of credibility and legitimacy in the eyes of offenders that are linked to key questions of transparency, firm and fair use of authority and respect for human dignity. These represent some of the challenges to which Nigel Stone referred (Stone, 1999). While there are no easy answers, there are possible ways to meet these challenges indicated in recent academic thinking around compliance and pro-social modelling, which will also be outlined in the introductory chapter.

Chapters 2 and 3 detail breach procedures in adult magistrates' court and special considerations in managing and enforcing orders in relation to young people, in the youth courts and Crown Courts. These three chapters together establish the essential knowledge and understanding required for proper and ethical enforcement practice.

Later chapters outline enforcement of adult orders through the courts, the range of youth justice orders and the role of the Parole Board and executive recall procedures in managing post-custody licences. The book finishes with an overview of parenting orders, measures relating to sexual and violent offenders and approved premises.

This volume could not hope to be the end word in terms of enforcement—the picture is too complex and both legal provisions and practice are constantly changing. However, we have endeavoured to bring together a clear and comprehensive guide to enforcement at this point in time which we hope will be of use to a wide range of practitioners, in terms of managing orders and licences effectively and in enforcing their conditions in ways that are fair and just.

BIBLIOGRAPHY

Attrill, G. and Leill, G. (2007) "Offenders' Views on Risk Assessment" In Nicola Padfied (ed.) *Who To Release? Parole, Fairness and Criminal Justice* (Cullompton: Willan)

Bottoms, A. (2001) "Compliance and Community Penalties" in *Community Penalties: Changes and Challenges* Bottoms, A., Gelsthorpe, L. and Rex, S. (eds), (Cullompton: Willan)

Bottoms, A., Gelsthorpe, L. and Rex, S. (2001) *Community Penalties: Changes and Challenges* (Cullompton: Willan)

Canton, R. (2007) "Compliance" in *The Dictionary of Probation and Offender Management* Canton, R. and Hancock, D. (eds), (Cullompton: Willan)

Canton, R. and Eadie, T. (2002) "Practising in a Context of Ambivalence: The Challenge For Youth Justice Workers" in *Youth Justice* Vol.2 No.1: 14–26

Canton, R. and Eadie, T. (2005) "From Enforcement to Compliance: Implications for Supervising Officers" in *Vista* Vol.9 (3): 152-158

Canton, R. and Eadie, T. (2007) "National Standards" in *The Dictionary of Probation and Offender Management* Canton, R. and Hancock, D. (eds), (Cullompton: Willan)

Canton, R. and Eadie, T. (2008) "Accountability, Legitimacy and Discretion: Applying Criminology in Professional Practice" in *Applied Criminology* Stout, B., Yates, J. and Williams, B. (eds), London: Sage

Cherry, S. (2005) *Transforming Behaviour: Pro-social Modelling in Practice* (Cullompton: Willan)

Cherry, S. (2007) "Pro-social Modelling" in *The Dictionary of Probation and Offender Management* Canton, R. and Hancock, D. (eds), (Cullompton: Willan)

Criminal Justice Joint Inspection (2008) *Aspects of the Enforcement of Court Orders* London: (HM Inspectorate of Court Administration)

Dept. of Constitutional Affairs (2006) *A Guide to the Human Rights Act 1998* 3rd edn, (London: Dept of Constitutional Affairs)

Drakeford, M. (1993) "The Probation Service, Breach and the Criminal Justice Act 1991" in *The Howard Journal* Vol.32(4): 291–303

Eadie, T. (2007) "Discretion" in *The Dictionary of Probation and Offender Management* Canton, R. and Hancock, D. (eds), (Cullompton: Willan)

Gelsthorpe, L. (2007) "Probation Values and Human Rights" in *The Probation Handbook* Gelsthorpe, L. and Morgan, R. (eds), (Cullompton: Willan)

Grapes, T. (2007) "Offender Management" in *The Dictionary of Probation and Offender Management* Canton, R. and Hancock, D. (eds), (Cullompton: Willan)

Hearnden, I. and Millie, A. (2004) "Does Tougher Enforcement Lead to Lower Reconviction?" *The Probation Journal* Vol.51: 48

Hedderman, C. and Hearnden, I. (2000) "The Missing Link: Effective Enforcement and Effective Supervision" in *The Probation Journal* Vol.47: 126

Hedderman, C. (2003) "Enforcing Supervision and Encouraging Compliance" in *Moving Probation Forwards: Evidence, Arguments and Practice* Chui, WH. and Nellis, M. (eds), (Harlow: Pearson Education)

HMIP (2006) *An Independent Review of a Serious Further Offence Case: Anthony Rice* (London: HMIP)

Home Office (1990) *Crime, Custody and the Community* (London: Home Office)

Home Office (1999) PC 3/99 *Enforcement* (London: Home Office)

Home Office (2000) PC 24/2000 *Guidance on Enforcement of Orders under National Standards 2000* (London: Home Office)

Home Office (2001) *New Choreography—A Strategic Framework 2001-4* (London: Home Office)

House of Commons Public Accounts Committee (2009) *Protecting The Public: The work of the Parole Board* (London: The Stationery Office)

Hudson, B. (2001) "Human Rights, Public Safety and the Probation Service: Defending justice in the risk society" *The Howard Journal* Vol.40 No.2

Loumansky, A., Goodman, A. and Feasey, S. (2008) "Enforcement and Compliance" in *Addressing Offending Behaviour: Context, Practice and Values* Green, S., Lancaster, E. and Feasey, S. (eds), (Cullompton: Willan)

Mair, G. and Canton, R. (2007) "Sentencing, Community Penalties and the Role of the Probation Service" in *The Probation Handbook* Gelsthorpe, L. and Morgan, R. (eds), (Cullompton: Willan)

May, C. and Wadwell, J. (2001) *Enforcing Community Penalties: The Relationship Between Enforcement and Reconviction* Home Office Research Findings 155

McIvor, G. (1992) *Sentenced to Serve: The Operation and Impact of Community Service by Offenders* (Aldershot: Avebury)

McIvor, G. (1995) *Working With Offenders* (London: Jessica Kingsley)

McNeill, F. (2003) "Desistance-focused Probation Practice" in *Moving Probation Forwards: Evidence, Arguments and Practice* Chui, WH. and Nellis, M. (eds), (Harlow: Pearson Education)

McNeill, F. (2008) "Desistance-focused Approaches" in *Addressing Offending Behaviour: Context, Practice and Values* Green, S., Lancaster, E. and Feasey, S. (eds), (Cullompton: Willan)

Ministry of Justice (2007) *National Standards for the Management of Offenders* (London: Ministry of Justice)

Ministry of Justice (2009) *Referral Order Guidance* (London: Ministry of Justice)

Ministry of Justice (2010) *Probation Instruction 04/ 2010 Community Compacts—For Use in the Community*

Moore, T. (2009) *Youth Court Guide* 3rd edn (Haywards Heath: Tottel Publishing)

Nash, M. (2005) "The Probation Service, Public Protection and Dangerous Offenders" in Winstone, J. ans Parks, F. (eds), *Community Justice: Issues for Probation and Criminal Justice* (Cullompton: Willan)

National Audit Office (2008) *National Probation Service: The Supervision of Community Orders in England and Wales* (London: National Audit Office)

National Probation Service (2000) PC 24/2000 *Guidance on Enforcement of Orders under National Standards 2000* (London: National Probation Service)

National Probation Service (2002) *Approved Premises Handbook* (London: National Probation Service)

National Probation Service (2004) PC 43/2004 *Managing Compliance and Enforcement of Community Penalties* (London: National Probation Service)

National Probation Service (2005a) PC 38/2005 *HM Court Service Effective Practice Guide on Enforcing Community Penalties* (London: National Probation Service)

National Probation Service (2005b) PC 25/2005 *Criminal Justice Act 2003: Implementation on 4 April* (London: National Probation Service)

National Probation Service (2005c) *Probation Circular 37/2005 The Role and Purpose of Approved Premises* (London: National Probation Service)

National Probation Service (2006) *Probation Circular 05/2006 Approved Premises: Drug Testing of Residents* (London: National Probation Service)

National Probation Service (2007) PC 10/2007 *Offender Engagement Good Practice Guide* (London: National Probation Service)

National Probation Service (2007a) *Performance Report 24 and Weighted Scorecard Quarter 4 2006/7* (London: National Probation Service)

National Probation Service (2007b) PC 29/2007 *Post-release Enforcement - Licence Conditions* (London: National Probation Service)

National Probation Service (2007c) PC 19/2007 *Implementation of National Rules for Approved Premises* (London: National Probation Service)

National Probation Service (2008) *Annual Report 2007/8* (London: National Probation Service)

National Probation Service (2008a) PC 05/2008 *Determining Unacceptable Absences* (London: National Probation Service)

National Probation Service (2008b) PC 14/2008 *Post-release Enforcement - Recall and Further Release* (London: National Probation Service)

National Probation Service (2009) PI 04/2009 *Recall of Prisoners on Licence: Sharing Information and Performance Monitoring.* (London: National Probation Service)

Newburn, T. (2003) *Crime and Criminal Justice Policy* 2nd edn (Harlow: Pearson Education)

Nicholls, G. (2007) "Enforcement" in *The Dictionary of Probation and Offender Management* Canton, R. and Hancock, D. (eds), (Cullompton: Willan)

NOMS (2006) *The NOMS Offender Management Model* (London: Home Office)

The Parole Board (2008) *Annual Report and Accounts of the Parole Board for England and Wales 2007/8* (London: The Stationery Office)

Rex, S. (1999) "Desistance from Offending: Experiences of Probation" *The Howard Journal* Vol.36 No.4:366

Scott, J. (2002) "Human Rights: A Challenge to Culture and Practice" in *Probation: Working for Justice* Ward, D., Scott, J. and Lacey, M. (eds), (Oxford: Oxford University Press)

Senior, P., Crowther-Dowey, C. and Long, M. (2008) *Understanding Modernisation in Criminal Justice* (Maidenhead: Open University Press)

Sentencing Guidelines Council (2005) *New Sentences: Criminal Justice Act 2003* (London: Sentencing Guidelines Council)

Sentencing Guidelines Council (2008) *Magistrates" Court Sentencing Guidelines* (London: Sentencing Guidelines Council)

Sentencing Guidelines Council (2009) *Over-arching Principles—Sentencing Youths* (London: Sentencing Guidelines Council)

Stone, N. (1999) *A Companion Guide to Enforcement* 3rd edn Ilkley: Owen Wells Publisher

Stone, N. (2008) *A Companion Guide to Life Sentences* 2nd edn (Crayford: Shaw and Sons)

Trotter, C. (2006) *Working with Involuntary Clients: A Guide to Practice* 2nd edn London: Sage

Underdown, A. (2007) "Effective Practice" in *The Dictionary of Probation and Offender Management* Canton, R. and Hancock, D. (eds), (Cullompton: Willan)

Wood, J. and Kemshall, H. with Maguire, M., Hudson, K. and McKenzie, G. (2007) *The Operation and Experience of Multi-Agency Public Protection Arrangements (MAPPA)* (London: Home Office) Online Report 12/07

Youth Justice Board (2007) *Release and Recall: Guidance for Youth Offending Teams* (London: Youth Justice Board)

Youth Justice Board (2008) *ISSP Management Guidance* (London: Youth Justice Board)

Youth Justice Board (2009a) *National Standards for Youth Justice Services 2009* (London: Youth Justice Board)

Youth Justice Board (2009b) *Case Management Guidance* (London: Youth Justice Board)

Youth Justice Board (2009c) *Youth Justice: The Scaled Approach* (London: Youth Justice Board)

Youth Justice Board (2009d) *Youth Rehabilitation Order with Intensive Supervision and Surveillance (ISS): Operational Guidance* London: Youth Justice Board

GLOSSARY OF ACRONYMS AND ABBREVIATED ACTS OF PARLIAMENT

ACO	Assistant Chief Officer, Probation Service
ACOP	Association of Chief Officers of Probation
ASBA 2003	Anti-social Behaviour Act 2003
ASBO	Anti-social Behaviour Order
C&DA 1998	Crime and Disorder Act 1998
CJA	Criminal Justice Act 1982
CJA 1991	Criminal Justice Act 1991
CJA 2003	Criminal Justice Act 2003
CJ&IA 2008	Criminal Justice and Immigration Act 2998
CO	Community Order
CPPC	Critical Public Protection Case
DCR	Discretionary Conditional Release (from custody)
DPP	Detention for Public Protection
DRR	Drug Rehabilitation Requirment
DTO	Detention and Training Order
ECtHR	European Court of Human Rights
ECHR	European Convention of Human Rights
FTR	Fixed Term Recall
HDC	Home Detention Curfew
HMIP	Her Majesty's Inspectorate of Probation
HRA 1998	Human Rights Act 1998
IPP	Imprisonment for Public Protection
ISS	Intensive Supervision and Surveillance
LJA	Local Justice Area
MAPPA	Multi-Agency Public Protection Arrangements
NOMM	National Offender Management Model
NOMS	National Offender Management Service
NPS	National Probation Service
OASys	Offender Assessment System
OM	Offender Manager
OMM	Offender Manager Model
PAROM1	Offender Manager's Parole Report
PC	Probation Circular
PD1	Pre-discharge Report
PI	Probation Instruction
PCC(S)A 2000	Powers of Criminal Courts (Sentencing) Act 2000
PPCS	Public Protection Casework Section (within NOMS)
PPO	Prolific or Other Priority Offender
PSO	Prison Service Order
RSHO	Risk of Sexual Harm Order
RO	Referral Order

SDS	Standard Determinate Sentence
SOA 2003	Sexual Offences Act 2003
SOPO	Sexual Offences Prevention Order
SPOC	Single Point of Contact
SSO	Suspended Sentence Order
VOO	Violent Offender Order
YJB	Youth Justice Board
YJ&CEA 1999	Youth Justice and Criminal Evidence Act 1999
YOI	Young Offender Institution
YOP	Young Offender Panel
YOT	Youth Offending Team
YRO	Youth Rehabilitation Order

Chapter 1
INTRODUCTION TO ENFORCEMENT

I. A brief history of the probation service and enforcement

The significance of the Criminal Justice Act 1991 (CJA 1991) for enforcement practice cannot be over-emphasised. Before that Act, the requirements of "being on probation" were much more loosely governed by section 2 of the Powers of Criminal Courts Act 1973. The supervising probation officer was responsible for determining appropriate levels of contact and he or she had a wide discretion in terms of responses to non-compliance. This resulted in considerable variations in practice that became less tenable as the 1980s progressed, particularly in the light of the increasing emphasis on managerial techniques and greater efficiency in public services (Senior et al, 2008). Furthermore, a more robust approach to offenders was being advocated by the political Right, and the probation service found itself having to justify its existence within a criminal justice climate significantly less sympathetic to its traditional ethos of advising, assisting and befriending offenders (Nash, 2005).

In the CJA 1991, the Home Office signalled its intention to create a more prominent role for the probation service within a "just deserts" framework based on administering punishment proportionate to the harm caused by specific offences. By the end of the decade, the loss of belief in rehabilitation and espousal of this justice model had already resulted in the probation order becoming more clearly identified as an alternative to custody. Additional requirements, such as attendance at a day centre or specified activities, were now available to magistrates to attach to orders (Mair and Canton, 2007). It was becoming clear that the service would have to adapt to a new role and to further changes ahead.

(i) Introducing National Standards

In the context described above, it was not surprising that the Home Office proposed measures that aimed to standardise key aspects of probation practice. A preliminary version of National Standards was first introduced for what was then known as Community Service in 1989. This represented a significant precedent in terms of a central direction from the Home Office about the implementation of court orders that was quickly followed up by more substantial legal provisions governing a broader range of probation service work.

Following on from the white paper *Crime, Custody and the Community* (Home Office, 1990), which coined the term "community penalties", the CJA 1991 changed the status of the probation order, so that it became for the first time a sentence of the court rather than an alternative to sentencing. By this stage, this was perhaps a symbolic rather than a substantive change (Mair and Canton, 2007). Nevertheless, it marked a shift for the probation service from its historic roots in social work towards a criminal justice role that encompassed punishment as well as rehabilitation and support.

The CJA 1991 ushered in a new sentencing framework that aimed to restrict the use of custody for the majority of offenders. Instead courts were expected to make greater use of probation, community service and new orders that combined the two, for offences that were "serious enough" to warrant that degree of intervention and/or restriction of liberty, but not "so serious" that only custody could be justified. Probation-managed sentences were thus located within the middle range of offence seriousness.

At the same time, the Act separated out serious violent and sexual offenders, allowing the normal principle of proportionality in sentencing to be waived if there were concerns about possible serious harm. This was the first clear articulation of the concerns about public protection and dangerousness that have since dominated criminal justice thinking and policy-making.

Section 15 of the Act also provided the legal basis for the Secretary of State to issue regulations governing the supervision of offenders and the functions of probation officers (and local authority social workers supervising juvenile offenders). These regulations appeared in 1992 as the first full version of National Standards. Their introduction was simultaneously intended to clarify expectations and improve consistency in practice and to increase both managerial and practitioner accountability.

Despite these evident benefits, the Standards met with resistance from a service that valued its autonomy and the degree of professional discretion it had hitherto enjoyed. Carol Hedderman (2003) notes ironically that these fears may not have been fully justified as the first Standards were expressed in ways that tended to regularise rather than eliminate the use of professional judgement. However, a revised set of Standards subsequently issued in 1995 did more explicitly limit practitioner freedom by stipulating tighter expectations of probation officers and the management of court orders (Home Office, 1995). Further editions of Standards have since been published, reflecting an increasingly tougher climate for offender management and a focus upon risk and public protection.

(ii) Putting the Standards into practice

Implementation of the 1992 National Standards and all subsequent versions has been supported by the Her Majesty's Inspectorate of Probation (HMIP).

Successive Quality and Effectiveness reports from the inspectorate in the 1990s continued to show poor rates of enforcement in terms of responses to non-compliance and prompt returns to court in line with National Standards.

In 1997, data from the HMIP indicated that only 30 per cent of offenders who should have been subject to breach proceedings in line with National Standards were actually prosecuted (Home Office, 1999). Consequently, by 1998, the Home Office introduced a Key Performance Indicator for the service, with a demanding expectation that breach proceedings would be initiated within 10 days of the last failure to comply in 90 per cent of cases. Guidance from the Home Office (PC 3/99) detailed the actions that services were expected to take to improve enforcement and the then Association of Chief Officers of Probation (ACOP) committed itself to a series of enforcement audits as part of its action plan (Hedderman and Hearden, 2000).

The first two editions of National Standards had allowed offenders two failures to comply with their orders before breach action would be instigated. A new and more stringent version of the Standards in 2000 reduced this to just one failure to comply for adults on community orders (a separate set of Standards for the reformed youth justice system being published alongside). The 90 per cent enforcement target remained in place but judged against this more rigorous Standard and with performance becoming cash-linked.

After initial struggles, enforcement and breach practices were beginning to improve significantly, with 92 per cent of orders enforced within the Standard in 2006/7 compared to only 53 per cent in 2001/2 (National Probation Service, 2007a). In a push to further increase performance, Probation Areas have been required to work with magistrates' courts to establish processes to expedite the listing and the handling of breach proceedings and to institute a fast track procedure for cases where there are significant concerns about risk of re-offending or of serious harm (National Probation Service, 2005a). Accordingly, a joint end-to-end enforcement target for Local Criminal Justice Boards has been in place since 2005/6 which stipulates that cases should move from second unacceptable failure to resolution of the case in an average of 35 days, with a target percentage achieved within 25 days — a typical indication of the increasingly joint nature of actions to achieve performance in the "joined up justice" framework of New Labour.

Arrangements for the enforcement of post-custody licences have undergone substantial changes also. Under the CJA 1991, breaches of licences in relation to short-term sentences (under four years) were prosecuted through the court. This was amended by s.103 of the Crime and Disorder Act 1998 (C&DA 1998) which removed powers from the court and required the Parole Board to deal with all matters relating to recall for adult sentences made in respect of offences committed after January 1, 1999. The situation has shifted again in the light of the new sentencing framework introduced by the Criminal Justice Act 2003 (CJA 2003). Currently, following that Act and further provisions in the Criminal Justice and Immigration Act 2008 (CJ&IA 2008), most recall procedures go through the Public Protection Casework Section in the National Offender Management Service (NOMS) Public Protection Unit. Slightly different arrangements exist in respect of licence periods relating to Home Detention Curfews, and the courts still deal with notices of supervision for under 21s on release from short sentences and under 18s subject to detention and training orders. This is a complicated post-custody enforcement landscape that will be detailed further in later chapters.

So there now exists a complex set of arrangements for the enforcement of court orders and post-custody licences, with National Standards spelling out demanding requirements of practitioners and managers for swift and effective action in response to non-compliance, particularly in high-risk situations. Additionally there are many dilemmas that may be thrown up by competing requirements that services also pay:

> "Due regard to the human rights, dignity and safety of offenders, victims and partners, and that services will be respectful and responsive to the diverse needs and circumstances encountered in correctional work."
>
> (Ministry of Justice, 2007: 3)

(iii) Effective practice

Of course, the focus on public protection and tight enforcement is not the only development that the probation service has encompassed over the past decade: the push for evidence-based practice and the need to demonstrate effectiveness have also clearly impacted upon the service. The term "effective practice" has often been used to refer to the "what works" literature or the body of research findings and academic writing that provides indications of practices associated with improved prospects of reducing re-offending (Underdown, 2007). Consequently a range of accredited groupwork programmes have been established, using cognitive behavioural methods and pro-social modelling techniques, in line with what the research literature suggests is most effective practice.

It is notable, however, that these two strands of probation practice have developed separately (Bottoms et al, 2001) and in some respects have worked in contradictory ways. Given that the research suggests that offenders who start but do not complete programmes are most likely to re-offend, there are questions about the role of strict enforcement and whether there are instances where it might undermine the rehabilitative efforts of the service (Hedderman, 2003; Mair and Canton, 2007).

Additionally, while National Standards have improved enforcement practice in terms of clarifying expectations and increasing consistency, there is no firm body of evidence that tough enforcement has a positive impact upon reconviction levels.:

- One early study by Gill McIvor (1995) looked at offenders on community service in Scotland and found that stricter approaches to managing attendance and clear communication about enforcement did improve compliance. An earlier publication on the same research showed also that the offenders most at risk of breaching their orders tended to have more unsettled backgrounds, including experience in the care system, and more previous convictions and periods in custody (McIvor, 1992).

- A subsequent Home Office study by May and Wadwell (2001) did find that offenders on community penalties who faced appropriate enforcement action tended to be reconvicted at rates lower than predicted in contrast to a higher rate for those who had unacceptable absences that did not result in enforcement action. However, the sample size for this study was small and there was an additional finding that enforcement action was more likely to be taken against offenders with a lower likelihood of reconviction, so raising questions about the key finding of the study (Loumansky et al, 2008).

- More equivocal findings were reported by Hearnden and Millie (2004) who carried out a follow-up study on the samples used in the second ACOP enforcement audit. Data was collected from 11 probation areas and these were identified as having high or low breach rates. There was no significant difference in reconviction rates for offenders from high or low breach areas, but it was found that those offenders who did face breach action had an increased likelihood of reconviction across both types of areas. They concluded that:

  "Based on whether an area has a high or low rate of breach at court, strictness of enforcement appears to have little impact on the overall reconviction rate. This suggests that offenders either disregard or are oblivious to strict probation enforcement strategies."

  (Hearnden and Millie, 2004: 54)

Although Hearnden and Millie recognise that tougher enforcement practices may improve sentencer confidence in community penalties, they too call for a shift in emphasis towards compliance. It is significant that it was shortly after this study was published that PC 43/2004 was issued on *Managing Compliance and Enforcement of Community Penalties* (National Probation Service, 2004) and a change in official focus became apparent.

(iv) Turning to compliance

For some time academics had being arguing for attention to shift from enforcement to compliance (for instance, Bottoms, 2001; Hedderman, 2003). Others had noted the focus in earlier versions of National Standards on responding to non-compliance rather than identifying actions that would encourage compliance (Canton and Eadie, 2005) — based effectively on negative assumptions about the deterrent power of threatened breach as opposed to a belief in positive engagement.

This concern was ultimately picked up by a Home Office awakening to the need for complementary efforts to reduce the numbers of offenders requiring enforcement actions. PC 43/2004, entitled *Managing Compliance and Enforcement of Community Penalties*, underlines the need to pay attention to compliance and, specifically, refers to a new compliance target for the probation service. Services have perhaps struggled to manage the tensions between these targets but, properly balanced, this dual approach offers opportunities for developing open relationships in which:

- the authority of the responsible officer is acknowledged;
- the demands and expectations of the court order are spelt out clearly; and
- there is negotiation around any practical or other problems that might affect ability to meet the requirements of the order.

A new Standard 3 in the 2007 National Standards addresses the offenders' experience of sentences and emphasises engagement and participation in sentence planning. Also, and significantly, Standard 3.2 states that the offender at the beginning of the sentence and at key review points should be helped to understand a range of issues including:

- the legal requirements, constraints and procedures applicable, including that any licence period forms part of the sentence;
- what is required of him or her and the sanctions for failing to comply;
- what he or she can expect from NOMS; and
- his or her rights, and how to complain if dissatisfied with his or her treatment.

(Ministry of Justice, 2007: 50)

Similarly the *National Standards for Youth Justice Services* require that young people are advised of the rights and responsibilities conferred by their order and that the requirements are fully understood, taking into account any issues with mental health, learning difficulties, speech, language and communication needs (Youth Justice Board, 2009a).

Embedding such practices may form a basis for securing engagement and compliance founded on the offender's informed consent to the work to be undertaken whilst under statutory supervision and understanding of the commitments that can be expected on both sides.

II. Human Rights and equalities

(i) The Human Rights Act

The Human Rights Act 1998 (HRA 1998) came into force on October, 2 2000, incorporating into English law arts 2–12, 14 and 16–18 of the European Convention on Human Rights and Fundamental Freedoms (ECHR) together with arts 1–3 of the First Protocol.

It is unlawful for a public body, including the probation service and other criminal justice agencies, to act in a way that is incompatible with the Act. If it does so an individual can bring a case directly to a domestic (UK) court rather than having to go to the European

Court of Human Rights (ECtHR).

(ii) Enforcement and the Act

Probation and youth offending team strategies and policies inevitably have implications for human rights which need to be integrated into decision-making processes in enforcement.

Breach proceedings brought in violation of the HRA 1998 would be rendered invalid. Some awareness of human rights issues is, therefore, critical for offender managers and Youth Offending Team (YOT) case managers. The following articles are of particular relevance:

> Art.6 — right to a fair trial
>
> Art.8 — right to respect for private and family life
>
> Art. 9 — right to freedom of religion

Competing rights often have to be balanced. As such the principle of proportionality is of significance to the court processes involved with enforcement, for example, in terms of how much restriction of liberty or how much intrusion into private life might be appropriate. For further information, see PC 59/2000, *Human Rights Act Guidance*.

(iii) Discrimination and the law

Services must also ensure that they do not discriminate against individuals on the basis of their personal characteristics in accordance with a range of legislation, such as:

- Sex Discrimination and Equality Acts
- Race Relations Acts
- Disability Discrimination Acts

This applies to all aspects of offender management, including enforcement practices which may be subject to challenge under this legislation and also the public sector equality duty introduced by the Equality Act 2010 when it comes into force.

(iv) A positive rights agenda

A positive rights agenda concentrates on promoting the civil or citizenship rights of all parties, including offenders, so that where key rights are limited or qualified, this is done with legitimate authority and in a proportionate way. Critically it does not assume that offenders forfeit all rights through their behaviours (Hudson, 2001). Rather, it aims to secure the inclusion and involvement of offenders and other marginal groups, seeking to make sure that their voices are heard and that they have a stake in society. It therefore means finding an appropriate balance of rights between offenders, victims and the public at large.

Striving to achieve such a balance is relevant to enforcement practice, where the tensions between prevention of offending and crime control and the needs and individual circumstances of the offender must be managed. It is not incompatible with the pro-social modelling approach described later in this chapter, and, as a critical underlying principle, would dictate that enforcement procedures should be clear and transparent and should throughout accord the offender dignity and respect.

III. Working within National Standards and guidance contained in Probation Circulars

(i)   The current National Standards

Since New Labour came into office in 1997, the criminal justice landscape has changed in dramatic fashion. These changes can be briefly summarised as:

(i)   the vigorous promotion of the concept and practice of "joined up justice" in which we see criminal justice agencies come together with other partners in new structures at both strategic and operational levels;

(ii)   the adoption of a stringent performance management framework, with partnership and single agency targets;

(iii)   the creation of the National Offender Management Service (NOMS), bringing prisons, probation and youth justice services under one organisational umbrella;

(iv)   the introduction of a new sentencing framework for adults through the CJA 2003 incorporating a generic community order as well as changes to short term custodial sentencing and longer term public protection sentences. New sentencing arrangements have also been introduced for children and young people;

(v)   the adoption of an Offender Management Model (OMM), with the aim of providing a consistent approach across all agencies, statutory, voluntary and private sector, involved in the management of offenders and;

(vi)   the establishment of the Youth Justice Board as a national overseeing body and youth offending teams (or youth offending services) in all local authority areas. This represents a separation of youth and adult justice services, with youth justice pursuing a strategic agenda for young offenders that (at least taking an optimistic view) dovetails with the children's services Every Child Matters priorities.

National Standards have necessarily been revised so as to reflect these changes. The most recent revisions were in 2005 to respond to the new CJA 2003 sentences, and in 2007 to take account of the OMM. This current version of the adult Standards was issued by NOMS and applies to all providers of offender management services, a much wider application than previous sets of Standards. However, the key guidance documents about working within Standards have had more longevity. These are:

- PC 24/2000   *Guidance on Enforcement of Orders under National Standards 2000;* and

- PC 43/2004   *Managing Compliance and Enforcement of Community Penalties.*

PC 43/2004 reissued the earlier probation circular but with an additional commentary that re-emphasised critical points, particularly in relation to a presumption that all absences would be treated as unacceptable until given proof otherwise.

PC 43/2004 has since been superceded by PC 05/2008, which underlines a revision in the 2007 National Standards that again allows practitioners a greater degree of discretion by stipulating that:

"The Offender Manager forms a view about the reasonableness or otherwise of any excuse provided by an offender for any apparent failure to comply. Judgements as to reasonableness take account of the nature of the failure, the circumstances of it and the circumstances of the offender."

(Ministry of Justice, 2007: 46)

The following sections will address issues raised by these probation circulars and will discuss findings from research and literature that might be helpful for practitioners in working within the Standards.

(ii) Discretion and accountability

While some bemoan the reduced room left for practitioners to use discretion, it nevertheless remains a crucial element in the management and enforcement of orders. This is recognised in PC 24/2000 in the following terms:

"In supervising offenders, probation staff will need to continue to use their professional discretion and judgement, taking into account all the circumstances of the case. ... Staff are accountable for the use of their judgement and in departing from the Standards (for instance, by reducing the frequency of contact or not breaching as required) discretion can be exercised only with the authority of a manager.

Discretion must be exercised on an individual, case by case basis....."

(Home Office, 2000: 2)

This conceives professionalism as the ability to exercise discretion and judgement in ways that can be reasoned and justified. It also requires that staff members are clear in recording where they have used their discretion and the reasons why. Far from doing away with discretion, this leaves the way open for developing good practice based on transparency and ethical values, where the use of discretion can be evidenced and explained.

Discretion is perhaps more circumscribed and structured within the present National Standards framework than previously, but Canton and Eadie (2007) recognise that policy-makers are seeking to strike a difficult balance between the needs for consistency and flexibility. The difficulties in practice emerge where managerialism has prioritised uniformity of treatment and application of rules over appropriate responses to the situation and circumstances of individuals, which may impact on both justice and legitimacy (Canton and Eadie, 2008).

Related to this, Canton and Eadie (2002) have developed a useful model to illustrate the interplay in youth justice between professional discretion and accountability in using the Asset assessment tool. They argue that the best professional practice has elements of both discretion and accountability, which can work in tandem. These points can be generalised to all offender management contexts. Practitioners and managers might well consider how they could move enforcement practices towards Quadrant A of this model, rather than Quadrant D which represents a more mechanistic, procedural approach.

Figure 1: Managing accountability and discretion in youth justice practice

(Adapted from Canton and Eadie 2002)

Within the contact requirements of National Standards, officers are able to make choices about how the order will be run. Based on assessment of risks and needs and objectives agreed in the sentence plan, these might include:

- the timing and venue of appointments;
- the sequencing of different interventions on the order;
- which partner organisations to involve (if these are not already stipulated as part of a requirement on the order);
- the content of work undertaken in one-to-one supervision to meet agreed objectives; and
- decisions to exceed National Standards contact levels on the basis of risk assessment.

Similarly, in terms of enforcement, the officer has discretion over:

- whether missed appointments are acceptable or not, and therefore whether warnings are triggered (subject to guidance);
- whether an offender's risk is such that he or she should be returned to court or recalled after only one absence;
- whether an offender's behaviour is such that it warrants a warning or breach action;

- whether to seek managerial authority not to breach on the second failure (community sentences) or third failure (post custody licences);

- the advice to be given to court about the advisability or otherwise of continuing a community order and appropriate amendments; and

- the advice to be given to court about whether or not to activate a suspended sentence.

(iii) Pro-social modelling

PC 43/2005 states that:

> "During supervision, it is important that the case manager uses a variety of motivational techniques and uses pro-social modelling to ensure that the offender is engaged and to maintain momentum."
>
> (National Probation Service, 2005: 3)

But what is meant by pro-social modelling? The main proponent of this approach is Chris Trotter, who has worked and researched in the social work and probation fields in Australia, focusing on constructive work with individuals in coerced or compulsory settings. In the United Kingdom, Sally Cherry offers a useful outline of the approach:

> "Working pro-socially is ethical and respectful, valuing offenders as individuals. It is optimistic about the possibility of change and seeks to engage them as partners in the change process. It is a strength-focused model, looking to reinforce what is right (often by using affirmations and rewards) before looking to sanction what is wrong. However, it is underpinned by values often demonstrated as rules, which are made transparent to the offender and reinforced constantly by the practitioner."
>
> (Cherry, 2007: 243)

Cherry's account of pro-social modelling does differ from the problem-based, deficit model often adopted by the probation service, in being focused on strengths and solutions. Two further aspects of pro-social modelling are of particular interest here. Firstly, the emphasis on clarifying and being explicit about the role and remit of the officer (Trotter, 2006; Cherry, 2005), including the authority invested in that role. Secondly, the legitimate use of authority, which Cherry argues should be exercised in ways that are:

- consistent;

- impartial;

- based on accurate information;

- open to correction or appeal; and

- ethical.

> (adapted from Cherry, 2005)

It is not a value-free approach, but is based on a clear stance about the unacceptability of certain forms of behaviour and the promotion of other, more pro-social behaviours. The worker can reinforce and encourage positive behaviours and can also model appropriate behaviours, demonstrating, for instance, how to challenge constructively or how to handle conflict. This is not without its difficulties and Sally Cherry refers to potential tensions in the workers' role:

> "The only answer to managing the tension between being client-focused yet working

within strict boundaries is to be very clear with yourself and your client about your role and the rules and the boundaries."

(Cherry, 2005: 43)

In terms of work within a correctional context, there should be clarity about rules and expectations from the initial point of the sentence, including what is negotiable and non-negotiable (Trotter, 2006). This is instructive in relation to compliance and enforcement, with the potential to establish a more open and constructive context within which to collaboratively address problems.

At this point the content of Standard 3.6 should be noted as this upholds many of the precepts of pro-social modelling and gives a clear — if rather aspirational — statement about the quality of the relationships that offenders have with the service and its staff:

"Offenders experience their relationship with staff as being characterised by:

- *courtesy, respect and the valuing of diversity*
- *enthusiasm and commitment*
- *the encouragement of compliance and co-operation*
- *recognition and reward for achievement and progress*
- *the firm, fair and legitimate use of authority*
- *behaviour that models pro-social and anti-criminal attitudes, cognitions and behaviours*
- *the teaching of problem-solving skills*
- *help to access wider community-based resources and facilities*
- *encouragement to take responsibility for behaviour and its consequences*

(Ministry of Justice, 2007: 52)

The core elements of the OMM — clear processes around assessment, planning and review, an offender-focus, individualised interventions, a team approach — could lend themselves to pro-social ways of working that respect individuals and achieve an appropriate balance between risks and rights. These principles are echoed in the recent case management guidance issued by the Youth Justice Board (YJB) covering all aspects of work with young people (YJB, 2009b). This has potential implications and some promise for the development of enforcement practices premised on securing compliance rather than dependent entirely on sanctions.

(iv)   Encouraging compliance

In essence, focusing on compliance means working to ensure that offenders are motivated and enabled to meet the legal requirements of their court orders. This represents a significant challenge for the service which Rob Canton identifies as:

"Peculiar to community sanctions and measures: community penalties require people to do things — to keep appointments as instructed, to participate in (or refrain from) activities, to work — which they might otherwise choose not to do. This creates the possibility of default ..... the more that is asked, the greater the opportunities for default and the proportion of orders breached has been increasing in recent years."

(Canton, 2007: 57)

11

Canton argues for a move away from enforcement and sanctions towards developing a more complex understanding of what may promote compliance. In doing so it is helpful to look at the framework developed by Anthony Bottoms (2001), which has been much quoted but nevertheless bears repetition:

A   Instrumental/prudential compliance

   (a) incentives

   (b) disincentives

B   Normative compliance

   (a) acceptance of a belief in a norm

   (b) attachment leading to compliance

   (c) legitimacy

C   Constraint-based compliance

   (a) physical restrictions

   (b) restrictions on access to target

   (c) structural constraints

D   Compliance based on habit or routine

Figure 2: An outline of the principle mechanisms outlining compliant behaviour

(from Bottoms, 2001: 90)

Normative compliance is perhaps more complex than the other types and possibly the most difficult to achieve (Hedderman, 2003). It involves a greater degree of change in the offender's beliefs and value systems, which is then reflected in altered behaviours. This is the area of compliance most relevant to pro-social modelling, where the practitioner establishes an empathetic relationship with the offender and through that seeks to influence beliefs, thinking and behaviours in a more pro-social direction. The attachment that the offender forms to the practitioner could itself be a motivator for change, and other key social relationships, with partner or parents for example, may also be significant.

Within normative compliance, legitimacy refers to the relationships or attachments between the offender and those in authority — perhaps specific individuals or the more general "powers that be" in society. Individuals with stronger social bonds and with greater degrees of trust in the legitimacy of the law as laid down in a democratic society are more likely to abide by the law, even where they may not personally agree with particular legal requirements. In his discussion, Anthony Bottoms (2001) uses attitudes to the speed limits on the roads as an example.

While instrumental motivations for compliance certainly have their place, they may work best when supported by normative and other influences (Canton and Eadie, 2005). Similarly, there is room for developing more positive rewards and incentives for offenders to comply, moving beyond short-term deterrent approaches towards practices more designed to securing longer term compliance with court orders but also with the law in general (Bottoms et al, 2001).

Clearly a focus on pro-social modelling and compliance would seem to offer some promise in terms of effective work with offenders. However, the extent to which this promise is realised is largely dependent on a willingness and ability of managers and practitioners to adopt principled approaches to enforcement and to how they carry out their role in engaging offenders and improving the likelihood of them fulfilling the responsibilities and commitments entailed in their court orders.

Chapter 2

A STEP BY STEP GUIDE TO ENFORCEMENT OF COMMUNITY ORDERS AND SUSPENDED SENTENCES (BREACH ACTION)

This chapter outlines the process to be followed in breach proceedings in the court for the adult community order and suspended sentence order. However, the basic processes apply also to youth justice orders (further details of which are covered in Chapter 3) and breach of young offender notices of supervision under section 65 of the CJA 1991.

(i) The court order

Enforcement or breach proceedings are taken on the basis of the terms of an order issued by a magistrates', youth or Crown Court. It is, therefore, important at the start of a sentence to check that all the details in the order are accurate, for instance, that the details of the requirements on the order are correct. If the order does not reflect what happened in court and the intentions of the court in sentencing, check the court records and ask for the order to be amended.

The order should also specify which local justice area (LJA) is responsible for the order. This is important for orders where the magistrates' court or youth court will deal with any breach action. Breach action should be commenced in the LJA where the offender resides if his or her address is known. If it is not known breach action should be commenced in the LJA specified in the order.

The order will specify a *responsible officer* but will not be name specific. In most cases this will be an officer of a local probation trust. Currently such an officer is known as an offender manager in the probation service and usually as case manager in youth justice.

(ii) Failures to comply

Breach action is taken on the basis of failures to comply *without reasonable excuse* with the requirements of an order. This includes failures due to inappropriate or unsafe behaviours whilst on probation premises or on placement. From May 1, 2010, expectations of behaviour must be spelt out at the beginning of a community order or period of licence supervision through use of Community Compacts (Ministry of Justice 2010). These may be supplemented by other agreements specific to a particular area or activity (for instance, an accredited programme).

There is an element of judgment as to what might constitute *reasonable excuse* and where explanations are given by the offender for an absence or other failure to comply, the responsible officer should record clearly whether the failure is judged to be acceptable or not.

The definition of *reasonable excuse* was challenged in the courts in the case of *West Midlands Probation Board v Sutton Coldfield Magistrates' Court and Sadler and Daly* [2008] EWHC 15 (Admin).

This case centred on whether the lodging of appeal against sentence could be considered a *reasonable excuse* for not attending appointments in relation to an unpaid work requirement. The Divisional Court ruled that it was not.

In his judgment, Dyson L.J. stated (at para.13) that:

> "It follows that, like any other sentence, a community order takes effect when it is imposed and it remains in full force and effect until and unless it is quashed on appeal or revoked or amended by order of the court. The lodging of an appeal does not in itself have any effect on the enforceability of an order."

(iii)   Warning

Where an offender has failed without reasonable excuse to comply with any of the requirements of an order, a warning must be given to the offender and the warning must be recorded.

A warning must:

(a) describe the circumstances of the failure;

(b) state that the failure is unacceptable; and

(c) inform the offender that if, within the next 12 months, he or she again fails to comply with any requirement of the order, he or she will be liable to be brought before a court.

It is important that any communication relating to the failure to comply is fully recorded and that any letters sent to or received from the offender are kept on file. This information may be used in later breach proceedings (see section (x)).

(iv)   Decision to breach

A further failure to comply without reasonable excuse within the 12 month period must result in breach action. There are targets for breach action and currently action must be taken within 10 working days of the failure or four working days in high-risk cases. A letter should be sent to the offender stating that he or she has breached the order a second time and that breach action will be commenced unless the offender can produce evidence that he or she had a reasonable excuse for the failure.

Breach action may also be commenced without a warning if an offender has been involved in a serious incident that indicates:

- an escalation in the risk of serious harm or likelihood of re-offending;
- a refusal to comply or;
- a breakdown of the order.

Where breach action is taken the prosecution need to satisfy two tests:

(a) The evidential test—this means there must be a reasonable prospect (more than 50 per cent) of being able to prove that:

- the offender was made the subject of the order;
- he or she was given instructions;

- he or she failed to comply; and
- he or she has no reasonable excuse.

It is worth noting that a breach of a community order, suspended sentence order or youth rehabilitation order is not in itself a criminal offence and therefore the Police and Criminal Evidence Act 1984 does not apply. As a result there is, for example, no requirement to caution the offender. However, the burden of proof in breach proceedings is the same as in any other criminal proceedings so it is important that evidence of instructions given, for example, is clear and unambiguous.

(b) The public interest test—this involves an assessment of whether the public interest would best be served by continuing with the prosecution or by dealing with the case in some other way. Factors to consider might include:

- age, mental and physical condition of the offender;
- the risk he or she poses;
- whether any further proceedings are pending;
- whether the offender is in custody; and
- any other factors relevant to the particular case.

The case should be kept under review and any information which is favourable to the offender should be disclosed whether or not the defence are aware of it.

(v) Obtaining the summons

Breach proceedings will be commenced in either the magistrates' court or the Crown Court depending upon where the order was made. Occasionally, a Crown Court order will direct that breach proceedings should be brought in the magistrates' court. The order must be in force otherwise breach action cannot be pursued.

The officer responsible for the case will need to notify the relevant court following a process known as "*laying an information*" (a specimen Information can be found in Appendix A).

Under section 127 of the Magistrates' Court Act 1980, an information must be laid within six months of the last failure to comply. In most instances, this is a technical point if National Standards are being followed, but it is nevertheless worth noting. The matter does not have to be dealt with within any defined period, although the powers of the court will reduce if responding to a breach case where the order has expired.

On receiving the information, the relevant court will then issue a summons directing the offender to appear at court at a specified time. (However, not all courts issue a summons. Some use a letter which has been agreed between the court and the local probation trust.)

The summons must then be served upon the offender either by the court or by the responsible officer, depending upon local practice.

In certain circumstances, a warrant for the arrest of an offender may be requested by the prosecutor rather than a summons. This may happen if, for example, the whereabouts of the offender are unknown or the offender poses a significant risk of further offending. In such instances, the responsible officer or court duty officer will be required to present the information to the court under oath.

The court will pass the warrant to the police (or civilian enforcement officer) to arrest the person named in the warrant and bring him or her before the relevant court.

(vi) Preparing the breach file

As soon as breach proceedings are being commenced, a breach file should be prepared and should contain:

- copy of the order;
- copy of the summons;
- certificate of service where appropriate (usually proof of postage);
- statement of facts or copy of the written information;
- instructions given to the offender;
- copy of warning letters sent;
- advance disclosure relating to the original offence;
- copy of up to date previous convictions;
- breach report; and
- any other information relevant to the case.

(vii) The first hearing and what may happen

(a) The offender may fail to appear in which case the court may issue a warrant for his or her arrest. This is known as a *bench warrant*, i.e. issued by the judge or magistrates.

(b) The case may be adjourned to another date because the case cannot proceed for some reason. Often the offender or his or her solicitor will make an application for an adjournment to enable the offender to prepare the case properly.

(c) The offender may admit the breach (see section (ix) below).

(d) The offender may deny the breach (see section (x) below).

(viii) Warrants

As noted earlier, it may be necessary for the probation service to apply for a warrant for the arrest of an offender on issuing breach proceedings or later in the proceedings if the offender fails to attend court.

A warrant is in effect an order from the court to the police (or civilian enforcement officer) to arrest the person named in the warrant, and if the warrant is not "backed for bail" to bring that person before the court without delay. If the warrant is a warrant with bail, the person executing the warrant arrests the individual, notifies him or her of the requirement to attend court at a particular date and time and releases him or her on bail.

It follows that the act of asking for a warrant is not to be undertaken without proper thought since the rights of the person arrested as a result of the warrant will be interfered with. If the interference is unlawful, that would represent a breach of his or her rights under the HRA 1998 and may give rise to a claim for damages. It would also damage the reputation of the person or organisation who sought the warrant.

All relevant facts should be made known when applying for a warrant. Factors which may influence the court to issue a warrant include that:

- the offender's whereabouts are unknown;
- the offender poses a significant risk of further offending;
- the offender has a history of not responding to summonses; or
- the offender may interfere with witnesses (although this is not particularly likely in enforcement cases).

Factors which may influence the court against issuing a warrant or to issue a warrant backed for bail include that:

- the offender has a settled address;
- the level of risk posed by the offender is low;
- the offender is infirm; or
- the offender has family commitments e.g. child care responsibilities or care of elderly relatives.

If the offender poses a high risk to the public or any section of it, it may be necessary to ask the court to "fast track" the application for and execution of the warrant. In any event, the "Offender Additional Information Sheet" or the agreed local equivalent should be completed and given to those who have to execute the warrant so they can locate the offender and arrest him or her safely and speedily.

(ix) Procedure where the breach is admitted

If the offender admits the breach, the probation service court duty officer will prosecute the case by outlining the facts in a fair and impartial manner. It is incumbent on the prosecution to draw the attention of the court to any points which favour the offender particularly where the offender is unrepresented. The magistrates are addressed collectively as "Your Worships", individual magistrates and court legal advisers as "Sir" or "Ma'am", as appropriate.

If the breach is being dealt with in the Crown Court counsel will prosecute the case.

Unlike other prosecutions, the court duty officer can offer advice to the court about what action to take on the breach. Normally a prosecutor would not play any part in the consideration of the sentence and there are tensions in these two roles that should be carefully managed.

The defence is then entitled to address the court in mitigation and offer a view on what action the court should take.

In cases involving adults, the court may amend the terms of the community order by imposing more onerous requirements, or it could deal with the offender as though he or she had just been convicted of the original offence. For a suspended sentence order the court may activate the prison sentence or impose more onerous requirements on the order.

(x) Procedure where the breach is denied

If the offender denies the breach, a date will be set for a pre-trial review or a trial and the case will be adjourned. The probation service will arrange for legal representation according to local practice, for instance, some trusts have in-house legal departments, some use the services of a local authority and others have arrangements with private firms of solicitors.

At trial the prosecution must prove the case beyond reasonable doubt. Case records and proof of communication with the offender are likely to be used to support the case. Witnesses will be called to give evidence of breaches of requirements and will be subject to cross-examination. The court can also require the witness to attend to give evidence and may do so if the offender is unrepresented.

Where possible, however, the attendance of witnesses should be avoided to save unnecessary inconvenience and expense. There are various options that may be considered.

- Written statements can be submitted in evidence if they are served on the offender at least seven days before the hearing date and if they comply with the requirements of section 9 of the Criminal Justice Act 1967. A specimen section 9 statement is set out in Appendix B.

  The offender can object to the statement and insist that the witness be called to give evidence but, if he or she does not, then the statement is admissible in evidence without the attendance of the witness. It has the same weight as oral evidence and is still subject to submissions which may be made by the defence.

- A written statement may also be admissible, under section 116 of the CJA 2003, provided that the interests of justice do not decree otherwise, if the person who made it is dead, ill or absent abroad.

- Admissions of facts may be made in writing under section 10 of the Criminal Justice Act 1967. In effect they can help to narrow down those facts which are admitted and those which are denied, and result in a saving of court time. They should be dealt with by the solicitor who is dealing with the case.

(xi) Withdrawal of proceedings

An information can be withdrawn before the offender has admitted or denied a breach (i.e. entered a plea.) A magistrate can do this if asked to do so by the responsible officer. In theory the allegation could be pursued again at a later date as a withdrawal of an allegation outlined in an information is not the same as a finding that the allegation is not proven.

Once the offender has entered a plea the information may not be withdrawn. If it is not considered to be in the interests of justice to pursue the case, the alternative is to offer no evidence and invite the court to dismiss the information. The dismissal of the information prevents the allegation from being the subject of a fresh prosecution at a later stage.

(xii) Breach reports

The responsible officer normally prepares a written report about a breach to assist the court. It should usually be sent to the court duty officer so that the responsible officer does not need to attend court.

The breach report is not considered until after a finding or admission of guilt, as it is not intended to assist the court in determining whether or not the offender has failed to comply with an order but rather to assist in deciding what to do with the offender.

In the breach report the responsible officer should:

- summarise the order and the period during which the author has held statutory responsibility;
- outline the failure/s to comply with the order including details of instructions given and any warnings. The failures must be limited to those set out in the information;
- indicate the extent of compliance with the order at the point where breach proceedings were commenced;
- explain the extent of the offender's compliance with the order since the prosecution was commenced;
- give a view about the viability of the continuation of the order with reasons;
- provide relevant personal information about the offender;
- provide an assessment of risk of both harm and re-offending;
- provide positive information where it exists; and
- give a view about how the order might be amended if it is to continue or what alternative sentence might be suitable for the offender. In the case of suspended sentence orders, the report should consider whether or not the custodial period should be activated in part or in full.

(xiii) Relevant legislation

Schedule 8 of the CJA 2003 governs breach of community orders and is reproduced in Appendix C.

Schedule 12 of the CJA 2003 governs breach of Suspended Sentence Orders and is reproduced in Appendix D.

Chapter 3
ENFORCEMENT OF ORDERS ON YOUNG PEOPLE UNDER 18

The basic procedures for breaches prosecuted within the youth court follow the steps outlined in the previous chapter. This chapter discusses in more detail some considerations particular to the youth court and cases involving young people, including considerations of welfare and age.

(i) Welfare and young people's rights

As with proceedings against adults, all enforcement cases involving young people must comply with the HRA 1998, particularly in relation to the right to a fair trial. In addition, the UN Convention on the Rights of the Child 1989 art.3 states that in all actions taken by public bodies, including courts of law, "the best interests of the child shall be a primary consideration." Furthermore, the UN Standard Minimum Rules for the Administration of Juvenile Justice (the Beijing Rules) requires in Rule 5.1 that "the juvenile justice system shall emphasise the well-being of the juvenile."

In domestic law, the welfare principle was established by section 44 of the Children and Young Persons Act 1933 which states that:

> "Every court in dealing with a child or young person who is brought before it, either as an offender or otherwise, shall have regard to the welfare of the child or young person."

However, regard to welfare must now be balanced with the principal aim set out for the youth justice system in section 37 of the C&DA 1998, which is the prevention of offending by children and young people.

This has caused debate about the downgrading of the welfare principle that has stood at the heart of the youth justice system for so long. However, it is still the case that the welfare of the young person is a consideration in all youth court proceedings, albeit not the prime consideration that it has been in the past, and proceedings should be conducted accordingly.

The Sentencing Guidelines Council (2009) point to the high incidence of welfare-related issues amongst young people (for instance, mental ill-health, learning difficulties or self-harming behaviours) and the need for courts to be alert to such issues. Appropriate information from and assessment by the youth offending team (YOT) or other agencies involved with young people will be critical in ensuring that sentencing is more able to achieve the difficult balance between the aims of prevention of offending and promoting/protecting the welfare of the young person.

(ii) Responding to the age of the young person

Court orders should be managed from the outset with the age and maturity of the young person in mind. This means explaining the requirements of the order and the expectations in clear language that the young person is able to understand. Written information should be appropriately worded and accessible to the young person. Parents, carers and other professionals should be involved according to the young person's age and needs.

If a young person fails to comply with the terms of an order, the responsible officer (YOT case manager) should make contact within one working day by telephone, letter or home visit to seek an explanation. If an explanation is judged not to be acceptable, a formal written warning should be issued within 24 hours. Written warnings should be clear and precise in stating the alleged non-compliance or unacceptable conduct. YOT case managers should bear in mind that a young person may have a very literal understanding of what he or she is allowed or is expected to do.

In terms of court proceedings, good practice suggests that the young person (and parents or carers, as appropriate) should be informed of the basis for the breach in a way that ensures as far as possible that he or she understands why the action is being taken and is able to make a decision about plea.

Once in court, the Magistrates' Court Rules require that the magistrates explain the nature and grounds for the proceedings to the young person in terms suitable to his or her age and level of understanding. In certain cases, this may be impracticable and so the parents or guardians may be informed instead. Although formally the prosecutor, the court officer may also be called upon to liaise with the defence solicitor or with parents.

In breach cases involving young people, court officers are more likely to be asked for relevant background information than in cases concerning adults. It is therefore important that court officers have this information available, particularly where they are not the responsible officer for the order themselves. It follows that breach reports on young people are likely to contain fuller information in order to guide the court in dealing with the case.

Again, the outcome of proceedings should be explained to the young person and parents by the court in simple language suitable to his or her age and understanding. However, it is often helpful for the court officer—once more switching roles—to talk to the young person and/or family before they leave the court precinct to make sure that he or she fully understands what the court has decided and what the next steps will be.

Youth rehabilitation orders (YROs) made in the Crown Court must be returned straight to the Crown Court in the event of breach, unless the order specifically states that failures to comply can be dealt with in the magistrates'/youth court. Crown Court proceedings are governed by a Practice Direction, *Trial of Children and Young Persons in the Crown Court*. This states that:

> "The court should explain the course of proceedings to a young defendant in terms he can understand, should remind those representing a young person of their continuing duty to explain each step of the trial to him and should ensure, as far as practicable, that the trial is conducted in language that the young person can understand."

It is important to recognise that appearing in the Crown Court may be a confusing and intimidating experience for a young person, in spite of any efforts that the court itself may make. It may additionally be more complex for YOT practitioners who are instructing counsel in relation to the case rather than conducting the prosecution themselves. Nevertheless, it is incumbent on all involved to try to help the young person participate in proceedings and to have his or her side of the case presented. While it is important for young people to be legally represented in the youth court, it is even more so in the Crown Court, where young people are at increased risk of custody.

(iii) Reaching the age of 18

Breach proceedings for orders made in the youth court will ordinarily be heard in the youth court. However, where the young person concerned is already aged 18 at the point where the allegation is made and the information is laid before magistrates, the case will commence in an adult magistrates' court.

(iv) Parental attendance at court

Where a child is age 15 or under, the court must require a parent to be present, and may require parents to attend for a young person who has reached the age of 16 or 17, unless it is considered unreasonable to do so. A summons for the parent is usually sent out alongside the summons for the young person.

These requirements normally relate to adults who have parental responsibility for the young person, as set out in the Children Act 1989.

Where a young person is in the care of the local authority, the authority has parental responsibility and the young person should be accompanied to court by a representative of children's social care.

Encouraging (or requiring) parents to attend court and to support their offspring is one means of reinforcing parental responsibility, which is a key objective of the youth justice system.

(v) Persistent offenders

Certain sentences are only available for young people who are identified as *persistent offenders*. These include a YRO with intensive supervision and surveillance or fostering requirements for 10–14 year olds and also the detention and training order (DTO) for young people aged 12–14.

The emphasis on persistent patterns of offending reflects a slightly different focus in relation for young people than for adult offenders, where there is a more obvious concern with dangerousness and public protection.

Although there is no legal definition of *persistent*, the Sentencing Guidelines Council suggests that the court might apply the following test:

> "(i) In most circumstances, the normal expectation is that the offender will have had some contact with authority in which the offending conduct was challenged before being classed as "persistent"; a finding of persistence in offending may be derived from information about previous convictions but may also arise from orders which require an admission or finding of guilt—these include reprimands, final warnings, restorative justice disposals and conditional cautions; since they do not require such an admission, penalty notices for disorder are unlikely to be sufficiently reliable;
>
> (ii) A young offender is certainly likely to be found to be persistent (and, in relation to a custodial sentence, the test of being a measure of last resort is most likely to be satisfied) where the offender has been convicted of, or made subject to a pre-court disposal that involves an admission or finding of guilt in relation to, imprisonable offences on at least 3 occasions in the past 12 months."

(Sentencing Guidelines Council, 2009: 11)

23

(vi) Young people and custody

Custody should be used cautiously in relation to young people, with regard for their welfare and developmental needs balanced with the proper concern for public protection. Both domestic law and international conventions have established that custody should be *a measure of last resort* in the sentencing of young people (Sentencing Guidelines Council, 2009). With very few exceptions, a young person can only be sent to custody or given an alternative to custody (YRO with intensive fostering or intensive supervision and surveillance) if the offence(s) before the court are judged to pass the custody threshold— the *so serious* criterion established by the CJA 1991.

Breach proceedings may place a young person at risk of receiving a custodial sentence. There is accordingly an onus on both courts and youth justice practitioners to be proactive in seeking to secure compliance and to use available options in the community to deal with breaches wherever possible.

Inevitably some young people will receive either immediate custodial sentences or custody as a result of breach proceedings. There are significant features to custodial arrangements for young people that distinguish them from adults. The main custodial sentence for under-18s is the detention and training order (DTO) which can be made for periods of up to two years in the youth court. While breaches of post-custody licences for adults are now almost exclusively dealt with by means of executive recall to prison, breaches of DTO are still heard within the court arena, where due process measures provide some degree of protection for young people and opportunity for the young person's circumstances and the reasons for non-compliance to be considered.

(vii) Contact levels under *The Scaled Approach*

The amount of contact required under National Standards will vary according to the intervention level judged as appropriate for the young person through the Asset assessment and under *The Scaled Approach* (which is the youth justice equivalent of the tiering system in the adult OMM). The minimum levels per month are:

Intervention Level	First 12 weeks	After 12 weeks
Intensive	12	4
Enhanced	4	2
Standard	2	1

National Standards for Youth Justice Services (YJB, 2009) stipulates that a contact is a planned face-to-face meeting between the young person and one or more of the following:

- the responsible officer;
- another member of the YOT;
- a member of another agency involved in the young person's supervision; and
- a volunteer approved to work with the young person.

These are minimum contact levels and the actual number of contacts may be significantly higher, particularly where the young person is a multi-agency public protection case and this has been agreed at multi-agency level as part of a risk management plan. It may also be higher where the young person is assessed as vulnerable or has particular welfare needs. In this latter case, some contacts above the minimum could be designated as voluntary contacts and would therefore not be enforceable.

Chapter 4
THE COMMUNITY ORDER

Legal basis for the order

Section 177 of the CJA 2003 establishes the community order which has been available to the courts since April 4, 2005 for offences committed on or after that date.

Section 148 of the CJA 2003 places restrictions on the imposition of a community sentence which can only be made where the court considers that:

    (a) the offence(s) are "serious enough" to warrant such a sentence;

    (b) the requirement or combination of requirements are the most suitable for the offender;

    (c) the restriction of liberty reflects the seriousness of the offence(s); and

    (d) the sentence for the offence is not fixed in law.

Section 150A provides a further restriction by stipulating that community orders can only be imposed where the offence(s) in question are punishable by imprisonment.

There are 12 requirements that can be part of a community order and each order must contain one or more of these requirements in combination:

- unpaid work requirement;
- activity requirement;
- programme requirement;
- prohibited activity requirement;
- curfew requirement;
- exclusion requirement;
- residence requirement;
- mental health treatment requirement;
- drug rehabilitation requirement;
- alcohol treatment requirement;
- supervision requirement; and
- attendance centre requirement (for offenders under 25 years).

The maximum length of a community order is three years. In making the order, the court must specify a date by which all requirements must be completed and may specify an earlier date or dates in relation to specific requirements.

I.   Requirements in the community order

Requirement	Unpaid Work	Sections 199 and 200

Duration: 40 to 300 hours, within a 12 month period (but see below)

Conditions that need to be met for this requirement:

The court must be satisfied that the offender is suitable to perform unpaid work and, if it thinks necessary, may first hear from an officer of the local probation trust as to suitability.

Special considerations

Where the offender is sentenced for two or more offences and is required to perform unpaid work for each of these, the court may direct that the hours can run concurrently or consecutively, providing the total number of hours does not exceed 300.

The specific requirement as spelt out in s.200(1) is that the offender:

> "must perform for the number of hours specified in the order such work at such times as he may be instructed by the responsible officer".

Paragraph 20 of Schedule 8 does permit a court to extend the period for completion of unpaid work hours.

The order will remain in force until the unpaid work hours are completed, unless revoked or the offender dies.

Requirement	Activity	Section 201

Duration: the requirement is expressed in number of days and must not exceed 60 days.

Conditions that need to be met for this requirement:

The court must be satisfied that it is feasible to secure compliance with the activity proposed and, in considering this, must consult an officer of the local probation board. The court must have the consent of any person other than the offender and responsible officer whose co-operation is required.

Special considerations

Under an activity requirement, an offender must:

(a)   present himself to a person or persons specified at a place or places so specified on a specified number of days; and/or

(b)   participate in activities specified in the order on a specified number of days.

This condition carries the authority for the offender to be required to attend activities or a probation centre programme. However, where the intention is to direct an offender to attend a specific accredited programme, a programme requirement should be used instead.

The actual dates, times and venue and other instructions will be specified by the responsible officer or others acting on his or her behalf, for instance, an officer in charge of a probation centre. It follows that instructions need to be detailed and specific, because this may be critical in the case of enforcement action. Often, for probation centre or similar programmes, instructions may be issued to offenders in the form of a weekly diary or calendar.

In most instances, the venue specified under s.201(a) will be a non-residential facility—referred to as a "community rehabilitation centre" in the legislation—either approved by the Secretary of State or by the local probation trust for use with offenders. Where this section is used, it also covers instructions to attend elsewhere for the purposes of participating in activities connected with the programme.

Section 201(9) requires the offender to participate in activities for the specified number of days and, whilst participating, to comply with instructions given by or with the authority of the officer in charge of the activities. Instructions may prohibit unacceptable behaviours and specify other expectations, such as not attending under the influence of alcohol and drugs.

The specified activity may consist of reparation activities, solely or in conjunction with other activities.

Requirement	Programme	Section 202

Duration: the number of days attendance required must be specified in the order

Conditions that need to be met for this requirement:

The court cannot make a programme requirement unless an officer of the local probation trust has recommended its suitability for the offender. It must also be satisfied that the accredited programme in question is available at the specified venue and must have the consent of any person whose co-operation is required other than the offender and responsible officer.

Special considerations

The programme requirement relates specifically to accredited programmes.

Section 202(6) requires the offender to participate in activities for the specified number of days and, whilst participating, to comply with instructions given by or with the authority of the officer in charge of the programme.

More than one programme requirement can be contained in one order. This may mean, for instance, that an offender has a requirement to attend a generic programme and a second requirement stipulating that this should be followed by an offence-specific programme.

Requirement	Prohibited activity	Section 203

Duration: 36 month maximum

Conditions that need to be met for this requirement:

The court must consult an officer of the local probation trust before including this requirement.

Special considerations

This requirement gives authority to order the offender to refrain from participating in specified activities or behaviours on specific dates or for a specified period. There may be particular enforcement difficulties with this requirement because defining or indeed detecting the prohibited behaviours may not be straightforward. Offender managers or court duty officers may therefore be required to assist the court in the appropriate wording of prohibitions and also to advise the court in relation to concerns about proportionality and offender rights.

This requirement should not be used to prohibit behaviour that is in any case illegal and will not normally relate to geographical restrictions that could be dealt with by an exclusion requirement. However, it can be used to prevent an offender carrying a firearm as defined by the Firearms Act 1967.

Requirement	Curfew	Section 204

Duration: between 2 and 12 hours per day for a period of up 6 months

Conditions that need to be met for this requirement:

The court must obtain and consider information about the place or places specified in the order for the curfew to take place and the attitudes of other people likely to be affected by the offender's enforced presence there (for instance, family members or partner).

Special considerations

Curfews can be reasonably flexible, so that the place specified or the hours of curfew can vary on different days of the week. Care should be taken to ensure that arrangements are not unnecessarily complicated but that they meet the needs of the offender, allowing for work and family commitments or religious observances. Curfews can be particularly useful for offenders whose criminal activities tend to take place at night, but they are not restricted to such offenders.

Under s.177(3) the court must impose a requirement that the curfew is electronically monitored unless:

(a) the court does not have the consent of an individual whose co-operation is needed to secure the monitoring (s.215(2)); or

(b) an electronic monitoring scheme is not available in the area in which the address for the curfew is proposed (s.218(4)).

Where an electronically monitored curfew is the only requirement on a community order, the responsible officer will be an employee of the approved contractor for the area in question. Otherwise the responsible officer will be an offender manager who will enforce this requirement alongside whatever other requirements are contained in the order.

Requirement	Exclusion	Section 205

Duration: 24 months maximum, but the Sentencing Guidelines Council suggest should normally be 12 months or less

Conditions that need to be met for this requirement:

None

Special considerations

This requirement prohibits the offender from entering a specified place for a specified period of time. A place can refer to an area, not necessarily a building or location, and this may be indicated to the offender on a map. The requirement can specify more than one place and these can be for different periods or different days of the week, for instance.

Where an electronically monitored exclusion is the only requirement on a community order, the responsible officer will be an employee of the approved contractor for the area in question. Otherwise the responsible officer will be an offender manager who will enforce this requirement alongside whatever other requirements are contained in the order.

It may not always be possible to monitor an exclusion electronically for technical reasons and, if this is the case, the question of enforceability should be considered.

Requirement	Residence	Section 206

Duration: up to 36 months

Conditions that need to be met for this requirement:

The court must consider the home circumstances of the offender before making this condition and, in practice, this will necessitate a standard delivery pre-sentence report. An offender can only be required to reside in hostels or other institutions where this has been recommended by an officer of the local probation board.

Special considerations

This requirement means that the offender must reside at a place specified in the order for a specified period of time. Usually this involves either approved premises or another kind of supported/rehabilitative environment and the offender will be expected to abide by any reasonable rules as to behaviours within that environment which, if specified in a written agreement or licence, would therefore be enforceable.

If worded appropriately, a residence requirement could allow the flexibility for the offender to stay somewhere other than the place specified in the order with the prior approval of the responsible officer.

Requirement	Mental Health Treatment	Section 207

Duration: up to 36 months

Conditions that need to be met for this requirement:

In order to make this requirement, the court must hear evidence from a registered mental practitioner (as specified by s.12 of the Mental Health Act 1983 as amended by the Mental Health Act 2007). The court must be satisfied that the mental condition of the offender requires and will be susceptible to treatment, and that neither a guardianship order nor hospital order is warranted. The court must also be satisfied that suitable arrangements for treatment have been made or can be made, including in-patient treatment.

The court must have the consent of the offender before making the treatment requirement. The court may also consider a full written report from the probation service but this is not mandatory.

Special considerations

The requirement will not specify the nature of the treatment but will specify one of the following:

(a) in-patient treatment at a named hospital or care home;

(b) non-residential treatment at a specified institution or place; or

(c) treatment by or under the direction of a named registered medical practitioner or chartered psychologist.

Whilst the offender is undergoing in-patient treatment, the responsible officer's role will be restricted to considerations of revocation or amendment of the order.

Section 208 allows the medical practitioner who is providing or directing treatment to change the place or institution where part of the treatment is being given with the consent of the offender, if this is considered better or more appropriate. Under s.208(2) this can include in-patient treatment, even where this was not specified in the original order. The responsible officer should be informed in writing of any such changes that are made.

See sections V and VI of this chapter in relation to revocation and amendments in relation to mental health treatment requirements.

Requirement	Drug Rehabilitation (DRR)	Section 209

Duration: Minimum of 6 months up to 36 months

Conditions that need to be met for this requirement:

Before making this requirement, the court must be satisfied that:

(a) the offender is dependent on or has a propensity to misuse drugs, AND

(b) the dependency or propensity requires or may be susceptible to treatment, AND

(c) arrangements have been made or can be made for the treatment specified in the order, including residential treatment.

The requirement must be recommended by an officer of a local probation trust, in most cases of medium or high offence seriousness in a standard delivery pre-sentence report. A full report will almost certainly be required where there is an additional mental health need.

The offender must also express willingness to comply with the requirement.

Special considerations

DRRs can be combined with other requirements which relate to the substance misuse' or other issues, such as domestic violence. Care should be taken to ensure that these are complementary and good practice suggests they should be negotiated with the treatment provider. Appropriate restriction of liberty is also a consideration.

Where "wrap-around" services—e.g. housing, employment, financial advice—are given as part of the treatment programme or structured day care, this will be included within the DRR requirement and no additional requirement will be needed. Where these services are not part of the commissioned treatment programme, a separate activity requirement may be needed.

Treatment may be residential or non-residential at a place specified in the order, but the nature of treatment will not be specified. Treatment will be by or under the direction of a specified person with the necessary experience and qualifications in relation to drugs work.

Where the treatment is residential and the residential facility is in another area, the order will be held in that new area. DRR cases cannot be transferred temporarily and held by the new area on a "care-taking" basis.

The offender will be required to give samples when and as determined by the responsible officer or person directing treatment, in order to prove or disprove the presence of particular substances in the body. The results of the tests must be communicated to the responsible officer.

In terms of National Standards contacts, collection of substitute medication and testing can both be counted.

Reviews of Drug Rehabilitation Requirements (DRRs)

The court in making an order with a DRR must order reviews for all DRRs lasting over 12 months and may order reviews for DRRs of 12 months or less. The court will set the frequency of review hearings at intervals of one month or more.

Usually the court that made the order will retain responsibility for reviewing the order. However, there will be instances where another court is named in the order because the offender does not live in the local justice area covered by the sentencing court and in these cases the named court assumes responsibility.

The responsible officer must provide a written report for each review, outlining the offender's progress and the results of the drug tests. This should also reflect the views of the treatment provider of the offender's response to treatment and testing.

In the first instance, the offender is required to attend review hearings. However, if at a subsequent review, the court considers that the offender is making satisfactory progress, it may direct that future reviews can place without him or her attending (s.211(6)). Subsequently, if the court sees that progress is no longer satisfactory, it may again require the offender to appear before it at a specific time and place (s.211(6)) and, on that occasion, may amend the order again to ensure that subsequent reviews are made at full review hearings.

At review hearings, the court has powers to amend the DRR (but cannot amend other requirements on the order). For instance, it can reduce the period of the DRR subject to the minimum term of six months or make alterations to treatment arrangements. The offender must give consent to the amendment in order for it to have effect. If consent is not given, the court may revoke the order and re-sentence for the original offence(s), taking into account the extent to which he or she has complied with the requirement.

Enforcement

A failure to report on a DRR is considered as an unacceptable failure only once in any one day, regardless of how many contacts have been arranged.

Refusal to provide a drugs test is considered a failure to comply, but a genuine inability to provide a sample for medical reasons would not be considered an unacceptable failure.

Failed drug tests—whether positive tests or refusals to give samples—are not grounds for breach proceedings in isolation, but are indicative of a failure to engage with a treatment programme. Consistent failures may nevertheless result in an order being returned to court because it is unworkable.

It may be that a medium-length DRR is proposed in cases where the offence is of low seriousness but where the offender has a high treatment need and wishes to access residential treatment. In such cases, where breach occurs, the court's attention should be drawn to the fact that the restriction of liberty is not commensurate with the original offence so that the court can respond appropriately.

Requirement	Alcohol Treatment	Section 212

Duration: minimum of 6 months up to 36 months

Conditions that need to be met for this requirement:

Before making this requirement, the court must be satisfied that:

    (a) the offender is dependent on alcohol; AND

    (b) the dependency requires or may be susceptible to treatment; AND

    (c) arrangements have been made or can be made for the treatment specified in the order, including residential treatment.

Significantly, the court does not have to be satisfied that the alcohol dependency caused or contributed to the offences of which the offender has been convicted.

The offender must express willingness to comply with the requirement.

Special considerations

Treatment may be residential or non-residential at a place specified in the order, but the nature of treatment will not be specified. Treatment will be by or under the direction of a named person with the necessary experience and qualifications in relation to alcohol work.

"Dependency" can be interpreted as rather broader than simply clinical dependency— physical and psychological—to include other hazardous or harmful drinking patterns.

Requirement	Supervision	Section 213

Duration: up to 36 months

Conditions that need to be met for this requirement:

None

Special considerations

The purpose of the supervision requirement is rehabilitation and this requirement may underpin the delivery of a varied set of requirements on a community order.

Legally, this requires the offender to:

> "attend appointments with the responsible officer or another person determined by the responsible officer, at a time and place determined by the responsible officer" (s.213(1)).

The simplicity of this requirement in law belies the complexity that may exist within a supervision process and the significance of this requirement in terms of promoting behavioural change in offenders and providing coherence to an intervention package. This requirement is central to operation of the Offender Management Model (OMM) in more complicated or high risk cases, with the responsible officer overseeing the sequencing and implementation of different requirements throughout the course of the order.

Requirement	Attendance Centre	Section 214

Duration: 12–36 hours

Conditions that need to be met for this requirement:

This requirement is only available for offenders under the age of 25.

The court cannot make this requirement unless there is an attendance centre available in the area and it is satisfied that it is reasonably accessible to the offender, given his or her circumstances and any means of transport available to him or her.

Special considerations

An attendance centre requirement is expressed in numbers of hours and must specify the centre where the hours will be spent. Activities, sports and social education are usually provided at the centres which have historically been run on a Saturday. An offender cannot be required to spend more than 3 hours at the centre on any one day.

Where the attendance centre is the only requirement on a community order, the responsible officer will be the manager of the specified centre. Otherwise the responsible officer will be an offender manager (OM) who will enforce this requirement alongside whatever other requirements are contained in the order.

II. Obligations of an offender under a community order

(i) keep in touch with responsible officer

Section 220(1)(a) requires that an offender on a community order or suspended sentence order *must keep in touch with the responsible officer in accordance with such instructions as he may from time to time be given by that officer.* "Instructions" can mean not only dates and times of appointments or work details but also standard sets of rules agreed with the offender at the start of an order, which allow the probation service to stipulate what would be considered inappropriate and therefore breachable behaviour or language whilst on probation premises or on activities related to the order.

(ii) notify the responsible officer of any change of address

These two obligations are enforceable as though they were a requirement imposed by the order.

In the case of *Richards v National Probation Service* [2007] EWHC 3108 (Admin), the Divisional Court considered the extent of the requirement to keep in touch.

Richards was ordered to undertake 100 hours of unpaid work and signed a set of rules provided by the probation service that set out his responsibilities. These included one rule which specified that, if he knew in advance that he would be unable to keep an appointment in relation to unpaid work, then he should inform the responsible officer as soon as possible, giving the reason. The next rule stated that he should provide the reason and supporting evidence to the responsible officer within seven days of the failure to comply.

Richards argued that the power in the CJA 2003 s.220(1) was a power to require the offender to keep in touch, not a power to require evidence after the event.

The Divisional Court held that it was entirely reasonable that an officer should require the reasons for non-compliance to be in writing and to be supported by third party evidence; it could not have been intended by Parliament that an officer should have to rely on the word of the offender alone.

III. Breach of community orders

The powers relating to breach, revocation or amendment of community orders are contained in Sch.8 of the CJA 2003. Appendix C contains the text of this Schedule.

Breach proceedings will be dealt with by the magistrates' court or Crown Court, depending on where the order was made. In some instances, the Crown Court in making an order will specify that breach matters may be dealt with by a magistrates' court. However, even where the magistrates' court is empowered to deal with the breach, the justices may still commit the offender to custody or release on bail until he or she can be brought before the Crown Court. An order made by the Crown Court on appeal from the magistrates' court is treated as a Crown Court order.

If the court is satisfied that an offender has failed *without reasonable excuse* to comply with any of the requirements of the order, the court may:

- **Amend the terms of the community order** so as to impose more onerous requirements. This may involve extending the duration of particular requirements, so long as the overall length of the order is not extended. Alternatively, new requirements may be imposed providing these were available to the court at the time the original sentence was made. These may be additional to existing requirements or as a substitute for them.

- **Revoke the order and re-sentence** in any way that the court could have done on the original sentencing occasion had the community order not been made.

The court may **not:**

- Fine the offender and allow the order to continue.
- Take no action.

When considering whether to amend or to revoke the order, the court must take into account the extent to which the offender has complied with the community order. Magistrates' court guidelines suggest that custody should be used as a last resort and reserved for those cases of deliberate and repeated breach where all reasonable efforts to ensure that the offender complies have failed (Sentencing Guidelines Council, 2008).

In line with this, the same guidelines also state that before increasing the onerousness of a community order, the magistrates should:

- take account of the offender's ability to comply; and
- avoid precipitating further breach by overloading the offender with too many or conflicting requirements.

(Sentencing Guidelines Council, 2008)

Ordinarily, where new requirements are added to an order or substituted for the previous requirements, the court cannot go outside the limits set for the requirement in the CJA 2003. The one exception to this is in relation to the unpaid work requirement, where the court is able to impose a 20-hour requirement for breach whereas the usual lower limit is 40 hours (CJ&IA 2008 s.38).

(i) Persistent and wilful refusal to comply

If the order has been made for imprisonable offences and the offender has persistently and wilfully refused to comply, the court may revoke and re-sentence to custody (para.9(4)). In these circumstances, the general restriction on imposition of a custodial sentence contained in s.152(2) of the CJA 2003 is waived, which means that the "so serious" threshold does not have to be met.

(ii) Powers of the court when the order has expired

Breach action may only be taken where the order is in force at the point where the information is laid. However, the order may have expired by the time the case is dealt with, particularly in cases where a warrant has been outstanding for a period. In this instance, the court does not have the power to amend the order as it no longer exists, but it may still re-sentence for the original offences. In doing so, it must take into account the extent to which the offender had complied with the order.

IV. Review of community orders

Section 178 of the CJA 2003 empowers the Secretary of State for Justice to enable courts to review community orders. This provision was trialled initially in the North Liverpool Community Justice Centre and the City of Salford Magistrates' Court but, by virtue of the Community Order (Review by Specified Courts) Order 2007, it has been extended to all of the 12 pilot community justice centres. The impact of conducting reviews will be evaluated and this provision may be rolled out to all courts in due course.

The intention of this section is for courts, in making an order, to be able to specify a periodic review of the order in order to monitor an offender's progress. At a review hearing, the court would be able to amend the order but could not impose different or more onerous requirements without the consent of the offender. The court would be unable to review a drug rehabilitation requirement because reviews of this requirement are already provided for under s.210 of the CJA 2003. However, any other requirements on the community order could be reviewed.

V. Revocation of community orders

The powers allowing courts to revoke orders in cases that do not involve breach are contained in Sch.8 paras.13 and 14 of the CJA 2003.

Either the offender or the responsible officer can apply to the court for the order to be revoked or for revocation and an alternative form of sentencing. The application will be heard in magistrates' or Crown Court depending on where the order was made or, in the case of a Crown Court order, whether a direction was included that breach matters were to be dealt with by a magistrates' court.

Revocation may take place where the court considers that it would be in the interests of justice having regard to the circumstances that have arisen since the order was made. This does not necessarily imply a change in circumstances. Indeed the circumstances being considered may involve a failure to change where change might have been anticipated or hoped for, for instance, where a sex offender attended a programme but maintained the same pattern of behaviour.

More positively, an application for revocation may be made where an offender has made good progress or has responded satisfactorily to treatment.

Revocation and resentencing may also be requested where an offender's situation has changed and the order has become impracticable. This may occur where an offender takes up a job travelling away from home or with a shift pattern that would make it difficult to complete the order. It may also include situations where an offender withdraws consent to a requirement relating to drug, alcohol or mental health treatment.

Where an application is made in these circumstances, it is generally understood that the court will not sentence to custody. However, the court has to balance the interests of the offender and the public.

VI. Powers to amend community orders

Under para.17 of Sch.8 to the CJA 2003, *the appropriate court*, on the application of the offender or the responsible officer, may amend a community order either by cancelling any of the requirements of the order or by replacing any of those requirements with a requirement of the same kind. That is, the court may substitute one activity for another or vary the conditions of an exclusion requirement, for example, but cannot substitute one requirement for another different requirement.

Appropriate court in this instance means:

(a) the court responsible for overseeing and reviewing any drug rehabilitation requirement;

(b) the Crown Court, where the order does not include a direction for failure to comply with requirements to be dealt with in a magistrates' court; and

(c) for all other orders, the magistrates' court acting for the local justice area (LJA) specified in the order.

The most basic amendment relates to changing the LJA where an offender has moved or proposes to change address. However, issues may arise where the new area does not have provision for carrying out a particular requirement. For example, a specific accredited programme may not be available there. In these circumstances, the court must cancel the requirement or make appropriate changes so that the offender will be able to complete the requirement in the new area. The court could, for instance, substitute one accredited groupwork programme for another. In doing so, it follows that the court should ensure that any altered requirement represents an equivalent restriction of liberty. This administrative procedure does not require the attendance of the offender at court but it would be good practice for him or her to attend and he or she should have notice of the application.

A medical practitioner responsible for drug, alcohol or mental health treatment conditions may find that treatment needs to be extended or perhaps alternative treatments offered. There may also be instances where an offender is found not to be susceptible to treatment. If the medical practitioner is of the opinion that the treatment requirement should be amended or is him or herself unwilling to continue to treat or direct the treatment of the offender for whatever reason, this should be reported in writing to the responsible officer who will then apply to the court under para.17.

The court cannot make amendments to mental health treatment, drug rehabilitation or alcohol treatment requirements without the consent of the offender. If consent is not given to a proposed amendment, under para.17 of Sch.8, the court then has the option of revoking the order and re-sentencing, and this may include a custodial sentence where the offence involved is punishable by imprisonment.

Under para.20, the standard 12-month period set by s.200 for completion of an unpaid work requirement can be extended. Again, in making a decision, the court must consider the interests of justice and the circumstances of the case.

The court cannot amend an order whilst an appeal is pending.

VII. Further convictions

Unlike suspended sentence orders, commission of a further offence during the currency of a community order does not in itself constitute a breach of the order.

In dealing with the new offence, the court will look at the existing order and consider what would be in the interests of justice, having regard to circumstances that have arisen since the order was made and taking into account the extent of compliance with the order.

The court may choose to leave the existing order in place and to sentence separately for the new offence. If the new sentence is another community order, the court must consider whether any new requirements would be compatible with the requirements on the original order.

However, in many instances, it may be more appropriate and less confusing for the offender to create one new sentence to cover both old and new offences. The court may therefore consider the viability of revoking the existing order and its powers in these circumstances can be summarised as:

Current order	New offence(s)	Court powers
Existing order made in Magistrates' Court	New offence(s) in Magistrates' Court	May revoke order or revoke and re-sentence
Existing order made at Crown Court	New offence(s) in Magistrates' Court	May commit to Crown Court, bail or remand defendant
Existing order made at Crown Court	New offence(s) in Crown Court	May revoke order or revoke and re-sentence
Existing order made in Magistrates' Court	New offence(s) in Crown Court	May revoke order or revoke and re-sentence

Chapter 5
THE SUSPENDED SENTENCE ORDER

Legal basis for the order

Section 189 of the CJA 2003 introduces the suspended sentence order (SSO) which has been available to the courts since April 4, 2005 for offences committed on or after that date.

The SSO allows the court, when it imposes a short custodial sentence, to suspend the period of imprisonment and to require the offender to comply with supervision in the community for a specified period. Breach or further convictions could result in the custodial sentence being activated.

The court can order the offender to comply with the same range of requirements available in relation to the community order. In this respect the SSO significantly blurs the distinction between community and custodial provisions. However, it remains a custodial sentence even where the offender complies with requirements in the community and so does not serve a period in custody. **The court must consider that the "so serious" threshold for custody has been met before it can make an SSO.**

In making an SSO, the court must determine three different time periods:

(a) the "*operational period*"—the length of time that the order is in force, which must be between 6 and 24 months;

(b) the "*supervision period*"—the period during which all the requirements must be completed. Again this is between 6 and 24 months and must fall within the operational period; and

(c) the "*custodial period*"—the maximum time that would be spent in prison if the custodial element is activated.

In the Crown Court the custodial period cannot exceed 12 months. If sentencing for more than one offence, the court can order custodial periods to be served consecutively, so long as these do not exceed an aggregate of 12 months.

The period that can be given for each individual offence in the magistrates' court is shorter, with a maximum custodial period of six months. However, magistrates can also give consecutive sentences for multiple offences up to an aggregate of 12 months.

When sentencing for multiple offences, the court cannot impose a community order at the same time as making an SSO.

The court must order the offender to comply with one or more requirement falling within s.190(i) during the supervision period. These requirements are:

- unpaid work requirement;
- activity requirement;
- programme requirement;

- prohibited activity requirement;
- curfew requirement;
- exclusion requirement;
- residence requirement;
- mental health treatment requirement;
- drug rehabilitation requirement;
- alcohol treatment requirement;
- supervision requirement; and
- attendance centre requirement (for offenders under 25 years).

In combining requirements, the court must be satisfied that they are compatible with each other and that they represent a proportionate restriction of liberty.

The details of these requirements are given in full in Chapter 4.

I. General observations

The Sentencing Guidelines Council guidelines indicate that the length of a custodial sentence should not be increased simply because it is suspended. They suggest that the custodial period should be the same as it would have been if an immediate term of imprisonment had been imposed, and that the operational period should reflect the length of sentence being suspended.

In looking at restriction of liberty, the Sentencing Guidelines Council is of the opinion that the custodial element is in itself a deterrent and punishment. Despite the fact that SSO's are likely to be made for offences which are more serious than community orders, this must be reflected in the range of community requirements imposed in the order:

> "Because of the very clear deterrent threat involved in a suspended sentence, requirements imposed as part of that sentence should generally be less onerous than those imposed as part of a community sentence. A court wishing to impose onerous or intensive requirements on an offender should reconsider its decision to suspend sentence and consider whether a community sentence might be more appropriate."

> (Sentencing Guidelines Council, 2005: 25)

Because the maximum length of an SSO is 24 months, the length of time certain requirements can run on an SSO is less than would be possible on a community order. For instance, a prohibited activity requirement can be imposed for a maximum of 24 months, whereas on a community order it could last for 36 months. The next section outlines the differences in more detail.

II. Requirements on the suspended sentence order

The general requirements in community orders to keep in touch with the supervising officer and inform him or her of any change of address apply equally to SSO's. The 12 additional requirements relating to the community order are detailed in Chapter 4. These are available for use on SSO's with the following amendments:

- Section 200(4) stipulates that an unpaid work requirement continues until the offender has worked the specified number of hours, but it cannot extend beyond the operational period of the SSO.

- The maximum duration of certain requirements is 24 months rather than 36, in line with the statutory maximum operational term for the SSO. This applies to the following requirements:

  - supervision;

  - prohibited activity;

  - residence;

  - alcohol treatment;

  - drug rehabilitation;

  - mental health treatment; and

  - exclusion (although it is unlikely that an exclusion requirement would be given for this maximum term).

III. Breach of suspended sentence orders

The distinctions between a community order and an SSO become most apparent when dealing with breach matters:

> "When sentencing for breach of a community order, the primary objective is to ensure that the requirements of the order are complied with. When responding to breach of a suspended sentence, the statutory presumption is that a custodial sentence will be activated."

(Sentencing Guidelines Council, 2008: 164)

In addition to this central difference in purpose, further convictions during the operational period represent a breach of an SSO, which is not the case for a community order.

Schedule 12 of the CJA 2003 contains the powers relating to breach or amendment of SSO's. Appendix D contains the text of this Schedule.

Unlike community orders, SSOs can be made subject to periodic review and, where this is the case, the court responsible for the review will also deal with breach matters.

Crown Court orders will ordinarily be returned to Crown Court although, in some instances, the Crown Court in making an order will specify that any breach of community requirements may be dealt with by a magistrates' court. However, even where the magistrates' court is empowered to deal with the breach, the magistrates may still commit the offender to custody or release on bail until he or she can be brought before the Crown Court, if they feel that their powers are insufficient.

If the court is satisfied that the offender has failed without reasonable excuse to comply with any of the requirements of the order or he or she is convicted of an offence during the operational period of the order (and the court has the power to deal with the SSO), the court may:

- order the offender to serve the whole of the custodial period that had been suspended; or

- order the offender to serve a custodial period shorter than the one originally suspended.

The presumption is that a custodial period will be imposed. However, under para.8(3), if the court considers this would be unjust in view of the all the circumstances, it must do one of the following:

- impose more onerous community requirements;
- extend the operational period (subject to the maximum of 2 years); or
- extend the supervision period (subject to the maximum of 2 years and providing it does not then exceed the operational period).

In deciding what action to take, the court must take into account the extent to which the offender has complied with the community requirements and, where the offender has been convicted of a subsequent offence, the facts of the offence.

The power of the court to make a custodial sentence is limited to the period specified when the SSO was made. The court cannot revoke and re-sentence as it can do with a community order and therefore the sanctions for breach may in fact be less punitive. This was confirmed in the case of *R. v Phipps* (2008) Crim. L.R. 398 in which the Court of Appeal commented that:

> "The lesson to be learned from all this is where a judge feels able to take a merciful course .... it is much better to pass a community order, spelling out to the offender the consequences of a breach, rather than a suspended sentence artificially low in its terms."

(i) Powers of the court when the order has expired

Once the operational period has expired, the court is unable to make amendments to an order. The court is also unable to re-sentence for the original offences. This means that in dealing with a breach when the SSO is no longer in force, the only action available to the court is to activate the custodial period in part or in full. In doing so, the court must take account of the extent to which the offender complied with the requirements of the SSO whilst it was in force. If the offender is in breach of the SSO through committing a new offence or offences, the court must take also consider the facts of the subsequent offence(s).

(ii) Breach by virtue of further conviction

Where the court dealing with the new conviction is also *the appropriate court* in relation to breach matters on the SSO, the process could be relatively straightforward as the court is able to decide how to proceed on both matters together.

The Crown Court, if convicting of new offences, can deal with an SSO made in magistrates' court. However, it is less simple where the situation is reversed. A magistrates' court has no powers in relation to an SSO breached by virtue of new offences, even where the Crown Court in making the order has given a direction that the magistrates' court is able to deal with breach of community requirements.

The issue of magistrates' court powers was clarified in two appeal cases, *R. v Majury* and *R. v Burbridge and Parkes* [2007] EWCA Crim 2968. The Court of Appeal confirmed that:

(a) where a Crown Court makes an SSO and directs that the magistrates' court can deal with any breach of community requirements, this does not extend to breaches comprising commission of a further offence; and

(b) para.11(2) of the CJA 2003 provides the means by which the Crown Court is made aware of further convictions in the magistrates' court, but cannot be used to commit new offences to be dealt with in Crown Court. Should the magistrates wish to do this, they may use the provisions of Powers of the Criminal Courts (Sentencing) Act 2000 (PCC(S)A 2000).

A question may also arise in cases where the new offences are unrelated to the offence or offences for which the SSO was made, and particularly where these are not imprisonable offences. This was the subject of appeal in *Nobbs v the Director of Public Prosecutions* [2008] EWHC 1653. The Divisional Court ruled that, although an excess alcohol offence, if sentenced in its own right, would not warrant custody, in this case it was significant that it was committed during the operational period of an SSO. The original sentencing court had also looked at the circumstances in the round and had recognised that the offender had patterns of alcohol-related offending and lack of commitment to the community requirements on the SSO, as well as breaches of previous community sentences. The Divisional Court therefore ruled that the custodial sentence was just and in line with sentencing guidelines.

(iii) Extent of compliance with community requirements

Clearly in determining what might be a just response to an enforcement case, the court may need to make complex judgments about the extent of compliance and the active participation or otherwise of an offender in interventions. It may be that the relevance of extent of compliance may differ between cases in breach because of further offending and those in breach through non-compliance.

In the case of *R. v Sheppard* [2008] EWCA Crim 799 the Court of Appeal considered the effect of compliance and how it might affect activation of the custodial element of a suspended sentence. Sheppard argued that he had complied in part with his SSO and that the court, at his third breach hearing, had been wrong in law to impose the whole of the original custodial term.

The Court of Appeal stated that the assessment of compliance is relevant to both the decision whether or not to activate and, separately, the decision about how much of the prison sentence should be served.

In this instance, the Court of Appeal did not consider it unjust to require the offender to serve a prison sentence. In terms of the second decision, it viewed the level of compliance as "dilatory, spasmodic and grudging". Therefore it was right not to reduce the prison term. Credit should not automatically be given for any extent of compliance. Coulson J. observed:

> "Community orders and suspended sentences are seen by some sections of the public as a soft alternative to prison. For the public to have confidence in them, they must be properly enforced by the courts. If there are repeated breaches, as there were in this case, then defendants must know they will face the probability that the full sentence originally imposed will be reactivated ..... it is also important that the probation service knows that the court may well impose full terms when community service orders and suspended sentence orders are breached; they can then give a clear message to those who are subject to such orders."

IV. Review of suspended sentence orders

In making an SSO, the court is able to stipulate that the order should be periodically reviewed. In most instances, the review will be the responsibility of the sentencing court, but in situations where, for example, the offender lives in a different area and will be supervised in that area, another court may be identified in the order for the purposes of review. Section 191(2) specifically precludes review of drug rehabilitation requirements because these are separately reviewed under the provisions of s.210.

At a review hearing, the court may:

- amend the community requirements on the order;

- impose different community requirements if the offender consents;

- amend mental health and alcohol treatment requirements if the offender consents;

- amend the supervision period subject to the six month minimum and two year maximum periods allowed; and

- adjust the intervals of periodic reviews.

The court cannot:

- alter the operational period of the order; or

- amend the order whilst an appeal is pending unless the offender consents.

In the first instance, the offender is required to attend review hearings. However, if at a subsequent review, the court considers that the offender is making satisfactory progress, it may direct that future reviews can take place without him or her attending (s.192(4)). Subsequently, if the court sees that progress is no longer satisfactory, it may again require the offender to appear before it at a specific time and place (s.192(5)).

Where a court holds a review hearing and is of the opinion that the offender has failed to comply with community requirements, s.192(6) allows the court to adjourn for the purposes of dealing with the case under para.8 of Sch.12.

V. Powers to amend suspended sentence orders

Under Sch.12 para.15, *the appropriate court*, on the application of the offender or the responsible officer, may amend an SSO either by cancelling any or all of the requirements of the order or by replacing any of those requirements with a requirement of the same kind. The court may substitute one accredited groupwork programme for another or vary the conditions of a prohibited activity requirement, for example, but cannot substitute one requirement for another different requirement.

Appropriate court in this instance means:

(a) the court responsible for overseeing and reviewing any SSO subject to review;

(b) the Crown Court, where the order does not include a direction for failure to comply with requirements to be dealt with in a magistrates' court; and

(c) for all other orders, the magistrates' court acting for the LJA specified in the order.

The most basic amendment relates to changing the LJA where an offender has moved or proposes to change address. However, issues may arise where the new area does not have provision for carrying out a particular requirement, for instance, a specific activity is not available there. In these circumstances, the court must cancel the requirement or make appropriate changes so that the offender will be able to complete the requirement in the new area.

A medical practitioner responsible for drug, alcohol or mental health treatment conditions may find that treatment needs to be extended or perhaps alternative treatments offered. There may also be instances where an offender is found not to be susceptible to treatment. Similarly, if the medical practitioner is of the opinion that the treatment requirement should be amended or is him or herself unwilling to continue to treat or direct the treatment of the offender for whatever reason, this should be reported in writing to the responsible officer who will then apply to the court under para.15.

The court cannot make amendments to mental health treatment, drug rehabilitation or alcohol treatment requirements without the consent of the offender. If consent is not given to a proposed amendment, under para.15(4) of Sch.12, the court then has the option of revoking the order and re-sentencing.

Under para.20, the standard 12-month period set by s.200 of the CJA 2003 for completion of an unpaid work requirement can be extended. Again, in making a decision, the court must consider the interests of justice and the circumstances of the case.

Chapter 6
SENTENCES OF IMMEDIATE IMPRISONMENT FOR ADULTS

I. Overview of custodial sentences and supervision on release

The range of custodial sentences currently being served by prisoners is complex. Although the sentencing framework was rationalised by the CJA 2003 and new public protection sentences introduced, many offenders who are serving longer sentences or who are under supervision on release from prison were sentenced under the previous arrangements. The CJA 1991 established a "just deserts" sentencing framework based on proportionality and the seriousness of the offences being sentenced. Proportionality still features in the CJA 2003, but there is a more varied mix of concerns amongst which risk and prevention of offending are much more prominent. Sentencing has moved from looking backwards at the harm caused by past offences to a focus on risk and prevention of future offences: the types of custodial sentences accordingly look strikingly different in line with this shift.

The CJA 2003 sentencing provisions became available on April 4, 2005, for offences committed on or after that date. The other critical dates to note in reading this and the next chapter are June 9, 2008 and July 14, 2008 when provisions in the CJ&IA 2008 relating to release and recall came into force.

This chapter begins with an account of all the sentences available for offenders aged 18 or over when convicted, and discusses the licences and licence conditions applicable on release. The following chapter moves on to outline the processes by which offenders can be recalled to prison and the changed role of the Parole Board in relation to the release of long-term prisoners and to recalled prisoners.

The chapter makes extensive reference to the National Offender Management Service (NOMS) Public Protection Casework Section (PPCS), details of which are available for probation staff via the EPIC system.

II. Short custodial sentences

(i)   Adult offenders

Legal basis for sentences under 12 months

The CJA 2003 provided for a new kind of short custodial sentence with extended supervision period ("custody plus") but, unlike SSOs, these provisions have not been implemented. This means that prison sentences of under 12 months are still dealt with under s.33 of the CJA 1991, which requires that prisoners are released at the half way point of their sentence and remain "at risk" for the remainder of the period. Therefore, if an offender commits another imprisonable offence before the end of the sentence (the sentence expiry date or SED) he or she will be liable to be returned to prison to serve the rest of the sentence.

Release on licence

Offenders released from these short sentences after their 22nd birthday will not be under any form of licence unless:

- released early on a home detention curfew (HDC); or
- returned to prison under s.40a of the CJA 1991 and the total period of recall + any sentence for the new offence is less than 12 months. In this relatively rare situation, the offender will be issued with a three month licence when re-released and will be under the supervision of the probation service.

Enforcement

Breach of a s.40A licence would be prosecuted through the courts.

(ii) Offenders aged 18–21

Legal basis for sentences under 12 months

Young offenders on short sentences are sentenced under the Powers of the Criminal Court (Sentencing) Act 2000 (PCC(S)A 2000) to Detention in a Young Offender Institution.

Release on licence

Unlike offenders over the age of 21, young offenders are automatically released into the supervision of the probation service. Supervision will be for a minimum of three months or until the young person's 22nd birthday if that falls before the end of the three month period. The supervision period may therefore extend beyond the end of the sentence.

Supervision can operate through two different mechanisms:

- A licence attached to an HDC.
- A notice of supervision under s.65 of the CJA 1991.

Where an HDC is to run for less than three months, a notice of supervision will be issued to cover the period after it expires until the three-month point. The basic conditions are the same in both but there are extra requirements in the HDC licence relating to the curfew.

Enforcement

Failure to comply with the conditions of the HDC can result in recall to prison, rather than a summons to court (see section V of this chapter).

Breach of notice of supervision is dealt with by the court which has the power to fine or to order a further custodial sentence of up to 30 days. The court can also recall the offender to prison if convicted of a new offence, in addition to any penalty imposed for the new offence (s.116 of the PCC(S)A 2000), providing the notice of supervision is still in force.

III. Determinate sentences over 12 months

(i)   Standard Determinate Sentences (SDS)

Legal basis for the SDS

The SDS was established by Ch.6 of the CJA 2003, replacing the previous arrangements that had been in place since the CJA 1991. This eradicates the differences in the previous system between sentences of less than four years and sentences of four years or more. SDSs can be made for any fixed period from 12 months upwards and have been available since April 4, 2005 for offences committed on or after that date.

Release on licence

Section 244 provides for SDS prisoners to be released at the halfway point of their sentence. They will then be subject to licence under s.249 until the sentence expiry date.

Previously HDC was only available for prisoners serving less than four years, whereas all prisoners are now considered for HDC unless they are ineligible.

Enforcement

Enforcement of SDSs is through the Secretary of State's powers of executive recall rather than through the courts by virtue of s.254 (and s.255 for those breaching HDC conditions).

(ii)   Discretionary Conditional Release (DCR)

Legal basis for the DCR scheme

There are still a considerable number of long-term prisoners in the prison system who are serving fixed term sentences of four years or more for offences committed before April 4, 2005 when the SDS became available. These prisoners are subject to the DCR scheme established by Pt II of the CJA 1991—the discretionary element relating to the possibility of an earlier release on parole depending on the prisoner's progress in custody and assessment of risk.

The release and licence arrangements for certain DCR prisoners were changed by the CJ&IA 2008, and these changes will be detailed after an overview of the original DCR scheme.

The DCR scheme as established by the CJA 1991

Release on licence

DCR prisoners are eligible for release on parole licence at the halfway point of their sentence (s.35(1)). If parole is not granted, the offender would be automatically released two-thirds of the way through the sentence and would be supervised on licence until the three-quarters point (ss.33 and 37(1)). From the three-quarter point to the end of the sentence, the offender would be in the "at risk" period and could be recalled to prison if convicted of further imprisonable offences.

The offender could therefore be subject to two different types of licence on release. A four-year (48-month) DCR sentence is illustrated below:

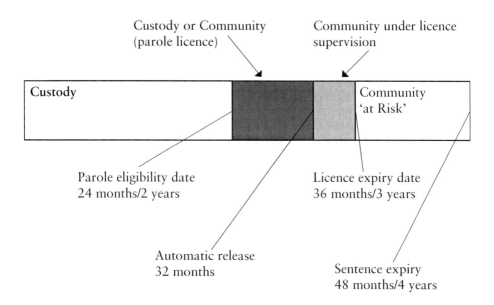

Custody or Community (parole licence)

Community under licence supervision

Custody

Community 'at Risk'

Parole eligibility date
24 months/2 years

Licence expiry date
36 months/3 years

Automatic release
32 months

Sentence expiry
48 months/4 years

Enforcement

The original CJA 1991 framework specified that enforcement and recall would be effected through the Parole Board during the period of parole licence. The standard supervision licence running from the end of parole to the licence expiry date would be enforced through the courts.

Changes to the DCR scheme

The arrangements described above are complicated and have been subsequently simplified by s.26 of the CJ&IA 2008. The changes apply to DCR prisoners who reach the halfway point of their sentence—or parole eligibility date—on or after June 9, 2008. These offenders will be automatically released at that half-way point and will be supervised on licence for the remainder of their sentence, unless recalled. This effectively eliminates the "at risk" period.

Prisoners who are serving sentences for sexual or violent offences specified in Sch.15 of the CJA 2003 are exempt from these new arrangements and, along with prisoners who have a parole eligibility date falling before June 9, 2008, will continue to be dealt with under the original DCR arrangements outlined above.

(iii) Extended sentences

Legal basis of extended sentences

Extended sentences essentially refer to extended periods of licence supervision, rather than longer periods in custody. These sentences are available in respect of sexual and violent offences under two separate sets of legal provisions.

Section 85 of the PCC(S)A 2000 (formerly s.58 of the C&DA 1998)

These provisions apply only to offenders convicted of a sexual or violent offence committed after September 30, 1998 and before April 4, 2005. They permitted judges to pass a custodial sentence proportionate to the offence but to add a further period on licence supervision where the court considered that the normal period of supervision under the CJA 1991 would not be adequate to prevent the offender committing further offences and to secure rehabilitation. Supervision therefore extends to the end of the sentence and throughout the extension period.

Section 85 could only be used for violent offences where the custodial term was four years or more but there was no lower limit in respect of sexual offences.

The maximum extension period for violent offences was 5 years and for sexual offences 10 years, but the court could not exceed the maximum penalty in law for the offence(s) in question.

Section 227 of the CJA 2003

The CJA 2003 put in place more substantial arrangements for extended sentences alongside the new sentence of imprisonment for public protection (s.225).

Sections 225 and 227 both refer to a lengthy list of "specified" sexual and violent offences contained in Sch.15 to the Act. The more restrictive s.225 sentences are applicable where the offender has been convicted of a *serious offence* and the court is of the opinion that there is a *significant risk of serious harm* through the offender committing further specified offences.

Serious offence is defined in s.224(2) as an offence punishable in the case of a person aged 18 or over by life imprisonment or by a determinate sentence of 10 years or more. *Serious harm* in s.224(3) refers to death or serious personal injury, whether physical or psychological.

Originally extended sentences could only be made where the conviction was for a *specified offence* but not a *serious offence*. However amendments introduced by the CJ&IA 2008 have ensured that:

- the provisions for extended sentences can now be applied where the conviction is for a serious *offence;*

- extended sentences should only be imposed where the seriousness of the offence would justify a custodial term of four years or more; and

- where the criteria are met, the court may rather than must impose an extended sentence.

The effect of this is to target the use of extended sentences at more serious offences and to allow more discretion in their use.

The court should determine the appropriate custodial term (not exceeding the maximum term in law for the offence(s) in question). It will then set the extended licence period which should be whatever length the court considers necessary for the purposes of protecting the public and preventing the offender committing further specified offences (s.227(2)). The extended licence period is determined more by assessment of potential future risk than by the seriousness of the offence(s) but should still be a proportionate response to risk with regard to the rights of the offender.

The maximum terms for the extension periods are 5 years for a specified violent offence and 10 years for a specified sexual offence. However, the total sentence including the extension period cannot exceed the maximum term in law permitted for that offence.

Release on licence

Prisoners serving extended sentences were originally only released on the approval of the Parole Board and, in theory, could be held until the end of their custodial term, being released for the extended licence period only. However, by virtue of the CJ&IA 2008, as of July 14, 2008, these prisoners are now released automatically half way through their custodial term.

Enforcement

Offenders on both types of extended sentence may be recalled to prison under the executive powers of the Secretary of State.

IV. Indeterminate sentences

(i)   Imprisonment for Public Protection (IPP) sentences

Legal basis for IPP sentences

IPP sentences were introduced by s.225 of the CJA 2003 and are available for offenders aged 18 and over convicted of *serious offences* committed on or after April 4, 2005. *Serious offence* is defined in s.224(2) as an offence punishable in the case of an adult aged 18 or over by life imprisonment or by a determinate sentence of 10 years or more.

The criteria for the sentence are:

- conviction for a *specified offence* contained in sch.15 of the Act;
- the offence is also a *serious offence*;
- the offence does not attract a mandatory life sentence and the court does not consider it sufficiently serious to justify a discretionary life sentence; and
- the court is nevertheless of the opinion that there is a *significant risk* to members of the public of *serious harm* through the offender committing further specified offences. *Serious harm* is defined in s.224(3) as death or serious personal injury, whether physical or psychological.

In these circumstances the legislation originally required the court to pass a sentence of an indeterminate period of imprisonment in order to protect the public from further serious harm (s.225(3)). However, from July 14, 2008, the court has had discretion to impose an extended sentence instead.

At the time of sentencing, the judge will determine the minimum term the offender will serve in prison, known as the *tariff*. For IPP sentences this should be at least two years (s.225(3b)). The prisoner cannot be released on parole until the tariff period has been served and may be held for considerably longer, depending on the assessment of risk. IPP prisoners are subject to the same processes as life sentence prisoners under the Generic Parole Process introduced on April 1, 2009.

Release on licence

An IPP prisoner will only be released under a direction from the Parole Board and will remain on licence for a minimum of 10 years. After this period, the licence may be revoked by the Secretary of State on the recommendation of the Parole Board, who must review the case annually.

As with life sentences, the supervision element can be suspended after the offender has experienced a minimum of four years "trouble-free existence in the community". However, this provision does not apply where the index offence is of a sexual nature.

Enforcement

Offenders on IPP sentences may be recalled to prison under the executive powers of the Secretary of State. The powers to do so are contained in s.32 of the Crime (Sentences) Act 1997 as amended by Sch.18 to the CJA 2003.

(ii) Discretionary and mandatory life sentences

Legal basis for life sentences

Life sentences are either mandatory, in the case of murder, or discretionary and the legal provisions vary according to the age of the offender at the time of conviction.

Briefly, the arrangements are as follows:

Mandatory life sentences

Over 21

Life imprisonment (s.1(1) of the Murder (Abolition of the Death Penalty) Act 1965).

18–20 at the time of conviction

Custody for life (s.93, of the PPC(S)A 2000). Prior to this Act, sentences would have been imposed under s.8(1) of the CJA 1982.

Under 18

Detention During Her Majesty's Pleasure (s.90, of the PPC(S)A 2000). Prior to this Act, the relevant legislation was s.53(1) of the Children and Young Persons Act 1933.

Discretionary life sentences

Over 21

Life imprisonment.

18–20 at the time of conviction

Custody for life (s.94, of the PPC(S)A 2000). Previously the legislation was s.8(2) of the CJA 1982.

Under 18

Detention For Life (s.91, of the PPC(S)A 2000). Prior to this Act, the relevant powers were contained in ss.53(2) and (3) of the Children and Young Persons Act 1933.

Under ss.225 and 226 of the CJA 2003 there is a statutory requirement for the court to pass a discretionary life sentence where the court considers this is justified by the gravity of the offence.

As with IPP sentences a tariff or minimum term to be served in prison will be determined at the time of sentencing by the judge. The lifer system is overseen by specialist teams within the PPCS in NOMS, who work with the Parole Board to ensure that prisoners serving life sentences and IPP sentences are reviewed appropriately and progress through the various stages of their sentence.

Release on licence

A life sentence prisoner is released on life licence which extends for the rest of his or her life unless it is revoked and the prisoner returned to prison. However, the supervision element of the licence may be suspended after a satisfactory period of progress in the community. Prison Service Order 4700 ("The Indeterminate Sentence Manual") para.13.9.2 suggests this should be a minimum of four "trouble-free" years but for lifers convicted of sexual offences will be for a minimum of 10 years (Sch.18, to the CJA 2003).

Provisions relating to licence release are contained in s.31 of the Crime (Sentences) Act 1997 which was amended to cover offenders sentenced under s.225 of the CJA 2003 by Sch.18 of that Act.

The supervision of indeterminate sentences is a complex business and is dealt with in more depth in *A Companion Guide to Life Sentences, 2nd edn* by Neil Stone.

Enforcement

Offenders on life licences may be recalled to prison under the executive powers of the Secretary of State. The powers to do so are contained in s.32 of the Crime (Sentences) Act 1997.

V. Home Detention Curfews

HDC provisions allow prisoners to be released earlier than their normal statutory release date and there are additional considerations where offenders are subject to these different licence arrangements.

Although HDC arrangements predate the CJA 2003, in practice most sentences currently involving HDC will do so by virtue of s.246 of the CJA 2003. This allows for certain prisoners to be released from prison subject to an electronically monitored curfew up to 135 days before the half-way point of sentence.

Most prisoners will be considered for HDC but categories of offenders who are ineligible include those who are:

- serving extended sentences for violent or sexual offences;
- subject to hospital orders and various provisions under the Mental Health Act 1983;
- subject to the notification requirements of the Sexual Offences Act 2003 (SOA 2003);

- serving a sentence imposed under Sch.8 of the CJA 2003 for failing to comply with a curfew requirement on a community order; and

- serving a sentence of four years or more under the CJA 1991.

Other offenders are not excluded by law but would usually be presumed unsuitable for HDC. These include offenders who:

- are serving a prison sentence of four years or more under the CJA 2003;

- have current offences indicating risk—e.g. cruelty to children, causing an explosion, possession of firearms with intent;

- are convicted of homicide or related offences, and

- have past sexual offences (excluding prostitution, soliciting and consensual adult homosexual activity in private).

Breach of HDC under s.255 of the CJA 2003 is notified to the relevant team in the NOMS PPCS by the monitoring contractor. Where an offender is under probation supervision, the offender manager should be notified also.

If an offender on HDC breaches not the HDC but another licence condition, the offender manager (OM) will initiate recall under s.254 of the CJA 2003 (or will lay an information before the court if the statutory supervision is by virtue of a young offender notice of supervision).

VI. Setting licence conditions—appropriate and enforceable?

All licences contain standard sets of conditions and these vary according to the type of sentence imposed and the age of the offender. Although a notice of supervision for young offenders (s.65 of the CJA 1991) cannot have extra conditions imposed, there are provisions that allow additional conditions to be added to licences under other legislative provisions. Such specific conditions should be proportionate to the risk involved in the particular case and should be justified on the grounds of public protection. This section will discuss these issues and also concerns about offender rights and legitimacy.

(i) Standard conditions for prisoners on determinate sentences

Licence conditions for SDS prisoners are set out by SI 2005/648 and this is used as guidance for licence conditions for DCR prisoners sentenced under the CJA 1991 also.

The standard conditions are as follows:

(a) To keep in touch with your supervising officer in accordance with any instructions you may be given.

(b) If required, to receive visits from your supervising officer at your home/place of residence (e.g. approved premises).

(c) Permanently to reside at an address approved by your supervising officer and notify him or her in advance of any proposed changes of address or any proposed stay (even for one night) away from that approved address.

(d) To undertake only such work (including voluntary work) approved by your supervising officer and notify him or her in advance of any change.

(e)   Not to travel outside the United Kingdom unless otherwise directed by your supervising officer (permission for which will be given in exceptional circumstances only) or for the purposes of complying with immigration deportation/removal.

(f)   To be well behaved, not to commit any offence and not to do anything that could undermine the purpose of your supervision, which is to protect the public, prevent you from re-offending and help you re-settle successfully into the community.

(ii)   Standard conditions for prisoners on indeterminate sentences

Life licences are issued under s.28(5) of the Crime (Sentencing) Act 1997 and IPP prisoners are also released under the provisions of the 1997 Act by virtue of Sch.18 of the CJA 2003.

The standard conditions are as follows:

(a)   He/she shall place himself/herself under the supervision of whichever supervising officer is nominated for the purpose from time to time.

(B)   He/she shall on release report to the supervising officer so nominated and shall keep in touch with that officer in accordance with that officer's instructions.

(c)   He/she shall, if his/her supervising officer so requires, receive visits from that officer where the licence holder is living.

(d)   He/she shall reside only where approved by his/her supervising officer.

(e)   He/she shall undertake work, including voluntary work, only where approved by his/her supervising officer and shall inform that officer of any change in or loss of such employment.

(f)   He/she shall not travel outside the United Kingdom without the prior permission of his/her supervising officer.

(g)   He/she shall be well behaved and not do anything which could undermine the purposes of supervision on licence which are to protect the public, by ensuring that their safety would not be placed at risk, and to secure his/her successful reintegration into the community.

(iii)   The *be of good behaviour* condition

This is a general condition that empowers the offender manager to respond to a variety of circumstances not covered by other licence conditions, including additional conditions that have been added.

PC 29/2007 describes this condition as:

"Designed to be a catch all condition that covers a pattern of behaviour or incident, whether foreseen or unforeseen, which gives rise to an increase in risk of serious harm or likelihood of reconviction and where no specific additional conditions have been included on the licence."

(National Probation Service, 2007b: 3)

One of the instances covered by this condition would be a failure to abide by hostel rules for an offender living in Approved Premises, so there is no necessity for an additional condition referring specifically to hostel rules and regulations.

Any offender found in possession of a Class A drug is automatically in breach of the *good behaviour* condition.

(iv) Additional licence conditions

Offender managers may recommend that additional conditions are added to the licence, or that existing additional conditions are deleted or varied. Even where suggested by a Multi-agency Public Protection Panel or by another agency, such recommendations must be channelled through the offender manager and endorsed by a senior manager from within the probation service.

Additional conditions must be justified as necessary:

- to ensure protection of the public;
- to prevent re-offending; and/or
- to secure the successful re-integration of the offender into the community.

They must also be lawful, that is, authorised by SI 2005/648 of 2005 and compliant with art.8 of the ECHR (right to respect for private and family life). As highlighted in PC 29/2007, this means that *a condition must be a necessary and proportionate measure for the purposes of ensuring public safety and/or prevention of crime* (National Probation Service, 2007b). Offender managers should consider whether the *good behaviour* condition would be sufficient to meet the purposes outlined above or whether more specific directions would help make expectations clearer and assist enforcement, where required.

Annex A of PC 29/2007 spells out the full range of additional conditions that may be requested. Briefly, these fall into the following categories:

(a) contact requirement;

(b) prohibited activity requirement;

(c) residency requirement;

(d) prohibited residency requirement;

(e) prohibited contact requirement;

(f) programme requirement;

(g) curfew requirement—currently this can be electronically monitored in only a limited number of areas across the range of offenders and nationally for offenders at MAPPA Level 3;

(h) exclusion requirement—this must specify a geographical area with road boundaries that can be marked on a map which is then given to the offender, prison governor and Parole Board, where appropriate, on release. Care should be taken to ensure that exclusions are not so restrictive that they breach ECHR art.8;

(i) supervision requirement;

(j) non-association requirement—this must name specific individuals rather than being a general prohibition on associating with other offenders.

It is also open to the Secretary of State to impose a drug testing condition on the licence of a Prolific or Other Priority Offender (PPO) where he or she has a substance misuse condition linked to offending and has served the current sentence for a trigger offence (primarily an acquisitive offence) specified in s.64 and Sch.6 of the Criminal Justice and Court Services Act 2000 (as amended). This provision can only be used where necessary and proportionate.

(v)   Judicial recommendations

Under s.238 of the CJA 2003, courts imposing an SDS or extended sentence may recommend additional conditions to be added to a post-release licence at the time of sentence. Information about such recommendations should be forwarded to the OM by the receiving prison shortly after sentence. The probation service has a responsibility to consider judicial recommendations before either standard release or release on HDC.

There is a presumption that such recommendations will be included in the licence, but it is recognised that circumstances or assessment of offender risk may change in the course of the sentence. If this is the case, then the OM should consult the NOMS Public Protection Casework Section and make a case for omitting the condition. Where the condition to be omitted relates to a victim, the victim contact team for the relevant Probation Trust should be involved in discussions.

If a decision is made not to include a judicial recommendation in a post-release licence, the sentencing judge should be informed in writing.

(vi) Requesting additional conditions

The process for requesting additional licence conditions before the offender's release differs according to the sentence being served and is outlined below:

- HDC—within the HDC3 Home Suitability Assessment Report and approved by the prison governor;

- SDS prisoners under the CJA 2003—within the PD1, unless the prisoner is to be released on HDC, and approved by the prison governor;

- extended sentences under the CJA 2003—within the PD1 report and initially approved by the prison governor after consultation with the Parole Board; and

- indeterminate sentences—within the PAROM1 report prepared by the OM and approved by the Parole Board.

The situation with DCR cases under the CJA 1991 differs according to whether the case is due for release under the original provisions or is subject to release at the half-way point under s.26 of the CJ&IA 2008.

For DCR prisoners under the new arrangements, additional conditions should be requested within the PD1 and will be approved by the prison governor. Otherwise:

- DCR prisoners serving less than 15 years—within the PAROM1 Report or, if the prisoner is being released at the non-parole date, the PD1 report prepared before release. Conditions must be approved by the Parole Board; or

- DCR prisoners serving 15 years or more—in the PAROM1 Report or PD1 if the offender is being released at the non-parole date. Conditions must be referred to the Parole Board for consideration who will make a recommendation to the NOMS Public Protection Casework Section which has the final decision.

Post-release the prison governor is responsible for authorising variations to additional conditions for prisoners serving SDSs. For all other prisoners, authorisation is by the PPCS in consultation with the Parole Board.

Full details are contained in Annex C of PC 29/2007. Further guidance and relevant forms in relation to life sentence and IPP licences are contained in Chapter 13 of the Indeterminate Sentence Maual (PSO 4700).

(vii) Bespoke conditions

There may be rare situations where the probation service, either alone or in conjunction with other agencies, considers that additional conditions not in the approved list (Annex A PC 29/2007) are necessary to manage the risk posed by an offender. Approval must be sought in the first instance from the PPCS who are available also to advise on the validity and practicality of monitoring and enforcing any proposed bespoke conditions. As with any additional condition, proportionality and impact on offender rights should also be considered.

(viii) Enforceability of licence conditions

Licence conditions should be clear and specific so that:

- the offender is aware of expectations on release and understands what behaviours or actions would be viewed as non-compliance;
- the conditions effectively address areas of known risk or concern, but are not unduly restrictive or punitive; and
- agencies involved in monitoring the offender are aware of what would represent a breach of the licence conditions and their role and responsibilities in terms of passing on relevant information to the OM.

All of the above are necessary in order to minimise confusion or ambiguity and also to stand the best chance of securing the offender's belief in the legitimacy of the restrictions imposed and therefore his or her compliance.

The specific wording of conditions clearly has a bearing on their enforceability. For example, a condition expressed as:

he shall not misuse substances

begs questions such as:

- what substances is this referring to?
- where does use become misuse?
- what level of drug/alcohol use would therefore be permissable?

This might be more clearly worded as:

he shall not enter licensed premises or consume alcohol

he shall not use Class A drugs

It is helpful for practitioners setting licence conditions to consider the following questions:

- Is it clear what behaviours or actions would constitute a breach of this condition?
- What means do we have of monitoring whether a breach has occurred?
- How would we be able to evidence that a breach has occurred?

For instance, it is relatively easy to see how a curfew condition could be monitored electronically or through staff at an approved premises. If breach action is taken, agency records could then be cited as evidence. Enforcement would be less straightforward at a private address where movements are not monitored in the same way and there are more evident questions about the consistency, timeliness and accuracy of information that might be received from family, partners or other third parties. The practicalities of enforcing a curfew condition in such circumstances would need to be thought through carefully and negotiated with the other individuals involved (including other professionals). This should help ensure that breach action, where warranted, can be effected, but also that the offender is protected against arbitrary and unfair allegations. There are situations, however, where it is preferable not to impose a condition, rather than to impose one that cannot be effectively and fairly enforced.

It is important that the OM fully explains the conditions to the offender at the point of release and outlines what the implications are for him or her, as well as discussing the purpose of each condition, particularly additional conditions. In doing so, it should not be assumed that offenders are necessarily in denial about their risk or unconcerned about managing risk. On the contrary, small scale studies of high risk sex offenders (Attrill and Liell, 2007; Wood and Kemshall, 2007) have shown that they share most of the professionals' concerns about predicting likelihood of re-offending and relevant risk factors.

Transparency and openness about assessment of risk and the decision-making process in setting the terms of conditions can help create a situation in which the offender is more likely to be encouraged to self-manage risk and, certainly, to make more efforts to stay within the perimeters of licence conditions. On the other hand, licence conditions which are poorly expressed and poorly thought out can have the opposite effect, with severe consequences where an offender is manipulative or overtly non-compliant.

The case of Anthony Rice is a salutary instance where a high risk offender was released on a licence containing additional conditions which were worded in an unclear and ambiguous way, creating problems in terms of enforcement and in terms of him challenging the legitimacy and fairness of the restrictions imposed. The sad result in this instance was the death of a young woman, Naomi Bryant. The HMIP report commented that certain licence conditions:

> "Were vulnerable to his challenge partly because they were unusually intrusive and partly because their rationale was unclear. The effect of all of this was to draw attention away from using licence conditions as an aid to effective management of Rice's risk of harm by taking up time debating their purpose and proportionality."

(HMIP, 2006: 38)

Good risk management and effective enforcement relies upon the right foundations being built before release. This involves identifying and including in the licence appropriate conditions with a clear purpose as well as work with the offender and with others involved in monitoring behaviour and progress to establish the legitimacy of licence conditions and to optimise the chances of co-operation and compliance.

Chapter 7
ENFORCING POST-CUSTODY LICENCES AND RECALL

I. Overview of enforcement and recall powers

The provisions for custodial sentences and release on licence detailed in the previous chapter are complex. So too are the various arrangements for the enforcement of licence conditions and recalls to prison, with a significant shift away from the courts and changes in the role of the Parole Board, in favour of powers of executive recall. This permits swifter action than would be possible under more deliberative procedures in line with the current public protection agenda. However, at the same time it raises professional and ethical dilemmas relating to proper processes, appropriate and proportionate actions and the respective rights of offenders, victims and communities.

II. Enforcement through the courts

The role of the magistrates' courts in enforcing licences is much reduced since the introduction of the CJA 2003. The court still deals with breach matters in relation to detention and training orders for offenders convicted under the age of 18 (see chapter 11). For the older age group, however, the enforcement functions of the courts in relation to shorter prison sentences have almost entirely transferred to NOMS, acting on behalf of the Secretary of State for Justice following the introduction of the standard determinate sentence (SDS) by the CJA 2003.

The court nevertheless has residual powers under the CJA 1991 to deal with the following:

* notices of supervision for young offenders aged 18–21 on release from custodial sentences of less than 12 months (s.65(5)); and

* s.40a licences for adult offenders.

Details of these provisions can be found in Chapter 6, Section I (i) and (ii).

This leaves a restricted role for the adult magistrates' court and its due process measures, which have been progressively abandoned in favour of more streamlined procedures and executive recall.

III. The role of the Parole Board

The Parole Board was established in 1968 under the CJA 1967 and became a Non-departmental Public Body in 1996. The Board's main role is to make risk assessments on certain categories of prisoners in order to determine when they are safe to release back into the community and to set the terms of licence conditions. However, its specific functions have expanded and altered as new custodial sentences have become available and also release and recall arrangements have changed.

The independence of the Board—and public confidence in the independence of its decision-making—is critical if it is to fulfil its role effectively. The standing and future of the Parole Board is currently being reviewed by the House of Commons Public Accounts Committee following a decision of the Court of Appeal in the case of *R. (on the application of Brooke) v Parole Board* [2008] EWCA Civ 29. The Court of Appeal upheld the declaration of the Divisional Court that the Parole Board was not sufficiently independent of the Secretary of State as required by both English common law and art.5(4) of the ECHR.

Currently the Parole Board has the following responsibilities:

Offenders on indeterminate sentences:

- Reviewing life sentence and IPP cases whilst in custody and directing release subject to risk assessment.

- Setting the conditions of licence for life sentence and IPP cases, with regard to the recommendations from the prisoner's OM.

- Consultation with the NOMS Public Protection Casework Section where there is a request for changes post-release to a life or an IPP licence.

- Determining the point at which an offender on a life or IPP sentence who has been recalled to prison can be re-released and directing re-release.

- Considering prisoners' representations with regard to their recall, where they wish to challenge the decision to recall or the process of recall.

Offenders on determinate sentences:

- Decisions about release on parole for prisoners on determinate sentences under the CJA 1991 not automatically released at the halfway point of sentence (see Chapter 6)—a decreasing area of work as the number of DCR prisoners continues to fall.

- Consultation with the NOMS Public Protection Casework Section where there is a request for changes post-release to a licence for an offender on a DCR sentence or extended sentence under the CJA 2003.

- Reviewing the cases of offenders on determinate sentences recalled to prison who are not subject to a Fixed Term Recall (FTR) (see Section VII (iii) of this chapter).

- Considering prisoners' representations with regard to their recall, where they wish to challenge the decision to recall or the process of recall.

The CJ&IA 2008 brought about significant changes for the Parole Board. In particular:

(a) Previously life licences could only be revoked on the recommendation of the Board, whereas this decision is now taken by the relevant team in the Public Protection Casework Section.

(b) The Board were required to consider and direct, where appropriate, the release of DCR prisoners at their parole eligibility date and also prisoners serving extended sentences under the CJA 2003 half way through their custodial terms—from July 14, 2008, both of these categories of prisoners have been released automatically at the half-way point.

The Act also introduced fixed-term (28 day) recalls for offenders assessed as lower risk.

The effect of this has been to focus the attention of the Parole Board on life sentence and IPP cases. This has meant a reduction in some aspects of the Board's work that had been dealt with administratively by paper panels and a move towards oral hearings. The Parole Board's Annual Report 2007–8 noted a 12 per cent increase in oral hearings over the previous 12 months, due almost entirely to offenders on IPP sentences. It commented that this is:

> "Increasingly turning the Board into a tribunal or court-based organisation with responsibility for the most serious and dangerous offenders."

(Parole Board, 2008: 4)

The same report indicates the implications of Parole Board hearings becoming more akin to court hearings in terms of process and the recording of proceedings, albeit with an inquisitorial rather than adversarial approach. This is necessarily more resource-intensive and lack of resources has become a significant issue for the Board, impacting on the timeliness and efficiency of its system of oral hearings. This is particularly so as the number of IPP prisoners in the system has been greater than predicted when the CJA 2003 was brought in (House of Commons Public Accounts Committee, 2009).

IV. The NOMS Public Protection Casework Section (PPCS)

Following restructuring within NOMS the PPCS has expanded and now comprises a number of specialist teams. The PPCS has taken over certain administrative responsibilities from the Parole Board and is the point of contact for recalls, thereby speeding up the process of recall particularly in emergency situations.

The current structure of the PPCS includes teams dealing with:

- case management of determinate and indeterminate prisoners before release;
- public protection advocacy (presenting officers who represent the secretary of state at oral hearings considering the re-release of recalled prisoners);
- review of determinate sentence prisoners on standard recall;
- breaches of HDCs and electronic monitoring; and
- 10 recall teams organised on a regional basis.

Details of these teams and relevant contacts are contained in Annex B of PC 14/2008 (National Probation Service 2008b) or, for probation employees, via EPIC.

V. Enforcement and recall procedures

(i) National standards

The initial procedures for enforcement are contained within National Standards 2007. In cases where the failure to comply is not assessed as representing a substantially greater risk to the public, Standard 2f.4 applies. This states that where an offender does not keep an appointment or fails to comply with a requirement of the sentence—as spelt out in the licence conditions—and has not provided an acceptable explanation in advance, he or she will be given a written warning. This should be issued by the end of the 10th working day following the failure to comply.

An offender may have more than one appointment or commitment in relation to licence conditions on any one day. If he or she fails to comply, then this will be treated as a single failure to comply although separate explanations should be sought for each appointment or other failure.

As with failures to comply with requirements of community sentences, the OM must make a judgment about whether any explanation received for a failure is reasonable or not. This decision and any related discussion with senior managers should be clearly noted on the case file.

An offender on licence may receive two written warnings before recall within any 12-month period. The Standard indicates that, on the third failure to comply, recall proceedings should be initiated through the relevant recall team within the PPCS. Any variation from this Standard must be authorised by a senior manager and the basis of any decision not to breach after the third failure to comply should be fully recorded.

However, enforcement action does not have to wait for the third failure to comply and can be started immediately where:

"The failure to comply is indicative of:

- a serious, gross, wilful or fundamental refusal to comply or breakdown of the licence, or;

- a significant rise in the risk of serious harm or likelihood of re-offending presented by the offender.

(MoJ, 2007: 46)

Standard 2f.3 states that where *the failure to comply that the public is at substantially greater risk*, then the OM should request an emergency recall. The appropriate assessment of risk is therefore critical and is discussed further in the following section.

Once the decision to recall has been made, the Request for Recall Form must be completed and submitted to the PPCS within 24 working hours.

(ii) Types of recall

From July 14, 2008, there are three types of recall:

- **Fixed Term** (FTR)—recall for 28 days under s.255A of the CJA 2003, if the offender is assessed as suitable and eligible.

- **Standard**—recall that could result in the offender remaining in custody until the end of sentence.

- **Emergency**—in situations assessed as high risk and for all offenders on indeterminate sentences.

In the Request for Recall Report the OM should identify whether the offender is eligible and suitable for a FTR although the final decision about the type of recall will rest with the PPCS. The presumption is in favour of FTR, but the offender will not be eligible if he or she:

- is serving a life, IPP or extended sentence;

- is serving a sentence for a specified offence under Sch.15 of the CJA 2003;

- has been recalled to prison having been released early on HDC or on compassionate grounds; or
- has been previously recalled on the current sentence and released on FTR.

Suitability must be judged in terms of the potential risk of serious harm and only offenders assessed as low or medium risk will be considered as suitable.

Offenders on determinate sentences who are ineligible or unsuitable will be subject to standard recall, except for the relatively few where emergency procedures are warranted. *However, all indeterminate sentence prisoners will be dealt with as emergency recalls.*

(iii) Request for Recall Reports

For standard recalls and FTRs, the OM must complete a Request for Recall Report which should be endorsed by the line manager and authorised by a senior manager (ACO or equivalent). From October 1, 2009, it has been mandatory for this to be sent to the relevant recall team within the PPCS by secure e mail. The request should be accompanied by specified sections of the Offender Assessment System (OASys), a list of previous convictions, pre-sentence report, a copy of the licence and charge sheet, where recall relates to new offences. From 1 April 2010, these supporting documents must also be sent by secure email.

National Standards specify that breach action should be initiated by the end of the 10th working day following the failure to comply that triggered breach action. The report and supporting documents should arrive with the recall team in the PPCS within 24 hours of the OM's decision to recall. The PPCS in turn should process the request within 24 hours, issuing a revocation order and notifying the nominated police force and prison establishment, if the offender is already in custody.

The Request for Recall Report should detail the grounds for recall—either the particular instances of non-compliance and the licence condition that has been breached, or the behaviours that have given rise to concern. General deteriorations in behaviour or attitudes that undermine the purposes of supervision may be covered within the *be of good behaviour* condition.

It is important that the grounds for recall are specific as the offender will be informed of the reasons for the recall and will have the right to challenge the decision and the process of recall. Both the decision and the processes that have been followed should therefore stand up to scrutiny and this is right and proper as the loss of a person's liberty is a serious matter.

For indeterminate sentence prisoners, the OM is required to detail in this report the particular behaviours or deterioration in compliance that have lead him or her to a view that the *risk of harm to life and limb* has increased to an unacceptable level, i.e. where it is now more than minimal.

(iv) Informing other agencies

The OM should contact the local police single point of contact (SPOC) at the same time as submitting the request for recall. A list of SPOCs is contained in Probation Instruction (PI) 04/2009 *Recall of Prisoners on Licence: Sharing information and performance monitoring* (National Probation Service, 2009).

In situations where the offender subject to recall is remanded in custody or is otherwise due to appear in court, the OM should ensure that the relevant court officer is aware that recall has been or is about to be requested, so that he or she can inform the court and ensure that the offender is not granted bail. If the offender is not in police or prison custody and fails to surrender to the court, the court duty officer should liaise with the Crown Prosecution Service with a view to the issue of a warrant not backed for bail.

PPO schemes or MAPPA co-ordinators should also be informed if involved with the offender being recalled.

VI. Assessing risk and powers of emergency recall

Provision exists for the emergency recall of offenders in situations where the OM has concluded that the offender presents as a risk of serious harm or that the risk of re-offending is unmanageable. The criteria against which the need for emergency recall should be judged are set out in PC 14/2008 and are:

- There is current evidence that the offender is considered to present a high or very high risk of serious harm to others.
- The offender is subject to Multi-Agency Public Protection Arrangements (MAPPA) at Level 3 or is a Critical Public Protection Case (CPPC).
- The offender's behaviour has deteriorated to such an extent that re-offending is believed to be imminent.

(National Probation Service, 2008b: 7).

This does require the exercise of skilled professional judgment; the decision whether or not to request emergency recall must be defensible and the probation service should be able to justify its decision fully.

The implementation guidance for Standard 2f.3 indicates that where the level of risk is not clear, the OM should adopt an investigative approach. This will involve seeking and analysing information from a range of sources in order to reach a more informed judgment, working in line with inter-agency protocols as appropriate. These might include:

- the offender;
- the offender's partner, family, friends or other people significant in his or her life;
- the offender's accommodation provider, if in a hostel or in social housing;
- other parts of the probation service or partner agencies involved in the offender's supervision;
- the police;
- information from the MAPPA process for MAPPA cases;
- other agencies involved with the offender; and
- the offender's employer or training provider.

Efforts should be made to ensure that information is accurate and up to date, but the initial indicators may be that the risk of serious harm occurring is imminent and action has to be taken before key information can be verified. Again, the urgency of a situation

65

is a matter of professional judgment and on occasions it may be considered safer to recall the offender and complete enquiries whilst he or she is held in custody.

If emergency recall is felt to be appropriate, the OM should contact the relevant recall team in the PPCS by telephone immediately. The PPCS is required to process a request for emergency recall within 2 hours, even where the situation is such that the probation service has given verbal information only. The OM should stay contactable until he or she has received confirmation that the recall has been processed. **The written Request for Recall Report should then be sent to the PPCS within 24 hours, with supporting documents.**

There is an out of hours facility for emergency recall for situations where the offender is believed to pose a high or very high risk of serious harm to others to such an extent that recall cannot safely wait until standard office hours. Following an out of hours contact, the Request for Recall Report and supporting documents should be sent to the relevant recall team in the PPCS within 24 working hours. The procedure for out of hours recall is outlined in Annexe G of PC 14/2008.

VII. Recall and re-release

(i) Recall of HDC cases

When an offender is returned to custody for breach of an HDC, the following arrangements for re-release will apply:

(a) Offenders aged 22 or over when first released and serving sentences under 12 months will be re-released at the half-way point of their sentence with no licence.

(b) Offenders aged under 22 and serving sentences of less than 12 months will be re-released at the half-way point of their sentences on a notice of supervision (s.65 of the CJA 1991). On re-release the offender will spend on supervision only the balance of the three months notice of supervision that remains.

(c) Offenders serving SDSs of 12 months or more breached under s.255 of the CJA 2003 (which is specific to HDC releases) will be re-released at the half- way point of their sentences and will be on licence until the sentence expiry date.

(d) Where SDS offenders are breached by their OM under the more general provisions of s.254 of the CJA 2003, they are treated as a standard recall which means they are liable to be held in prison up to the end of sentence subject to review.

(ii) Fixed Term Recall

FTR prisoners will ordinarily be released from prison after a standard 28 days on licence until the end of their sentence. However, on recall, the offender has the right to make representations to the Parole Board who may recommend immediate release.

The Secretary of State also has powers to release the prisoner at an earlier point, so long as he is satisfied that this would not compromise public protection. If the OM considers this would be appropriate, he or she should contact the PPCS and provide a short written report indicating any changes in the arrangements that can be made for the offender that impact positively on either motivation to comply with supervision or risk of further offending.

Because of the short term nature of the recall, the OM will not be required to produce a written report for the consideration of re-release. Therefore, if the OM wishes to recommend additional conditions for the licence on re-release, the details should be included in the Request for Recall Report. This information will then be forwarded to the receiving prison.

(iii) Standard recall—determinate sentences

In theory, a standard recall prisoner could remain in custody for the remainder of his or her sentence but in practice the question of re-release will be considered at periodic reviews. To assist this process, the OM should prepare a written report to inform the PPCS and Parole Board within 14 days of the offender's recall to custody. The format for this is contained in Annex H of PC 14/2008, entitled *Report for Review of Pre-release by the PPCS/Parole Board*, and this should be submitted to the PPCS with an updated Offender Assessment System (OASys) Risk Management Plan (R 11.12).

For SDS and DCR sentences, the Secretary of State has executive powers to release prisoners within the first 28 days of recall if he is satisfied that release will not compromise public protection. This power will be exercised on his behalf by the PPCS, informed by the OM's report which must contain:

- a review of assessments completed on the offender;
- further information relevant to the offender's risk;
- a risk management/sentence plan; and
- a clear recommendation on release that is supported by evidence and the OM's judgment about whether the offender can be managed in the community.

The PPCS must refer to the Parole Board any SDS or DCR prisoner who has not been released at the end of 28 days. Any prisoner on an extended sentence must be referred immediately.

After a review of available evidence including the OM's assessment, the Parole Board can:

- recommend immediate release on licence;
- fix a date for the offender's release within 12 months of the decision; or
- make no determination about release.

If an offender remains in custody, the case must be reviewed annually but the PPCS can refer the case back to the Board for further consideration within the year should assessments of risk or circumstances change. This process will be overseen by the PPCS who will periodically request updated information and assessment from the OM to assist in further reviews.

The Secretary of State has executive powers to release SDS and DCR prisoners at any time if he is satisfied this will not compromise public protection. DCR prisoners who were originally released on licence under CJA 1991 provisions will be re-released with a CJA 2003 licence which will last until the end of their sentence.

Prisoners on extended sentences can only be re-released on the recommendation of the Parole Board. The PPCS on behalf of the Secretary of State must act on any such recommendation.

(iv) Standard recall—indeterminate sentences

The Parole Board is responsible for reviewing cases of recalled prisoners on indeterminate sentences and often this will be carried out through an oral hearing, either at the request of the offender or the PPCS. If the decision is that the offender must remain in prison for reasons of public protection, the Parole Board must set the next review date within 24 months.

Offenders on indeterminate sentences are by definition more likely to pose a risk of serious harm and here the key consideration for the Parole Board in determining whether or not to direct release will be:

- whether the *risk to life and limb* posed by the offender is no more than minimal; and
- whether the risks the offender presents are manageable in the community.

Information from the OM in the home area could be critical in these decisions and it is therefore important that the OM remains engaged wherever possible with prisoners even where they are recalled for long periods. A Report for Review of Pre-release must be prepared within four weeks of the recall and submitted to the PPCS with an updated OASys Risk Management Plan. Where the prisoner is a MAPPA case, a MAPP meeting should be held as soon as possible after the recall and information from this meeting should be incorporated into the Risk Management Plan. Similar reports will be required for further reviews whilst the offender is held in custody along with a Sentence Plan Review.

The key factors that the Parole Board will consider are:

- likely future compliance with licence conditions and supervision; and
- how the case might be managed in the community, including additional licence conditions requested, accommodation, employment or training placements and so on.

The OM should outline any practical concerns in putting together a successful re-release risk management plan. He or she should indicate, for instance, when accommodation or a place in residential rehabilitation might become available if not available immediately.

The OM should also indicate what work the offender might need to do whilst in custody in order to prepare for a safe re-release. These suggestions should be realistic and achievable, with a clear rationale. It therefore follows that details of such work should be as specific as possible with timescales, if known.

The OM's report should also contain a clear recommendation as to whether the offender should remain in custody or should be released on the basis of the risk management plan either immediately or at some defined point in the future. The recommendation should be endorsed by the OM's line manager and authorised by a senior manager (ACO or equivalent).

VIII. Prisoners' rights on recall

Swift and effective powers of recall must be balanced by mechanisms for offenders to challenge decisions and actions taken over recall. There are an increasing number of prison law cases, many of which relate to reviews of prison recalls and their impact on human rights (particularly arts.5 and 6 of the ECHR).

Article 5(4) of the ECHR provides that:

"Everyone who is deprived of his liberty by arrest or detention shall be entitled to take proceedings by which the lawfulness of his detention shall be decided upon speedily by a court and his release ordered if the detention is not lawful."

A prisoner can ask for his or her case to be brought to judicial review immediately following recall, although this would be a rare course of action when mechanisms are in place for the Parole Board to review the recall of prisoners, either statutorily or on application. Many prisoners, however, have challenged delays by the Parole Board in recall cases. In *R. (on the application of Cooper) v Parole Board* [2007] EWHC 1292 it was held that the Parole Board had a duty to ensure that cases were dealt with speedily in accordance with art.5(4).

When apprehended by the police and returned to prison, prisoners must be informed of the reasons for their recall and their right to make representations to the Parole Board in respect of their recall. Prisoners must also be supplied with copies of the OM's Report for Review of Pre-release and it is the OM's responsibility to ensure that these are sent to the offender at the holding prison for initial and all subsequent reviews.

Where the Parole Board has decided not to release a recalled prisoner, the prisoner can request a review of the decision. The Parole Board does not have to agree to a prisoner's request for an oral hearing but, if granted, the prisoner is entitled to legal representation and may call witnesses to be examined at the hearing. Significantly, appeals were upheld in the case of *R. (on the application of Smith) v Parole Board* and *R. (on the application of West) v Parole Board* [2005] UKHL.1, where the prisoners had argued that the Board should have offered an oral hearing at which they could present their argument against recall. While this judgment does not bestow an automatic entitlement to an oral hearing, it gives a clear direction that oral hearings should be held in a greater number of cases. Bingham L.J. commented that:

"It is difficult to see that there will be many cases where denial of an oral hearing is consistent with the principle of fairness when the Board is minded to require the prisoner to remain in custody and the prisoner asks for a hearing."

However, the scope for prisoner representation has been narrowed again by the Parole Board (Amendment) Rules 2009 where r.12(2) provides for the prisoner to request an oral hearing, rather than requiring a hearing to take place.

There have been challenges also in relation to the process of Parole Board hearings and the burden of proof required, which is founded on the basis of probability rather than the standard required in criminal proceedings. Relatedly, Parole Board Rule 19(2) states that:

"The panel shall avoid formality in the proceedings and as far as possible shall make its own enquiries in order to satisfy itself of the level of risk of the prisoner; it shall conduct the hearing in such manner as it considers most suitable to the clarification of the issues before it and generally to the just handling of the proceedings."

(Parole Board, 2009)

This reflects the responsibilities of the Board in relation to public protection and prevention of future offending, in contrast to court processes which are more focused on proving and responding to allegations of past actions (whether offences or instances of non-compliance).

The shift of power towards the Executive and the changes in the way the Parole Board works have profound implications for offender rights. For probation practitioners involved with the review processes discussed in this chapter, there will no doubt be pressures to be cautious in recommendations to the PPCS and to the Parole Board. The challenge is to ensure that good quality information is provided and defensible judgments are made, with a view to offender rights and proportionate responses to the risks that exist.

Chapter 8

REPARATION AND REFERRAL ORDERS

I. First tier penalties

This chapter deals with first tier penalties for young people who are convicted of an offence before their 18th birthday. These are penalties that fall below the threshold for community sentences and include fines and discharges as well as the referral and reparation orders which are the subject of this chapter.

The discretion of youth courts in dealing with young people at an early stage of their offending was narrowed with the introduction of the reprimand and final warning schemes and, subsequently, referral orders. These have limited both the number of pre-court disposals and the sentencing options available for young people on the first occasion they appear in court with guilty pleas. These changes have resulted in a significant reduction in the number of reparation orders being made. Consequently, in 2007/8, 5,008 reparation orders were imposed compared to 28,475 referral orders (Youth Justice Board, 2009). This number is likely to reduce further as the YRO becomes established and also following further expansion of referral orders.

This chapter addresses reparation orders first before tackling the more complex arrangements in relation to referral orders (RO's), which have undergone significant changes since they first became available in 2002. In different ways, both of these orders were intended to reflect the principles of restorative justice that were so important in New Labour's reform of the youth justice system around the turn of the century.

II. Reparation orders

Legal basis for the order

Originally introduced by the C&DA 1998, the governing legislation is currently the PCC(S)A 2000.

Under ss.73 and 74, a reparation order can require a young person to make reparation either to the community at large or to a specified person or persons. This may be a victim or person otherwise affected by the offence. The order is expressed in terms of hours up to a maximum of 24 hours which must be completed within a three month period.

A reparation order cannot be imposed:

* at the same time as an RO or a YRO; or
* whilst a YRO (unless the YRO is revoked when the reparation order is made).

The court must consider a written report from the youth offending team (YOT) detailing the type of work that will be undertaken and confirming its suitability for the offender. The report should also indicate the attitude of the victim or victims to the requirements that will be included in the order. The young person cannot be ordered to make direct reparation to any person without his or her consent.

The requirements included in the order should be proportionate to the offence or offences and commensurate with their seriousness. Reparation can take a variety of forms but should not involve payment of compensation (s.73(3)). It should be organised so as to avoid any conflict with the offender's religious beliefs or interference with work or education (s.74(3)(a) and (b)).

The responsible officer can be a probation officer, local authority social worker or, in most cases, a YOT officer, and reparation will take place under his or her direction.

(i) Requirements of a reparation order

The order will contain the basic requirements to keep in touch with the case manager from the YOT responsible for the order and to inform him or her of any change of address. Additional requirements should relate specifically to reparation activity and should be worded as clearly and unambiguously as possible.

At the start of the order young people should be given explicit instructions about the activity or the work they will perform and what will be expected of them (punctuality, standards of behaviour and so on). The plan for reparation activity should be agreed and put in writing with a copy given to the young person and victim, where appropriate. The reparation should be proportionate and realistic for the young person to complete within the period of the order.

If the victim has consented to reparation, he or she must be contacted by the responsible officer within five days of the order being made to discuss arrangements. If the young person then fails to comply with direct reparation, National Standard 9.51 (YJB 2009) requires that the responsible officer informs the victim of what enforcement action is being taken within two working days.

(ii) Breach of reparation orders

Powers relating to breaches, amendments and revocations of reparation orders are contained in Sch.8 of the PCC(S)A 2000, as amended by Sch.4 of the CJ&IA 2008.

Breach action is initiated by the responsible officer (YOT case manager) making an application to *the appropriate court*, rather than laying an information (see chapter 2). *The appropriate court* in this instance is the youth court acting for the LJA named in the order, which will ordinarily be the area where the young person resides. The young person must be present in court for a breach hearing (Sch.8 para.6(1)) although other applications can proceed in his or her absence. Applications should be specific about the grounds for breach and the instances of non-compliance. It should be noted that a further offence does not in itself constitute a breach of a reparation order.

Where the court is satisfied that the order is still in force and that the young person has failed without reasonable excuse to comply with its requirements, the court may:

- order the young person to pay a fine up to £1,000 (£250 if the young person is aged under 14).

If the order was made in youth court (or on appeal from a youth court) the court may also:

- allow the order to continue with or without amendment; or
- revoke the order and re-sentence.

If the order was made in Crown Court (or on appeal from the Crown Court) the magistrates may then:

- remand the young person in custody or release on bail until he or she is brought before the Crown Court, who has the power to revoke and re-sentence.

In dealing with the young person, the court should take into account the extent to which he or she has complied with the requirements of the order.

The 2004 version of the Youth Justice National Standards stated that victims should never be cited in breach hearings. Although this requirement has not been included in the 2009 National Standards for Youth Justice Services, good practice suggests that the principle should still apply. It therefore follows that victims cannot be asked to give evidence or be called as witnesses in breach hearings.

(iii) Amendment or revocation of reparation orders

Revocations and amendments are dealt with under para.5(1) of Sch.8 which allows the appropriate youth court, on the application of the young person or the YOT case manager, to:

- revoke the order;
- cancel any provision within the order; or
- insert provisions, either in addition to or substituting for existing provisions.

The reference to provisions rather than requirements means that this paragraph could be used to change the administrative aspects of the order (LJA or responsible officer, for instance) as well as the details of reparation activities.

If requirements are to be inserted into the order, the young person must be in attendance but other matters can be dealt with in his or her absence.

III. Referral orders

Legal basis for the order

Although established by the Youth Justice and Criminal Evidence Act 1999 (YJ&CEA 1999) the governing legislation for the RO is currently found in ss.16–32 of the PCC(S)A 2000. This has been substantially revised and expanded by provisions in the CJ&IA 2008.

ROs are the main sentencing provision for first time offenders in the youth court or magistrates' court. The Crown Court, in contrast, has all sentencing options open to it when dealing with first offenders. Significantly, this includes ROs but only where the judge decides to proceed under s.66 of the Courts Act 2003 and exercises the powers of a district judge.

In essence, the RO permits the court to delegate its decision-making powers to a young offender panel (YOP) involving volunteers from the community. This is intended to divert young people from formal court proceedings and to provide a more deliberative forum with greater opportunity to engage the young offender in reparation and in problem-solving. The legal basis of the order is established by the court and non-compliance with the order must be brought back to the court to be dealt with, as the YOP itself has no legal status.

ROs are either mandatory or discretionary. The order will require the young person to attend meetings of a YOP and to agree a contract with the panel which will last for a period specified by the court, between 3 and 12 months.

If a young person is under 16 the court *must* order a parent or guardian to attend panel meetings and *may* do so for a 16 or 17 year old, unless the court considers that it would be unreasonable in the circumstances (section 20).

Under section 16 (a) and (c) ROs can only be made where:

- the sentence for the offence or offences is not fixed by law, AND
- the court is not proposing to deal with the young person by means of:
  - an absolute discharge; or
  - a custodial sentence; or
  - a hospital order under the Mental Health Act 1983.

This is a precondition for all ROs and will be assumed in the outline of circumstances where ROs can be made below.

Mandatory referral orders

The court must make an RO where the young person:

- is under 18; and
- has pleaded guilty to an imprisonable offence; and
- has no previous convictions in a UK court.

Originally ROs were mandatory for all first offenders pleading guilty in court, but this brought a large number of summary motoring offences within the RO ambit. This was considered unnecessary and impractical and resulted in the introduction of the imprisonable offence criteria.

Discretionary referral orders

The court may choose to make an RO where the young person:

- is under 18; AND
- has no previous convictions in a UK court; AND
- has pleaded guilty to one but not all the offences being sentenced i.e.
- has entered mixed pleas; OR
- has pleaded guilty to a non-imprisonable (summary) offence.

Referral orders are not available where the young person has pleaded not guilty to all the offences before the court.

Discretionary ROs also may now be made where a young person:

- has one previous conviction in a UK court but was not made subject to a referral order on that occasion; OR

- has more than one previous conviction in a UK court but has only had one RO made against him or her—even then a new RO can only be made if the court considers that there are exceptional circumstances and if a YOT officer recommends its suitability for the young person.

Additional orders

When making an RO, the court may impose at the same time:

- a parenting order (s.34 of the CJA 2003);

- a compensation order;

- an order for costs.

It may not at the same time impose:

- a youth rehabilitation order;

- a reparation order;

- a fine;

- a conditional discharge; or

- a parental bindover.

(i) General observations

Effectively, in making an RO, the court is requiring the YOT to set up a Young Offender Panel (YOP) to consider the young person's case and to agree the specifics of the intervention that will take place. The court's role in determining what will happen to a young person on the court order is therefore more limited than it would be for many community sentences, for instance.

Section 18 of the PCC(S)A 2000 states that the RO shall:

- specify the responsible YOT;

- require the young person to attend each meeting of the YOP established in respect of his or her case by the YOT; and

- specify the period that the contract agreed between the young person and the panel will have effect. This could range from a minimum of three months to a maximum of 12.

Where the court has dealt with multiple offences and has made two or more ROs to run either concurrently or consecutively, the young person will still be referred to one YOP and will agree one contract. The only difference where the orders are consecutive is that the period that the contract will last (the compliance period) will be longer, being an aggregate of the months stipulated for each RO, up to a maximum of 12 months (s.18(5)).

The length of the RO stipulated by the court determines the *compliance period*. Unlike other orders, this does not start as soon as the order is made, but runs from the date that a contract between the young person and the YOP is signed. The order will remain in force until the end of the compliance period.

IV. Young offender panels (YOPs)

(i) Roles and responsibilities

Panels are made up of a member of the YOT and a minimum of two trained community volunteers, one of whom will chair the meeting.

YOT members advising a panel will be expected to:

- support the panel process and panel members—in general, the YOT member should not lead discussion but it may be appropriate to intervene if communication is difficult or if the meeting is not making progress;

- provide information and advice on available services and interventions;

- advise the panel in terms of the appropriateness and proportionality of proposed elements in a contract;

- ensure that the panel is responding appropriately to public protection concerns;

- assess and monitor risk to the safety and well being of all participants in the panel process; and

- ensure that the requirements in contracts are worded clearly so that they are understandable to the young person and are enforceable.

Outside the panel meeting, the YOT will also have responsibility for:

- contacting victims and either relaying their views or facilitating their involvement in the panel;

- ensuring that the panel is made aware of any comments made by the sentencing court in making the RO (this may be particularly relevant where the young person was on the custody threshold);

- assessing the young person and providing a written report for the consideration of panel members. This should be made available to the young person in advance of the meeting and to parents, except where this would be inappropriate; and

- ensuring that the young person is aware of the panel process and what will be expected of him or her in terms of compliance with the contract and how it will be monitored.

The young person does not have legal representation at a panel meeting so it is important that the YOT member is prepared to intervene constructively to ensure that the conduct of the panel is fair and balanced. Because this falls outside of the court process, the young person has no right of appeal against contracts or elements of contracts which are disproportionate or inappropriate (although the young person can refuse to sign and therefore trigger a referral back to court). It follows that YOT members should be proactive in ensuring that contracts are put together with due care and as far as possible with the active participation of the young person (and parent(s), if present), guarding against undue pressure to agree to elements which are unduly onerous or potentially degrading.

(ii) Attendance at panel meetings

In addition to the community volunteers, YOT panel member and young person, the following may be present at panel meetings:

- a parent, carer or other adult supporter for the young person;
- victim—this may be an individual direct victim or representative of a corporate victim, for instance. A victim may bring another person with him or her as support;
- for any looked after young person, a member of children's social care;
- other individuals important to the young person (for instance, from school or the youth service);
- other members of the YOT who may have knowledge of the young person or who may inform the setting of the contract.

Solicitors cannot attend as legal representatives, although there may be occasions where a solicitor might attend as parent, carer or support for a young person.

The young person is required to attend panel meetings. If he or she fails to attend a panel meeting, the meeting must make a decision as to whether to reconvene another meeting or to refer the young person back to court. Information from the YOT about attempts to secure attendance in advance of the meeting may be critical in this decision.

V. Contracts

(i) Setting conditions

The two core elements of any referral order contract are:

- (a) reparation to the victim and/or community; AND
- (b) a programme of interventions delivered or organised by the YOT which addresses the factors associated with risk of re-offending.

Contracts must take into account the young person's school or work commitments and any religious observance, and it is important to clarify these commitments either before or at the panel meeting.

The aim of interventions should be to prevent the young person re-offending and a wide range of activities or interventions could contribute to that aim. A programme can therefore be varied and tailored to the risks and needs of the young person. It should also be proportionate and realistic for the young person to achieve.

Reparation should be included in every contract in some form, but direct reparation can only be included in a contract with the consent of the victim or other person affected (s.23(4)).

While the contract may require a young person to stay away from particular places or persons, it may not impose any physical restraints. Nor can the contract include electronic monitoring (s.23(3)).

(ii) The Scaled Approach

Alongside the YRO, the Youth Justice Board (YJB) is introducing The Scaled Approach—effectively a youth justice version of the tiering in terms of risk already established in the adult criminal justice system.

This sets three levels of intervention based on assessed risks and needs:

- **LOW** likelihood of re-offending or risk of serious harm
- **MEDIUM** likelihood of re-offending or risk of serious harm
- **HIGH** likelihood of re-offending or risk of serious harm

Because ROs are used widely for young offenders on the first occasions they appear in court, young people on ROs could be assessed at any of these three levels.

Within this approach, where young people are assessed as higher risk, this should be reflected in their contracts. This may mean:

- more elements on the contracts, stipulating more interventions;
- interventions which last longer or are more intensive; or
- more restrictions on a young person.

Reports prepared by the YOT for initial panel meetings should state clearly the assessed level of risk for the young person and the appropriate level of intervention. The guidance on ROs and young offender panels (MoJ, 2009) states that in the highest risk cases on the custody threshold, an intensive contract must provide an adequate and robust response to the offence and the risk factors present in the case. This may mean up to 25 hours of intervention, although unlike Intensive Supervision and Surveillance (ISS), this cannot include electronic monitoring. This must be accompanied by a swift referral back to court where the young person either does not agree a satisfactory contract or fails to comply.

Caution should be exercised in setting intensive contracts, because the need to manage risk must be balanced with other factors, such as the welfare needs, vulnerability and maturity of the young person. Some young people may already have significant contact with other agencies such as children's social care, Connexions or the Child and Adolescent Mental Health Services (CAMHS). Care should be taken to establish contracts which are realistic and which take account of the full range of agencies that might be involved with the young person. The sequencing of interventions may also be important in helping a young person progress successfully through an order and to gain maximum benefit from interventions—again dovetailing YOT interventions with the work of other agencies.

On the other hand, it may be that a young person has welfare or developmental needs which are not being addressed and here the RO may act as a means of engaging another appropriate agency or prompting another agency to fulfil statutory duties in relation to him or her. Ensuring that unmet needs are addressed is important in terms of the long term welfare and development of the young person. However, it may also have positive benefits for encouraging compliance with the conditions of an RO contract by:

- being responsive to a young person's needs and circumstances; and
- dealing with issues that may affect ability to comply such as homelessness or problematic family relationships.

(iii) Voluntary conditions

The RO contract may include conditions which are voluntary as well as conditions which the young person is required to comply with. This may allow for extra flexibility in dealing with sensitive areas or with welfare or developmental needs outside the scope of the RO. They also allow the young person some choice over engagement with key interventions.

An example of positive use of voluntary conditions might involve contact with a substance misuse worker. A contract might require a young person to undergo an assessment by the YOT substance misuse worker and this would be enforceable if the young person did not attend the interview. However, any follow up contact or intervention could be made voluntary and the young person can make his or her own decision about whether or not to continue.

This sort of arrangement might also be appropriate for other activities, involvement with youthwork interventions or counselling, for instance. An element of compulsion can be helpful in establishing the first contact, thereby getting over the initial resistance or reluctance, but then allowing the young person some control over what then happens is often appropriate and constructive.

(iv) Agreeing contracts

Contracts will normally be agreed at the initial panel meeting and the compliance period will start from the point that the contract is signed by the young person and member of the panel (s.24(2) of the PCC(S)A 2000).

The contract should be expressed in ordinary language so that the young person can understand what it requires him or her to do and the consequences of not complying. If necessary, this may mean reading the contract to the young person.

When signed, the young person should be given a copy. Copies should also be given to:

- parent or carer;
- representative of children's social care, where appropriate;
- any other individual/agency who may be assisting the young person in complying; and
- the victim, where consent has been given.

If a contract is not agreed at the first meeting, the panel should seek a further meeting within 10 days, unless it appears that there is little or no prospect of reaching a satisfactory agreement, in which case the YOP may refer the case back to court immediately (s.25(2)). Again, information from the YOT and the professional opinion of the YOT panel member may be important in this decision.

(v) Progress meetings

The YOP should be reconvened at least every three months to review the young person's progress on the RO. The YOT should prepare a written report for the panel's consideration focusing on compliance but also highlighting any difficulties that have impacted on progress.

The YOP may call a meeting at any stage if it feels the need to do so in order to review the order or to deal with any other matter in connection with the contract (s.26(2)). In practice this would normally be triggered by information from the YOT case manager. The young person may also request that a meeting is called to consider variation of the contract or a referral back to court for revocation of the order.

Review panels have the ability to vary the conditions of contracts and, where good progress has been made, to refer the case back to court for revocation.

Review panels should also take account of any instances of non-compliance, short of breach, and seek to re-engage the young person in order to secure future compliance.

At the end of the compliance period, a final review meeting should be held. If this meeting agrees that the RO has been satisfactorily completed, the order will be discharged when the compliance period expires. However, if the panel is of the view that the contract has not been satisfactorily completed it may refer the offender back to the appropriate court (s.27(4)).

(vi) Varying the contract

A variation of the contract may be requested by the YOT or the young person for the following reasons:

(a) a difficulty with a specific element of a contract (for example, arranging direct reparation);

(b) a change in circumstances that makes compliance with elements of the contract problematic (for example, starting a college course); or

(c) the contract as it stands is too onerous.

If the contract conditions are amended, a new contract must be signed. If the young person refuses to sign the revised contract without good reason, the panel may refer the case back to court (s.26(8)).

(vii) Extensions to the compliance period

Where a young person has been unable to comply with the order for reasons outside of his or her control (for example, illness, bereavement) then the panel may refer the case back to court to ask for the compliance period to be extended for up to three months in the interests of justice (s.27B and Sch.1 para.9ZD)).

The total compliance period including the extension cannot exceed the maximum 12 months.

VI. The effect of further offences

If a young person subject to an RO is convicted of further offences before his or her 18th birthday, Sch.1 Pt II of the PCC(S)A 2000 makes provision for ROs to be extended.

If the further offences occurred before the RO was made, the court may deal with the new offence or offences by extending the compliance period for the order. However, the total period may not exceed the maximum 12 months (Sch.1 para.11).

The court may also extend the RO where the new offences were committed after the RO was made. This can only happen where it is satisfied on the basis of a report from the YOP dealing with the young person that there are exceptional circumstances that mean that, in spite of the re-offending, the extension is likely to help prevent further re-offending (para.12).

In all other cases, when the court sentences for the new offence, this has the effect of automatically revoking the RO and any associated orders. It may also re-sentence for the offences relating to the RO, taking into account the extent of any compliance with the RO contract (Sch.1 para.14).

VII. Referrals back to court

(i) Actions of the YOT regarding compliance

If a young person does not comply with his or her contract by:

- not attending a panel (including a review panel);
- not agreeing a contract; or
- not complying with one or more conditions in the contract.

The YOT case manager must follow this up either by face-to-face contact or by telephone within one working day. If no acceptable reason is given and the non-compliance is significant, a YOP must be convened within 10 working days.

The YOT does not have the power to refer the young person back to court directly in the event of breach. This can only be decided and effected by the panel meeting.

The YOT will provide the panel with full details of the non-compliance and any relevant information about the young person's attitudes and current circumstances.

Where the panel agrees that the young person is in breach and wishes to refer the young person back to court, the YOT member must report to the court on the referral back within 10 working days.

(ii) Actions of the young offender panel regarding non-compliance

Where a review panel is convened to deal with non-compliance, the YOP will consider the allegations of non-compliance and all other information put before it, including what the young person or parents may say by way of explanation. This should be a more deliberative process than a breach hearing in court, and the emphasis should be more on establishing how to move forward than necessarily proving the breach or otherwise.

In some instances, the panel may agree that there was an issue with the contract that made it difficult to comply. Perhaps the conditions were inappropriate, too onerous or impractical in some way. In these circumstances, the YOP may amend the order accordingly by deleting or varying specific conditions.

However, where the young person is unable to offer a reasonable explanation for not complying, the panel must send the young person back to court for re-sentencing. The reasons for doing so should be presented to the court in a written report via the YOT.

In most instances the panel will refer the young person back to the youth court for the local justice area where the young person lives. However, where a young person has reached the age of 18, the matter would be dealt with in a magistrates' court.

(iii) Powers of the court in relation to breach

When the court receives a report from the YOP with details of the breach, it will issue either a summons or a warrant to cause the young person to appear before it. At this stage the young person will have the right to legal representation because he or she is back in the more formal court arena.

There may be several outcomes in court under Sch.1 paragraphs 5–9 of the PCC(S)A 2000:

(a) The court agrees that the young person is in breach and revokes and resentences.	All sentencing options are open to the court except another referral order.
(b) The court agrees that the young person is in breach but chooses not to revoke and re-sentence.	The young person is sent back to the YOT/YOP to complete the contract.
(c) The court does not agree that the young person is in breach and the order remains in force.	The young person is sent back to the YOT/YOP to complete the contract.
(d) The court does not agree that the young person is in breach and the compliance period has expired.	The order and any associated orders are discharged.
(e) The court takes the view that the contract conditions have been satisfactorily completed.	The order and any associated orders are discharged.

The court may only revoke and re-sentence where the young person is present in court. However, it may still re-sentence even where the compliance period has expired if it is satisfied that the contract was not complied with (Sch.1 para.5(6)). In re-sentencing, the court should have regard to the circumstances of the referral back to court and, where a contract has been agreed between the young person and the YOP, the extent of any compliance with the contract (Sch.1 para.5)).

(iv) Revocation for reasons other than breach

A RO may be revoked early by up to three months if the YOP considers the young person has made demonstrably good progress (s.27A of the PCC(S)A 2000).

Early revocation (and re-sentencing, where appropriate) may also take place where there has been a change in the young person's circumstances that makes it impractical to continue with the order. This may happen where a young person is being taken abroad by family, for instance.

In either of these cases, the YOP would refer the young person back to court and provide a written report detailing the situation and the actions it feels appropriate.

(v) Summary of provisions for referral back to court

A YOP may refer a young person back to court in the following circumstances where there is no reasonable explanation:

- failure to attend a panel meeting;
- failure to agree either an initial or a revised contract;
- failure to sign either an initial or a revised contract;
- failure to comply with one or more conditions of a contract, including attending appointments with the YOT; or
- unsatisfactory progress towards completing the contract.

And also for early revocation:

- to recognise good progress; or
- in the interests of justice where a young person's circumstances have changed.

In addition a referral back may be used to request an extension to the compliance period of an order in the interests of justice.

VIII. Parental involvement

Under s.20 of the PCC(S)A 2000, a court can require a parent or guardian to attend meetings of a referral panel convened for a young person. If the parent fails to attend, the YOP may send a report back to the court, primarily the youth court, who can issue a summons or a warrant requiring the parent to appear before it (Sch.1 para.9C of the PCC(S)A 2000).

The court may make a parenting order if it is satisfied that the parent has failed to comply with the s.20 order and that a parenting order would be desirable to prevent the young person offending further (Sch.1 para.9D(1)). If the young person is under 16, the court must consider information about the family circumstances and the likely effect of the parenting order on those circumstances. In practice, the court will look to the YOT to provide such information (Sch.1 para.9D(6)).

Chapter 9
THE YOUTH REHABILITATION ORDER

The legal basis for the order

Section 1 of the CJ&IA 2008 establishes the youth rehabilitation order (YRO) which has been available to the courts since November 30, 2009 for offences committed on or after that date.

The YRO is a community sentence and replaces the previous community orders available for young people. Section 148 of the CJA 2003 places restrictions on the imposition of a community sentence which can only be made where the court considers that:

- the offence(s) are "*serious enough*" to warrant such a sentence;
- the requirement or combination of requirements are the most suitable for the offender;
- the restriction of liberty reflects the seriousness of the offence(s); or
- the sentence for the offence is not fixed in law.

Section 150A of the CJA 2003 provides a further restriction by stipulating that community orders can only be imposed where the offence(s) in question are punishable by imprisonment. When proposing to make a YRO, the court must also consider the young person's family circumstances and how they might be affected by the YRO (para.28 Sch.1 of the CJ&IA 2009).

The court is not permitted to impose a YRO whilst a previous YRO or a reparation order is still in force. If it wishes to make a new YRO, it must first revoke the pre-existing order (Sch.1 para.30(4)). However, by virtue of Sch.1 para.30(2), a YRO can be made during the currency of a detention and training order (DTO). In this instance, the court is permitted to order that the YRO will come into force either when the community part of the DTO commences or on the expiry of the DTO.

The court is able to impose more than one YRO on the same sentencing occasion for multiple offences. These would take effect from the same date but, if they contain the same requirements, the court may order these to run either concurrently or consecutively, providing the specified period or number of hours does not exceed the maximum permitted by law (Sch.2 para.31(4). If two or more fostering requirements are imposed these must run concurrently.

There are 16 requirements that can be part of a community order and each order must contain one or more of these requirements in combination:

- supervision requirement;
- activity requirement;
- unpaid work requirement for young people over 16 years;

- programme requirement;
- attendance centre requirement;
- prohibited activity requirement;
- curfew requirement;
- exclusion requirement;
- residence requirement;
- local authority residence requirement;
- mental health treatment requirement;
- drug treatment requirement;
- drug testing requirement;
- intoxicating substance treatment requirement;
- education requirement; and
- electronic monitoring.

There are also more restrictive requirements enabling the court to impose a period of Intensive Supervision and Surveillance (ISS) or to order a period of residence in a foster placement. Under s.1(4) such requirements are only available where the court is of the opinion that the offence or offences before the court are *so serious* that they meet the custody threshold, so that in effect they represent alternatives to custody. ISSs are not addressed in this chapter but are covered separately in Chapter 11.

The maximum length of a YRO is three years. In making the order, the court must specify a date by which all requirements must be completed and may specify an earlier date or dates in relation to specific requirements.

The YRO is an all-purpose order and can be used at different intervention levels within the Youth Justice Board's *Scaled Approach*, varying the number of requirements and their intensity or duration to suit the particular case. It is important, where two or more requirements are combined in one order, that they are compatible with each other and also that the young person's commitments on the order are both realistic and proportionate.

The responsible officer for a YRO will normally be a member of a youth offending team (YOT)), but under s.4(2)(b) can be an officer of the local probation trust. This allows for instances where a young person has reached the age of 18 whilst the order is in force and the supervision is taken over by the probation service (this will be subject to local agreement). However, in the interests of clarity, the responsible officer is referred to throughout this chapter as the YOT case manager.

I. Requirements in the YRO

The details of requirements that can form part of a YRO are contained in Sch.1 of the CJ&IA 2008.

Requirement	Activity	Paragraphs 6–8

Duration: the requirement is expressed in number of days and must not exceed 90 days.

Conditions that need to be met for this requirement:

The court must be satisfied that it is feasible to secure compliance with the activity proposed and that the relevant provision is available in the local justice area (LJA). In considering this, it must consult a member of the youth offending team or an officer of the local probation trust. The court must have the consent of any person other than the offender and responsible officer whose co-operation is required.

Special considerations

Paragraph 6(1) stipulates that under an activity requirement, an offender must:

(a) participate in activities at a specified place or places for a specified number of days; OR

(b) participate in an activity or activities specified on the order for a specified number of days; OR

(c) participate in one or more residential exercises for a continuous period or periods for a specified number of days; OR

(d) engage in activities in accordance with instruction of the responsible officer on a specified number of days.

The actual dates, times and venue and other instructions will be specified by the YOT case manager or others acting on his or her behalf, for instance, an officer in charge of an activity centre. It follows that instructions need to be detailed and specific, because this may be critical in the case of enforcement action. Where a young person has a number of commitments, it may be helpful to issue instructions in the form of a weekly diary or calendar.

Paragraph 6 requires the offender to participate in activities for the specified number of days and, whilst participating, to comply with instructions given by or with the authority of the officer in charge of the activities. Instructions may prohibit unacceptable behaviours and specify other expectations, such as not attending under the influence of alcohol and drugs.

The specified activity may consist of reparation activities, solely or in conjunction with other activities (para.8(2)).

Residential exercises

If required to participate in a residential exercise under para.6(1)(c), the order should specify either the place where this will be held or the activity. The young person will be required to present him or herself at that place at the beginning of the time period and reside there or to participate in the activity for the specified number of days. During the period of residence or whilst on activities, the young person must comply with instructions given by or under the authority of the officer in charge.

Engage in activities in accordance with the instructions of the responsible officer

Instructions given under para.6(1)(d) may require the offender to participate in any activity specified in the instructions or to present him or herself to a person or persons specified in the instructions. Instructions can also require a young person to participate in a residential exercise but only with the consent of parents and for a maximum period of 7 days.

Requirement	Supervision	Paragraph 9

Duration: up to 36 months

Conditions that need to be met for this requirement:

None

Special considerations

Legally, this requires the offender to *"attend appointments with the responsible officer or another person determined by the responsible officer, at a time and place determined by the responsible officer"*.

This sounds deceptively simple, but in reality the supervision requirement may be even more critical in underpinning a package of interventions in a YRO than in an adult community order. It should help give purpose and coherence to the order and the relationship between the young person and YOT case manager can be a significant motivating factor.

Requirement	Unpaid Work	Paragraph 10

Duration: 40 to 240 hours, within a 12-month period (but see below)

Conditions that need to be met for this requirement:

The young person must be 16 or 17 at the time of conviction.

The court must be satisfied that the offender is suitable to perform unpaid work and, if it thinks necessary, may first hear from a member of a YOT or an officer of the local probation trust as to suitability. The court must also be satisfied that such work is available in the LJA where the young person lives.

Special considerations

Where the offender is sentenced for two or more offences and is required to perform unpaid work for each of these, the court may direct that the hours can run concurrently or consecutively, providing the total number of hours does not exceed 240.

The specific requirement as spelt out in subpara.10(5) is that the offender *"must perform for the number of hours specified in the order such work at such times as the responsible officer may specify in instructions"*.

Paragraph 17 of Sch.2 does permit a court to extend the period for completion of unpaid work hours.

The order will remain in force until the unpaid work hours are completed, unless revoked or the offender dies.

Requirement	Programme	Paragraph 11

Duration: the number of days attendance required must be specified in the order

Conditions that need to be met for this requirement:

Programme is defined as a "systematic set of activities" by subpara.11(2). The court cannot make a programme requirement unless a member of a YOT or an officer of the local probation trust has recommended its suitability for the offender. It must also be satisfied that the programme in question is available at the specified venue and must have the consent of any person whose co-operation is required other than the offender and responsible officer.

Special considerations

Paragraph 11 requires the offender to participate in activities in a specified place or places for the specified number of days and, whilst participating, to comply with instructions given by or with the authority of the officer in charge of the programme.

More than one programme requirement can be contained in one order. This may mean, for instance, that an offender has a requirement to attend a generic programme and a second requirement stipulating that this is followed by an offence-specific programme.

Requirement	Attendance Centre	Paragraph 12

Duration: 12–36 hours if the young person is 16 or 17 at the time of conviction

12–24 hours if the young person is 14 or 15

No more than 12 hours if the young person is under 14

Conditions that need to be met for this requirement:

The court cannot make this requirement unless there is an attendance centre available in the area and it is satisfied that it is reasonably accessible to the young person, having regard to the means of access available to him or her and any other circumstances.

Special considerations

An attendance centre requirement is expressed in numbers of hours and must specify the centre where the hours will be spent. Activities, sports and social education are usually provided at the centres which have historically been run on a Saturday. An offender cannot be required to spend more than three hours at the centre on any one day.

The specific requirement, spelt out in subpara.12(7) is to:

(a) attend the centre at the beginning of the period, and

(b) during that period to engage in occupation or to receive instruction, under the supervision of and in accordance with instructions given by, or under authority of, the officer in charge of the centre, whether at the centre of elsewhere.

Where the attendance centre is the only requirement on a YRO, the responsible officer will be the manager of the specified centre. Otherwise the responsible officer will be a YOT case manager who will enforce this requirement alongside whatever other requirements are contained in the order.

| Requirement | Prohibited activity | Paragraph 13 |

Duration: 36 month maximum

Conditions that need to be met for this requirement:

The court must consult a member of a YOT or an officer of the local probation trust before including this requirement.

Special considerations

This requirement gives authority to order the offender to refrain from participating in specified activities or behaviours on specific dates or for a specified period. There may be particular enforcement difficulties with this requirement because defining or even detecting the prohibited behaviours may not be straightforward. YOT case managers or court duty officers may therefore be required to assist the court in the appropriate wording of prohibitions and also to advise the court in relation to concerns about proportionality and young people's rights.

This requirement should not be used to prohibit behaviour that is in any case illegal and will not normally relate to geographical restrictions that could be dealt with by an exclusion requirement. However, it can be used to prevent an offender carrying a firearm as defined by the Firearms Act 1967.

| Requirement | Curfew | Paragraph 14 |

Duration: between 2 and 12 hours per day for a period of up 6 months

Conditions that need to be met for this requirement:

The court must obtain and consider information about the place or places specified in the order for the curfew to take place and the attitudes of other people likely to be affected by the offender's enforced presence there (for instance, family members).

Special considerations

Curfews can be reasonably flexible, so that the place specified or the hours of curfew can vary on different days of the week. This can, for instance, help accommodate the needs of a young person whose parents live separately and who spends time with each parent. Care should be taken to ensure that arrangements are not unnecessarily complicated but that they meet the needs of the young person, allowing for education, training or work commitments, family circumstances or religious observances.

Under s.177(3) the court must impose a requirement that the curfew is electronically monitored unless the court considers it inappropriate to do so OR:

(a) the court does not have the consent of an individual whose co-operation is needed to secure the monitoring (para.26(3)); or

(b) an electronic monitoring scheme is not available in the area where the address for the curfew is proposed (para.26(6)).

Where an electronically monitored curfew is the only requirement on a community order, the responsible officer will be an employee of the approved contractor for the area in question. Otherwise the responsible officer will be a YOT case manager who will enforce this requirement alongside whatever other requirements are contained in the order.

| Requirement | Exclusion | Paragraph 15 |

Duration: 3 months maximum

Conditions that need to be met for this requirement:

None

Special considerations

This requirement prohibits the offender from entering a specified place for a specified period of time. A place can refer to an area, not necessarily a building or location, and this may be indicated to the young person on a map. The requirement can specify more than one place and these can be for different periods or different days of the week, for instance.

An exclusion requirement must be electronically monitored unless the court considers that the circumstances of the case make it inappropriate to do so or is unable to do so because the necessary arrangement cannot be made.

| Requirement | Residence | Paragraph 16 |

Duration: up to 36 months

Conditions that need to be met for this requirement:

The court must consider the home surroundings of the offender before making a requirement to reside at a specified place and in practice this will necessitate a full pre-sentence report. The young offender must also be 16 or 17 at the time of conviction.

A young person can only be required to reside in hostels or other institutions where this has been recommended by a member of a YOT or an officer of the local probation trust.

Special considerations

This requirement means that the offender must reside either with a specified individual or at a place specified in the order for a specified period of time. This latter instance is known as a "place of residence requirement".

If worded appropriately, a place of residence requirement could allow the flexibility for the offender to stay somewhere other than the place specified in the order with the prior approval of the YOT caseworker.

| Requirement | Local authority residence | Paragraph 17 |

Duration: up to 6 months

Conditions that need to be met for this requirement:

The court must be satisfied that:

(a) the behaviour that constituted the offence was due to a significant extent to the circumstances in which the young person was living; AND

(b) that the requirement will assist the young person's rehabilitation.

The court must consult with the young person's parent or guardian, unless it is impracticable

THE YOUTH REHABILITATION ORDER

to do so. It must also consult the local authority who will receive the young person and who will be named on the order.

In most circumstances, the requirement can only be made if the young person has been legally represented during the proceedings.

The residence requirement will cease when a young person reaches the age of 18.

Special considerations

This requirement means that the offender must reside in accommodation provided by or on behalf of a local authority named in the order for a specified period of time.

Requirement	Live with local authority foster parent	Paragraph 18

Duration: up to 12 months, but not beyond the young person's 18th birthday

Conditions that need to be met for this requirement:

Section 1(4) places restrictions on the use of this requirement which is only available where:

(a) the court is dealing with the young person for an imprisonable offence; AND

(b) the court is of the opinion that the offence (or offences) is *so serious* that a custodial sentence would be appropriate (or for a young person aged under 12, would be appropriate if he or she were aged 12); AND

(c) if the young person is aged under 15 at the age of conviction, the court is of the opinion that he or she is a *persistent offender* (see Chapter 3).

In effect, this means that the fostering requirement is an alternative to a custodial sanction.

Additionally, the court must be satisfied that:

(a) the behaviour that constituted the offence was due to a significant extent to the circumstances in which the young person was living, and

(b) that the fostering requirement will assist the young person's rehabilitation.

The court must consult with the young person's parent or guardian, unless it is impracticable to do so. It must also consult the local authority who will receive the young person and who will be named on the order.

In most circumstances, the requirement can only be made if the young person has been legally represented during the proceedings.

NB: arrangements to deliver this requirement may not be available in all local authority areas.

Special considerations

The order will specify the local authority who will place the young person with a foster parent under s.23(2)(a) of the Children Act 1989, normally the local authority area where the young person lives.

Under para.4(4) the court must impose a supervision requirement alongside a fostering requirement, which should provide support and oversight of the fostering placement and assist in the management of the placement.

If no foster placement is available or the YOT case manager is proposing to apply for variation or revocation of the order, the young person will be required to live in local authority accommodation for the interim period.

Requirement	Mental health treatment	Paragraph 20

Duration: any specified period whilst the supervision order is in force

Conditions that need to be met for this requirement:

This requirement can only be included after assessment by a registered medical practitioner has indicated that the young person has a medical condition that may be susceptible to treatment. The young person must express willingness to comply (para.20(3)(c)). The court must be satisfied that suitable arrangements are available for the treatment to be carried out.

Paragraph 20(1) specifies that the requirement is for the young person to submit to treatment by or under the direction of a registered medical practitioner and/or chartered psychologist with a view to the improvement of his or her mental condition.

Special considerations

Treatment can be medical or psychological intervention and can include in-patient treatment. The order will not specify the treatment, but will specify the medical establishment or practitioner involved. Breach action will therefore be based on failure to attend appointments or therapy sessions that form part of the treatment, for example, rather than a failure to participate or make progress in treatment.

Paragraph 21 permits the medical practitioner or chartered psychologist directing treatment to carry out that treatment in an institution or place not named in the order, providing the young person has expressed his or her willingness to comply with the new arrangements. However, if the treatment proposed is as an in-patient, the medical practitioner or chartered psychologist must notify the YOT case manager in writing, specifying the institution or place where the treatment will be carried out.

When a young person attains the age of 18, the treatment condition will no longer be in force.

Requirement	Drug treatment	Paragraph 22

Duration: Minimum of 6 months up to 36 months

Conditions that need to be met for this requirement:

Before making this requirement, the court must be satisfied that:

(a) the young person is dependent on or has a propensity to misuse drugs; AND

(b) the dependency or propensity requires or may be susceptible to treatment; AND

(c) arrangements have been made or can be made for the treatment specified in the order, including residential treatment.

The requirement must be recommended by a member of a YOT or an officer of a local probation trust, in most cases of medium or high offence seriousness in a full pre-sentence report. A full report will almost certainly be required where there is an additional mental health need.

The young person must also express willingness to comply with the requirement.

Special considerations

Treatment may be residential or non-residential at a place specified in the order, but the nature of treatment will not be specified. Treatment will be by or under the direction of a specified person, with the necessary experience and qualifications in relation to drugs work.

Requirement	Drug testing	Paragraph 23

Duration: the treatment period as specified in the drug treatment requirement

Conditions that need to be met for this requirement:

When making this requirement the court must also make a drug treatment requirement, so by definition the court must be satisfied that

(a) the young person is dependent on or has a propensity to misuse drugs; AND

(b) the dependency or propensity requires or may be susceptible to treatment; AND

(c) arrangements have been made or can be made for the treatment specified in the order, including residential treatment.

Arrangements must be in place for the testing to be carried out and these may not be available in all YOTs. The offender must also express willingness to comply with the requirement.

Special considerations

By virtue of this requirement, the young person must "provide samples in accordance with instructions given by the responsible officer or the treatment provider" (para.23(1)). The order will specify the minimum number of samples to be provided each month and may specify the times and circumstances in which the YOT case manager or treatment provider may require samples to be provided. The order may also specify descriptions of the samples that may be required (e.g. urine samples).

Paragraph 23(5) stipulates that the results of tests must be communicated to the YOT case manager.

Requirement	Intoxicating substance treatment	Paragraph 24

Duration: Any specified period up to 36 months

Conditions that need to be met for this requirement:

Before making this requirement, the court must be satisfied that:

(a) the offender is dependent on or has a propensity to misuse intoxicating substances; AND

(b) the dependency or propensity requires or may be susceptible to treatment; AND

(c) arrangements have been made or can be made for the treatment specified in the order, including residential treatment.

"Intoxicating substance" is defined in para.24(5) as alcohol or "any other substance or product (other than a drug) which is, or the fumes of which are, capable of being inhaled or otherwise consumed for the purpose of causing intoxication". This covers solvents and other substances that do not fall within the classifications in the Misuse of Drugs Act 1971.

The requirement must be recommended by a member of a YOT or an officer of a local probation trust. The offender must also express willingness to comply with the requirement.

Special considerations

Treatment may be residential or non-residential at a place specified in the order, but the nature of treatment will not be specified. Treatment will be by or under the direction of a specified person, with the necessary experience and qualifications in relation to work with individuals with a dependency or propensity to misuse intoxicating substances.

Requirement	Education	Paragraph 25

Duration: any specified period whilst the YRO is in force

Conditions that need to be met for this requirement:

The young person must be of school age and the court, having consulted with the education authority, must be satisfied that efficient arrangements can be made for full time education suitable to the young person's age, ability and aptitude and any special educational needs. The court must also be satisfied that the requirement is necessary for securing the good conduct of the young person or for preventing further offending.

The actual requirement is for the young person to comply with arrangements for education made by his or her parents, so long as they are approved by the local education authority.

Special considerations

A local education authority must be named in the order and this must be the authority where the young person lives.

II. Obligations of a young person on a YRO

Section 5(5) of the CJ&IA 2008 contains the basic underpinning requirements of the YRO which are:

(i)   *keep in touch with responsible officer*

This requires a young person who is subject to a YRO to "keep in touch with the responsible officer in accordance with such instructions as he may from time to time be given by that officer". "Instructions" can mean not only dates and times of appointments or work details but also standard sets of rules agreed with the young person at the start of an order, which allow the youth offending team to stipulate what would be considered inappropriate and therefore breachable behaviour or language whilst on their premises or on activities related to the order.

(ii)   *notify the responsible officer of any change of address*

These two obligations are enforceable as though they were a requirement imposed by the order.

III. Breach of a YRO

The process

The powers relating to breach, revocation or amendment of the YRO are contained in Sch.2 of the CJ&IA 2008. Appendix E contains the text of this Schedule.

Because YROs are used for young people rather than adults, the legislation allows greater flexibility, with breach action following the third unacceptable failure to comply, rather than the second as is the case with the adult community order. This is some recognition of the difference in maturity and typically more disorganised lifestyles of many young offenders, but it still represents a strict enforcement regime.

An information alleging breach should normally be sent in the first instance to the youth court for the LJA in which the young person lives or the magistrates' court, if the young person has already reached the age of 18 at the time of the allegation. The information should be specific about the requirement(s) with which the young person has failed to comply and the grounds for breach action. The magistrates will then issue a summons or a warrant to cause the young person to be brought before them or before the Crown Court. Local arrangements, however, may be in place expediting this process and allowing the YOT to set a court date and advise the young person directly.

Refusal to undergo any surgical, electrical or other treatment involved in a mental health, drug or intoxicating substance requirement will not be treated as a failure to comply, if the court is of the opinion that the refusal was reasonable in the circumstances (Sch.2 para.9).

If the order was made in the youth court, the breach will be dealt with in the youth court or the magistrates' court if the young person has reached the age of 18.

If the order was made in the Crown Court, it must be returned to the Crown Court unless, in making the order, the Crown Court directed that future proceedings relating to the order could take place in a youth court or other magistrates' court under Sch.1 para.36 of the CJ&IA 2008.

Even where the youth/magistrates' court is empowered to deal with the breach, the magistrates may still commit the offender to custody or release on bail until he or she can be brought before the Crown Court. This will primarily take place where the magistrates feel that re-sentencing may be appropriate and that that their own powers in that regard are not sufficient.

Powers of the court

If the court is satisfied that an offender has failed *without reasonable* excuse to comply with any of the requirements of the order, the court may:

- impose a fine of up to £1000 (£250 if the young person is aged under 14);

- amend the terms of the YRO so as to impose requirements in addition to or as substitution for the existing requirements. The choice of requirements available is limited to those that could have been made part of the order when it was originally made. This does not include a fostering requirement or intensive supervision and surveillance (ISS) requirement unless the order already includes such a requirement; or

- revoke the order and re-sentence in any way that the court could have done on the original sentencing occasion had the community order not been made.

95

In contrast to the adult community order, the court is able to take no action and to allow the order to continue without amendment if it feels this is justified in the circumstances.

When considering whether to amend or to revoke the order, the court must take into account the extent to which the young person has complied with the YRO.

Ordinarily, where new requirements are added to an order or substituted for the previous requirements, the court cannot go outside the limits set for the requirement in the CJ&IA 2008. There are two exceptions to this in relation to the YRO:

(a) The unpaid work requirement—the court is able to impose a 20 hour requirement for breach whereas the usual lower limit is 40 hours (para.6(7)).

(b) The fostering requirement may be extended beyond its normal 12 month limit up to 18 months from the date it was first imposed (para.6(9)).

As with the adult community order, sentencing guidelines stipulate that the primary objective in sentencing for breach should be to ensure that the subject of the order completes the requirements set by the court (Sentencing Guidelines Council, 2009); this is an important consideration for YOT case managers in advising the court about whether YROs should be amended and how.

Rather than amending the YRO, the court may choose to revoke the order and to re-sentence by means of a custodial sentence. The Sentencing Guidelines Council (2009) suggest that before doing so the court should be satisfied that the YOT and other local authority services have taken all the steps necessary to ensure that the young person has been given appropriate opportunity and support necessary for compliance. This is intended to ensure that custodial options are treated as a *measure of last resort* and are not used in a punitive way where other ways of responding to the breach might be appropriate and effective. It puts an onus on the YOT to work to secure compliance and to be able to advise the court about the young person's level of engagement and any arrangements that the YOT has made to accommodate his or her needs or circumstances.

(iii) Persistent and wilful refusal to comply

Where a young person has persistently and wilfully refused to comply with a YRO, the court has additional powers. In determining whether a young person has *persistently and wilfully* breached an order, the Sentencing Guidelines Council suggest that the court should use the *persistent offender* criteria:

> "In particular, almost certainly a young person will have 'persistently' breached a youth rehabilitation order where there have been three breaches (each resulting in an appearance before a court) demonstrating a lack of willingness to comply with the order."

> (Sentencing Guidelines Council, 2009: 21)

In these circumstances, the court may revoke the YRO and:

- impose a YRO with an ISS requirement even where the offence(s) before the court are not imprisonable (para.6(13)). For young people under 15, the persistent offender criteria in s.1(4)(c) would still apply (see Chapter 3);

- where the order is a YRO + ISS made in breach proceedings by virtue of para.6(13), impose a custodial sentence. However, if the original offence(s) were not imprisonable, the custodial term is limited to a four-month Detention and

Training Order (DTO) (para.6(15)); and

- impose a custodial sentence. In these circumstances, the general restriction on imposition of a custodial sentence contained in s.152(2) of the CJA 2003 is waived, which means that the "so serious" threshold does not have to be met (para.6(14).

(iv) Powers of the court when the order has expired

Breach action may only be taken where the order is in force at the point where the information is laid. However, for a variety of reasons, the order may have expired by the time the case is dealt with by the court. This limits the court's options because it does not then have the power to amend the order as it no longer exists. It may impose a fine and may still re-sentence for the original offences. In doing so, it must take into account the extent to which the offender had complied with the order whilst it was in force.

IV. Review of YROs

Schedule 1 para.35 of the CJ&IA 2008 empowers the Secretary of State to make provisions for the review of YROs by courts. At the time of writing this has not yet been implemented although it is being piloted with adult community orders and may become established practice in the future.

V. Revocation of YROs

The powers allowing courts to revoke orders in cases that do not involve breach are contained in Sch.2 paras.11 and 12 of the CJ&IA 2008.

Either the young person or the YOT case manager can apply to the court for the order to be revoked or for revocation and an alternative form of sentencing. The application will be heard in *the appropriate court*. This will be the youth court for the LJA named in the order or magistrates' court, if the young person has reached the age of 18. This will usually be the area where the young person resides. Applications in respect of Crown Court orders will be heard in the Crown Court unless, at the time the order was made, a direction was included that future proceedings relating to the order could take place in a youth court or other magistrates' court under Sch.1 para.36 of the CJ&IA 2008.

The young person is unable to make an application whilst an appeal against sentence is taking place.

If an application for revocation with or without re-sentencing is dismissed by the court, no further application can be made by any party without the consent of *the appropriate court* for a period of three months from the date of dismissal.

Revocation may take place where the court considers that it would be in the interests of justice having regard to the circumstances that have arisen since the order was made. This may involve the young person making good progress or responding satisfactorily to treatment.

Revocation and resentencing may also be requested where an offender's situation has changed and the order has become impracticable. This may occur where a young person's education or family situation has altered significantly or where a young person has moved to another area with only a short period of the order remaining.

VI. Amendment of YROs

Under paras 13 and 14 of Sch.2 of the CJ&IA 2008, *the appropriate court* (see above) on the application of the young person or the responsible officer, may amend a YRO either by cancelling any of the requirements of the order or by replacing any of those requirements with an requirement of the same kind. That is, the court may substitute one programme for another or vary the conditions of an activity requirement, for example, but cannot substitute one requirement for another different requirement. This may be needed, for instance, where a young person moves area and a specific programme is not available in the new area. The court may then cancel the existing requirement or substitute another programme, if it is satisfied that the new programme is suitable for the young person and corresponds closely to the programme originally specified in the order (para.15(4)).

Paragraphs 13(2) and 14(2) allow the court to amend the order by substituting a new LJA for the area specified in the order if the young person is living or is proposing to live in the new area. The court must amend the order in this way if the application is made by the responsible officer.

The court cannot impose a mental health treatment, drug treatment or drug testing requirement without the consent of the young person. If the young person does not express willingness to comply with such a requirement, under para.16(4), the court then has the option of revoking the order and re-sentencing. In doing so, the court must take account of the extent to which the young person has complied with the order.

Under para.17, the standard 12-month period set by Sch.1 para.10 for completion of an unpaid work requirement can be extended. In making a decision, the court must consider the interests of justice and have regard to circumstances that have arisen since the order was made.

VII. Effect of further convictions

Commission of a further offence during the currency of a YRO does not in itself constitute a breach of the order.

Under paras 18 and 19, the court may revoke or revoke and re-sentence for the offences relating to the existing order if it considers that it would be in the interests of justice to do so, having regard to circumstances that have arisen since the order was made. Such circumstances could include imposition of a custodial sentence for the new offence(s). In making its decision, the court must also take into account the extent to which the young person has complied with the YRO.

The court is unable to make a new YRO whilst an existing YRO is in force and therefore, if it wishes to impose a YRO for the new offences, it must first revoke the existing YRO. In most instances, a fresh YRO will be made to cover both the new and the "old" offences.

The court has few sentencing options available if it wishes to leave the existing YRO in place. It could impose a fine or compensation order and could conditionally discharge the young person, but would be unable to make a reparation order.

Chapter 10
ENFORCING POST-CUSTODY LICENCES FOR YOUNG PEOPLE

I. Overview of custodial provisions for young people

This chapter will focus on the main custodial sentence for young people, the detention and training order (DTO) which is available in both the youth court and the Crown Court. Young people are released on a notice of supervision, normally to a youth offending team (YOT), until either the sentence expires or the young person is returned to prison. Breaches of such licences are prosecuted through the courts. Longer custodial sentences subject to executive recall are covered also in this chapter but with reference to Chapters 6 and 7 on adult custodial sentences.

There are currently three types of establishment where young people may be placed whilst serving a custodial sentence. These are:

- local authority secure children's homes (LASCHs);
- secure training centres; and
- young offender institutions (YOIs).

YOIs are run by the prison service or by private companies under contracting out arrangements. In practice, the majority of young males in custody are in YOIs. Young men may be placed in a YOI if aged 15 or over on the date the custodial sentence is imposed, unless deemed to be vulnerable. They may also be transferred there mid-sentence having reached the age of 15. A smaller number of young women aged 17 are also housed in dedicated units within establishments jointly designated as adult prison and YOI for women. There are significant differences in staffing levels and extent of welfare orientation between these types of establishment and these are reflected in the sentence planning and pre-release processes.

As with adult post-custody licences, various conditions may be added to the standard conditions on a young person's licence. This may include a requirement to undergo Intensive Supervision and Surveillance (ISS). ISS is an intensive and varied package of intervention available for young people with persistent or serious patterns of offending, whilst on bail, as a requirement of a community sentence or as a condition on a post-custody licence. In the interests of clarity, ISSs are dealt with separately in Chapter 11.

II. Restrictions on impositions of custodial sentences

There are general restrictions on the use of custodial sentences for young people in addition to specific age-related restrictions.

Firstly, under s.83 of the PCC(S)A 2000, the court may not pass a custodial sentence on a young person who is not legally represented. The exceptions to this are where:

- the young person had been granted a right to representation funded by the Legal Services Commission as part of the Criminal Defence Service which was later withdrawn because of his or her conduct; OR

- the young person was informed of the right to apply for such representation and had opportunity to do so, but refused or failed to apply.

Secondly, before passing a custodial sentence, the court must consider that the offence or combination of the offence and one or more offences associated with it are *so serious* that neither a fine nor community sentence can be justified (s.152(2) of the CJA 2003). The custody threshold may only be disregarded in extremely limited circumstances.

Thirdly, in making a determination about seriousness, the court must obtain and consider a written pre-sentence report. However, it does not need to order a new pre-sentence report where one or more previous reports are available and the court has regard to the information contained therein (s.156(5)).

Furthermore, the Sentencing Guidelines Council state that:

"Before deciding to impose a custodial sentence on a young offender, the court must ensure that all the statutory tests are satisfied—namely

(i) That the offender cannot be properly dealt with by a fine alone or by a youth rehabilitation order

(ii) That a youth rehabilitation order with intensive supervision and surveillance or with fostering cannot be justified, and

(iii) That custody is the last resort

And in doing so should take account of the circumstances, age and maturity of the young offender."

(Sentencing Guidelines Council, 2009: 23)

III. The detention and training order

The legal basis for the DTO

Originally introduced by the C&DA 1998, the present legislation governing DTOs is the PCC(S)A 2000. This permits a youth court to impose periods of custody up to 24 months, which is substantially longer than the maximum period available in the magistrates' court.

In addition to the general restrictions on the use of custody detailed above, if the young person is over 12 but under the age of 15 when convicted, the court can only impose a DTO if it is of the opinion that the young person is a persistent offender (s.100(2(a))—the definition of a persistent offender is discussed in Chapter 3. The DTO is not currently available for young people who are still 10 or 11 years old when convicted.

Under the DTO, a young person may be sent to custody for periods of 4, 6, 8, 10, 12, 18 or 24 months and will serve half that period in custody and half in the community subject to a notice of supervision. Periods spent on remand in custody or local authority accommodation will not be deducted from the sentence, but, in determining the length of the DTO, the court should have regard to time spent on remand. Home Detention Curfews (HDCs) are not available but alternative provisions for early release also apply so the actual period spent in custody may be reduced.

Where the young person is sentenced for more than one offence, the court may order DTO terms to be served consecutively but only up to a maximum of 24 months.

IV. Early release

Section 102 of the PCC(S)A 2000 allows a young offender to be released before the half-way point of sentence:

- 1 month early for DTOs 8—under 18 months; and
- 1 or 2 months early for DTOs 18–24 months.

Currently, the system operates with a presumption in favour of release which is electronically monitored. Amendments in the Offender Management Act 2007 have also introduced more flexibility so that young people may be released up to one or two months early rather than exactly one or two months. Early release is conditional on having an appropriate address at which the monitoring equipment can be installed. This may require the consent of an appropriate responsible adult at the proposed address.

Certain offenders will be ineligible for early release and these include young people convicted of offences involving violence or endangering others. Early release will also be denied in cases where a young person has behaved in a dangerous or violent way towards others during the sentence or has made exceptionally poor progress against the sentence plan objectives because of a failure to co-operate or take responsibility for his or her behaviour.

In most other cases the young person will be released under the early release arrangements and will be subject to curfew. Any breach of the curfew conditions will be notified to the YOT case manager by the contractor and this will include tampering with the equipment and committing or threatening violence against any employee of the contractor as well as absence from the premises during curfew hours. Such breaches will be dealt with by the court.

If a young person breaches any condition of the notice of supervision not related to the curfew this will be dealt with in the usual way.

V. Obligations of young people on notice of supervision

There are six standard conditions in a notice of supervision which require a young person:

- to keep in touch with their supervising officer (i.e. YOT case manager) in accordance with any instructions given;
- if required, to receive visits from their supervisor at home;
- to reside permanently at an address approved by the supervisor and to notify the supervisor of any stay away;
- to undertake only work approved by their supervisor and to notify him/her in advance of any proposed change;

101

- not to travel outside the United Kingdom without prior permission of the supervisor; and

- to be well behaved and not to commit any offence or do anything that could undermine the purpose of their supervision.

As YOT case managers typically have more regular contact with young people in custody than is the case with adult prisoners, there is more opportunity for building relationships and seeking to secure compliance before the point of release. The pre-release meeting which will be held around 10 working days before release should discuss the notice of supervision conditions, including recommendations for additional conditions, and underline what will be expected of the young person. The notice will be explained to the young person and he or she should sign it before release. The young person should report to the responsible YOT on the day of release and the conditions and expectations of licence should then be confirmed. If a young person is living with parents, they should also be made aware of the conditions and their co-operation sought in assisting the young person to comply.

Additional conditions

If the circumstances of the case or the public protection issues involved suggest that it would be warranted, additional conditions may be included in the notice of supervision. These may include:

- an electronically monitored curfew;

- a period on ISS (see chapter 11); or

- any of the additional conditions that may be added to adult standard determinate sentence licences as detailed in pc 29/2007 and covered earlier in Chapter 6.

Where additional conditions are agreed at the young person's Final Review before release, these should be confirmed by the responsible officer and sent to the establishment in Form T1:FR.

Care should be taken over the wording of additional conditions to ensure they are realistic and understandable to the young person, as well as enforceable. They should also be proportionate and it is important to consider the potential for unintended consequences that might have implications for the development and well-being of the young person. Restrictions on mixing with other people, for instance, should be thought about carefully; they may appear sensible in terms of reducing peer influences on offending, but they may also prevent a young person engaging in pro-social activities such as football or youthwork activities.

VI. Breach of notice of supervision

DTOs are enforced in line with the National Standards for youth rehabilitation orders (YROs), as spelt out in National Standard 9.55 (YJB, 2009). Under this Standard, YOT case managers are required to follow up all failures to attend within one working day by telephone, home visit or letter to determine whether the reason is acceptable or otherwise. If no reason is given or the reason is not acceptable, then a formal written warning must be issued within 5 days.

The young person is allowed a maximum of two formal warnings within a 12-month period. On the third failure to comply the YOT case manager must initiate breach action unless exceptional circumstances apply in which case the YOT manager may authorise a decision to delay breach action. This should be clearly recorded with details of the reasons supporting this decision.

On the other hand, breach action may be taken immediately if the breach represents a serious matter or the young person is judged to pose a high risk of serious harm to others.

The YOT case manager will lay an information before the relevant court in the same way as for a YRO, irrespective of whether the order was made in youth court or the Crown Court. This will be the youth court acting for the LJA where the young person resides in the majority of cases, or the magistrates' court if the young person is aged 18 at the time of the allegation. The court will then issue a summons or a warrant to cause the young person to be brought before it.

Under s.104(3) of the PCC(S)A 2000, the powers of the court on a finding of guilt are restricted to:

- imposing a fine of up to £1000 (£250 if the young person is under 14); or
- ordering the offender to be returned to custody for either three months or the remainder of the term of the DTO, whichever is the shorter.

If the notice of supervision has expired by the time the breach is dealt with in court, the court's powers are limited to the imposition of a fine.

VII. The effects of further offences

Where a young person subject to a DTO notice of supervision is convicted of a new imprisonable offence, the court may order the young person to be detained in custody for a period not greater than the period between the commission of the offence and the end of the DTO. The court will also be able to sentence separately in respect of the new offence and this may include a custodial sentence. In this case, the court may direct that the two periods in custody are served either concurrently or consecutively.

VIII. Long-term determinate sentences for young people

While the majority of custodial sentences for young people are DTOs, there are provisions available in the Crown Court for sentences lasting longer than the maximum two years permitted for the DTO. This section will focus on sentences for determinate periods and the next section will address arrangements relating indeterminate sentencing. Use of such sentences is controversial and raises a number of issues in terms of young people's rights and their treatment within the criminal justice system. There are consequently tight legal safeguards around the availability of these sentences. Nevertheless, their use is increasing and YOT case managers need to familiarise themselves with the practices and procedures for executive recall already well established within the adult custodial framework.

Legal basis of long-term determinate sentences

Under s.91 of the PCC(S)A 2000, the Crown Court may impose a sentence of detention in respect of:

- an offence punishable in a person aged 21 or over with imprisonment for 14 years or more, but not an offence with a sentence that is fixed by law; and

- an offence under ss.14 or 15 of the Sexual Offences Act 1956 (indecent assault).

And, for a young person who is over 14 but under 18 when convicted, in respect of:

- an offence under ss.1 or 3A of the Road Traffic Act 1988 (death by dangerous driving and death by careless driving whist under the influence of drink or drugs).

The court may do so only where it is of the opinion that none of the other methods by which the case may be dealt with are suitable. It may impose any period up to the maximum term available for that offence. For certain offences, such as rape, this means that this section can be used to impose what is in effect a discretionary life sentence. At the other end of the spectrum, there is no statutory minimum and, in theory, s.91 sentences can be imposed for periods of less than two years.

Release on licence

For s.91 sentences with a determinate length, release is automatic at the half-way point. For any sentence over 12 months, a standard determinate sentence licence will apply (see Chapter 6) until the end of the sentence.

On rare occasions, a s.91 sentence may be made for a period of less than 12 months in which case the young person will be released subject to a notice of supervision for three months under s.65 of the CJA 1991.

In addition, a young person who reaches the age of 18 during his or her sentence can be released early on HDC if the eligibility criteria are met. He or she will therefore be subject to HDC licence for the HDC period.

Enforcement

Section 65 notices of supervision are enforced through the courts while other licences, including HDC, are dealt with through the recall arrangements outlined in Chapter 7.

IX. Extended sentences

Legal basis of extended sentences

As for adults, extended sentences for young people essentially refer to extended periods of licence supervision, rather than longer periods in custody.

Section 228 of the CJA 2003

The CJA 2003 put in place the arrangements for extended sentences for adults (s.227) alongside the new sentence of imprisonment for public protection (s.225). The equivalent arrangements for young people are contained in ss.226 and 228.

Sections 225–228 all refer to a lengthy list of "specified" sexual and violent offences contained in Sch.15 of the Act. Some of these offences are also *serious offences*. A *serious offence* is defined in s.224 (2) as an offence punishable in the case of a person aged 18 or over by life imprisonment or by a determinate sentence of 10 years or more. *Serious harm* in s.224(3) refers to death or serious personal injury, whether physical or psychological.

Extended sentences under s.226 are applicable where a young person under 18 has been convicted of a *specified offence* and the court is of the opinion that there is a *significant risk of serious harm* through the offender committing further specified offences. Originally extended sentences could only be made where the conviction was for a *specified offence* but not a *serious offence*. However amendments introduced by the CJ&IA 2008 have ensured that the provisions for extended sentences may now be applied where the conviction is for a *serious offence*.

This change increases the potential use of extended sentences and is intended to reduce the use of indeterminate sentences of detention under s.226.

However, extended sentences should only be imposed where the seriousness of the offence would justify a custodial term of four years or more. Moreover, even where the criteria are met, the court *may* rather than *must* impose an extended sentence.

The effect of this is to target the use of extended sentences at more serious offences and to allow more discretion in their use.

The court should determine the appropriate custodial term (not exceeding the maximum term in law for the offence(s) in question). It will then set the extended licence period which should be whatever length the court considers necessary for the purposes of protecting the public and preventing the offender committing further specified offences (s.228(2)). The extended licence period is determined more by assessment of potential future risk than by the seriousness of the offence(s) but should still be a proportionate response to risk with regard to the rights of the young person.

The maximum terms for the extension periods are five years for a specified violent offence and eight years for a specified sexual offence. However, the total sentence including the extension period cannot exceed the maximum term permitted by law for that offence.

Release on licence

Young people serving extended sentences were originally only released on the approval of the Parole Board and, in theory, could be held until the end of their custodial term, being released for the extended licence period only. However, by virtue of the CJ&IA 2008, as of July 14, 2008, these young people are now released automatically half way through their custodial term unless the Parole Board directs otherwise.

Enforcement

Young people subject to the licence period of an extended sentence may be recalled to prison under the executive powers of the Secretary of State (see Chapter 7).

X. Indeterminate sentences for young people

Life sentences

Legal basis for life sentences for young people under 18

For murder, s.90 of the PCC(S)A 2000 requires the court to sentence the young person to be detained during Her Majesty's Pleasure. For other offences, s.91 empowers the court to pass what are in effect discretionary life sentences.

Release on licence

Release is at the discretion of the Parole Board and subject to licence. See Chapter 6 for further details.

Enforcement

Young people on life licences may be recalled to prison under the executive powers of the Secretary of State. The powers to do so are contained in s.32 of the Crime (Sentences) Act 1997 as amended by Sch.18 of the CJA 2003.

Detention for public protection (DPP)

Legal basis for detention for public protection sentences

DPP sentences were introduced by s.226 of the CJA 2003 and are available for young people aged under 18 convicted of *serious offences* committed after April 4, 2005. *Serious offence* is defined in s.224(2) as an offence punishable in the case of an adult aged 18 or over by life imprisonment or by a determinate sentence of 10 years or more.

The criteria for the sentence are:

- conviction for a *specified offence* contained in Sch.15 of the Act;
- the offence is also a *serious offence;*
- the offence does not attract a mandatory sentence of detention during Her Majesty's Pleasure and the court does not consider it sufficiently serious to justify a s.91 sentence, and
- the court is nevertheless of the opinion that there is a *significant risk* to members of the public of *serious harm* through the offender committing further specified offences. *Serious harm* is defined in s.224(3) as death or serious personal injury, whether physical or psychological.

At the time of sentencing, the judge will determine the minimum term the offender will serve in prison, known as the *tariff*. For DPP sentences this should be at least two years (s.225(3b)). The prisoner cannot be released on parole until the tariff period has been served and may be held for considerably longer, depending on the assessment of risk.

Release on licence

A DPP prisoner will only be released following a direction from the Parole Board and will remain on licence for a minimum of 10 years. After this period, the licence can be revoked by the Secretary of State on the recommendation of the Parole Board, who must review the case annually.

Enforcement

Young people on DPP licences may be recalled to prison under the executive powers of the Secretary of State. The powers to do so are contained in s.32 of the Crime (Sentences) Act 1997 as amended by Sch.18 of the CJA 2003.

XI. Licences for young people on long-term sentences

The standard conditions for young people released on licence from longer term sentences are as follows:

(i)   **Standard conditions relating to determinate sentences (including extended sentences)**

    (a) to keep in touch with your supervising officer in accordance with any instructions you may be given;

    (b) if required, to receive visits from your supervising officer at your home/place of residence;

    (c) permanently to reside at an address approved by your supervising officer and notify him or her in advance of any proposed changes of address or any proposed stay (even for one night) away from that approved address;

    (d) undertake only such work (including voluntary work) approved by your supervising officer and notify him or her in advance of any change;

    (e) not to travel outside the United Kingdom without prior permission from your supervising officer (permission for which will be given in exceptional circumstances only); and

    (f) to be well behaved, not to commit any offence and not to do anything that could undermine the purposes of your supervision, which are to protect the public, prevent you from re-offending and help you re-settle successfully into the community.

(ii) **Standard conditions relating to indeterminate sentences**

    (a) he/she shall place himself/herself under the supervision of whichever supervising officer is nominated for the purpose from time to time;

    (b) he/she shall on release report to the supervising officer so nominated and shall keep in touch in accordance with that officer's instructions;

    (c) he/she shall, if his/her supervising officer so requires, receive visits in his or her home;

    (d) he/she shall reside only where approved by his/her supervising officer;

    (e) he/she shall work only where approved by his/her supervising officer and shall inform that officer at once if that job is lost; and

    (f) he/she shall not travel outside the United Kingdom without the prior permission of his/her supervising officer.

(iii) Additional conditions

Additional conditions can be included in the licence. Youth Justice Board guidance indicates that these should be justified on the grounds of public protection and risk management. Conditions that address welfare concerns that do not relate to the offence and associated risk factors should not be added (YJB, 2007), although it may be appropriate to address these needs as part of post-custody supervision. Proportionality and developmental issues are also critical considerations in setting licence conditions, as well as the implications for the young person's rights.

The sentencing court may have specified particular conditions to be included in the licence and, if so, these should be included unless there is good reason not to do so.

As with adults, conditions should be selected from an approved list detailed in Annex A of PC 29/2007 and also Chapter 13 of the Indeterminate Sentence Manual (PSO 4700). These are reproduced in the YJB's *Case Management Guidance* (YJB, 2009b). Conditions may include an electronically monitored curfew and/or Intensive Supervision and Surveillance (addressed in Chapter 11).

For determinate sentence cases, before release the YOT case manager should receive a PD1 form from the secure establishment and this is the vehicle by which additional conditions may be requested (unless the young person is being released on HDC in which case the Home Suitability Assessment Report will be used).

The YOT case manager should liaise with the local police, victim liaison worker from the probation service and MAPPA structures, as appropriate. As with DTO cases, the pre-release meeting held in the secure establishment should also discuss and formulate recommendations for additional conditions, which the YOT case manager will then include in the PD1.

If a young person is held in a YOI, the additional conditions will normally be approved by the prison governor. For longer term prisoners (over four years) and those serving extended sentences, the Parole Board must approve licence conditions. Where release is not automatic but is at the discretion of the Parole Board, the YOT case manager will prepare a Parole Assessment Report at requested intervals and, if release is being proposed, requests for additional conditions should be contained in this report.

There are differences where the young person is about to be released from a local authority secure children's home or secure training centre, as the directors or managers of these establishments do not have the same authority as a prison governor. In this case, the YJB's Placement and Casework Service will be involved in the process of preparing licences and approving additional licence conditions. Contact details are available on the YJB website (http://www.yjb.gov.uk).

XII. Recall procedures

The recall procedures are dealt with in Chapter 7 and these apply to young people as well as to adults. There are additional considerations for young people:

- When recall is requested, the YJB Placements and Casework Service should be notified and a copy of the recall request report should be forwarded to them.

- YOT officers requesting recall should be aware of the potential emotional impact upon the young person and should communicate any concerns about the welfare and vulnerability of the young person to other professionals involved in the recall process.

- All requests for recall should be authorised by the YOT manager or other individual with delegated authority.

Fixed-term recall procedures apply to eligible young people and under these arrangements a recalled young person may be re-released after 28 days (see Chapter 7).

Chapter 11

INTENSIVE SUPERVISION AND SURVEILLANCE (ISS)

I. Introduction

ISS is a complex beast, an intensive programme established initially as the Intensive Supervision and Surveillance Programme, for young people with persistent patterns of offending. More recently it has also encompassed young people accused or convicted of serious offences and more recently still has developed strands appropriate for younger offenders (junior ISS) and for older young offenders in full-time employment or training.

What is interesting and rather curious about ISS is that in itself it had no legal standing before the YRO provisions in the Criminal Justice and Immigration Act 2008 (CJ&IA 2008) came into force. It was set up to operate at various stages in the criminal justice process as:

- a condition of bail;

- a requirement of a community order; and

- an additional condition on a post-custody licence or DTO notice of supervision.

The CJ&IA 2008 in creating an "extended activity requirement" that can be attached to a YRO, places the ISS on a statutory footing for the first time.

ISS significantly blurs the boundary between community and custodial provision. In theory a young person could commit one offence and follow the sequence outlined below:

(i) Eligibility and suitability for ISS

As ISS is a highly restrictive intervention, it is important that safeguards are in place to ensure that it is used only for those cases where the nature of the offence(s) or patterns of offending warrant such intervention.

- In terms of sentencing this means that the offence or offences before the court must be considered to meet the custody threshold (the *so serious* criterion).

- For bail cases the young person must be at risk of remand to custody or to local authority accommodation.

- For post-custody cases, the decision about whether the young person should participate in ISS will be based on assessment of risk and needs.

Further details are given later in this chapter.

As well as being eligible, the young person must be assessed as suitable for the programme and its demands. Such assessment should be based on the Asset Core Profile and Risk of Serious Harm form, where appropriate. Good practice would suggest that assessment should be a jointly conducted by the case manager and ISS scheme, with involvement from secure establishments in post custody cases.

Relevant considerations include the following:

- It should be realistic for the young person to comply with the varied elements of the programme. This may be difficult for young people with mental health or substance misuse needs, for instance.

- The programme should have sufficient goals to work towards with the young person and this may be an issue for some young offenders who have few criminogenic needs. In these instances, the restrictions and potentially punitive elements of the programme may not be counterbalanced by the positive aspects of rehabilitation and support; YOT case managers may therefore consider that other sentencing options may be more appropriate.

- Case managers should be aware of the possibility of "up-tariffing" the young person and should be actively considering whether other less restrictive options may be appropriate—so that in effect ISS is reserved for those young people with highest criminogenic needs and/or most at risk of custody and that it is used as *a measure of last resort*.

- ISS should not be used for vulnerable young people with welfare needs that do not relate to their offending. It is not appropriate to deal with these by a court-mandated route that puts the young person at increased risk of custody in the event of breach.

- Where a young person poses a risk of serious harm, ISS should only be used where a thorough assessment has indicated that the risk can be effectively managed in the community using ISS resources and involvement from other agencies (which may be agreed through a multi-agency meeting, for instance, in MAPPA cases).

These points about suitability are important because the intensive intervention and surveillance that is integral to ISS creates multiple opportunities for non-compliance and, as an explicit alternative to custody, ups the stakes in terms of a young person receiving a custodial penalty for breach. Any decision to propose ISS in court or as a condition of licence/notice of supervision should be defensible and supported by evidence.

(ii) Components of ISS programmes

The core elements of ISS are:

- restorative justice/ reparation;
- education/training/employment;
- interventions relating to offending and associated risk factors;
- family support;
- assistance in developing inter-personal skills; and
- surveillance.

111

Intervention should be tailored to the young person's needs and may therefore include varied elements relating to such areas as substance misuse, constructive use of leisure, accommodation and budgeting.

Relevance to the young person and responsiveness to needs is clearly significant in encouraging engagement and increasing compliance with the programme. Quality of relationships and openness in planning processes, using pro-social modelling, can assist with this.

(iii) Curfews and electronic monitoring

All ISS requirements should be supported by a night-time curfew, which will be electronically monitored in all but exceptional cases.

For young people under the age of 16, the maximum length of curfew is three months. For those aged 16 or over, a period of up to six months may be stipulated in line with the type and intensity of ISS being proposed (see below).

During the currency of a YRO with a curfew requirement that is electronically monitored, the YOT case manager may apply to the court for the curfew conditions to be altered, if a change in the young person's circumstances warrants such action.

Enforcement of the curfew will rest with the YOT case manager, except in bail cases. It is therefore important to establish good channels of communication with the local contractor. The YOT is also required to establish a single point of contact via the Secure eMail system to receive notifications of violations. In the event of violation, the YOT case manager should seek an explanation and will be responsible for any decision about whether the reason for the violation is legitimate or whether to issue warnings or initiate breach action, in line with the *National Standards for Youth Justice Services* (YJB, 2009a).

(iv) Types of ISS

The development of different forms and intensities of ISS reflects the political popularity of the programmes and their flexible combinations of care and control elements.

The following types and levels of intensity of ISS interventions are available and should be used in accordance with assessment using the Asset tool and the Scaled Approach.

Type	Criteria	Duration		Contacts	
Extended	Very high risk of serious harm and/or high likelihood of offending (Asset score 33–64)	12 months	1–4 months 25 hours	5–6 months 15 hours	7–12 months 5 hours
Intensive Band 1	High risk of serious harm and/or likelihood of offending (Asset score 24–32)	6 months	1–3 months 25 hours	4–6 months 5 hours	
Medium Band 2	Low risk of serious harm and likelihood of offending (Asset score under 24)	6 months	1–2 months 20 hours	Month 3 10 hours	4–6 months 5 hours
Junior	Young person must be aged 13 or younger	6 months	1–3 months 12.5 hours	4–6 months 5 hours	

Employment–based	Young person must be able to provide proof of "legitimate" employment of at least 35 hours pw	6 months	1–3 months 7 hours, at least one contact each day	4–6 months 3 hours
Training–based	Young person must be on a fulltime training course or apprenticeship of at least 35 hours pw	6 months	1–3 months At least one contact each day	4–6 months 5 hours

The extended ISS is obviously very intrusive and employs a high degree of surveillance and control. It should therefore be used in exceptional circumstances only, in most cases as a requirement on a YRO.

Attendance requirements are strict and two items from the 2009 National Standards for Youth Justice Services (YJB, 2009a) should be noted:

- Where young people do not attend due to sickness during the intensive phase of ISS, that intensive phase should be extended to take account of the absences so that the number of days' activity originally designated for the intensive phase is still achieved.

- The same principle should apply to other absences not authorised by the ISS scheme.

Where a young person is on an employment or training-based ISS package and loses his or her job or placement, his or her timetable should be reviewed immediately and the programme should increase to full intensity (at Band 1, 2 or extended whichever is appropriate).

(v) Case management

Because of the intensive nature of the programme and its multiple commitments, young people may rapidly find themselves in a position of breach. Appropriate and swift application of the procedures is necessary, particularly where young people may pose a risk of serious harm to others or have extensive patterns of offending. However, it is not in the interests of justice nor of public protection to proceed with inappropriate and unnecessary breach actions, and this may work counter to the effective engagement of young people.

Good practice therefore suggests that ISS practitioners should:

- make efforts to ensure that young people have clear written information about their appointments and other commitments (which may be presented in a weekly timetable, for example);

- inform parents and relevant other professionals of the young person's appointments and commitments as appropriate, so they are in a position to support compliance;

- be proactive and creative in finding ways of securing compliance—some young people may wish to receive telephone calls or texts in advance of appointments, for example;

- be similarly proactive and creative in terms of overcoming obstacles to compliance and use resources to best effect—providing weekly bus passes, for example, rather than reimbursing bus fares;

113

- be prepared to designate some aspects of the programme as voluntary activities —for instance, on-going contact with a drugs worker, counselling, youthwork activities. these can then count towards the programme hours without being enforceable (however, if a young person does not attend they can be quickly replaced by enforceable activities);

- make careful judgments about the acceptability or unacceptability of explanations for failures to comply, taking into account the young person's circumstances and knowledge of him or her gained through the programme. accurate recording of these decisions is critical as they must stand up to scrutiny and be defensible; and

- use pro-social modelling techniques to tackle issues of compliance and expectations head on, but in ways that acknowledge the efforts the young person might be making to comply and seek to adopt a collaborative problem-solving approach.

This is essentially good practice that could be used in the management of any order, but these points are particularly relevant to ISS in order to enhance its supportive and rehabilitative potential with an often chaotic and needy constituency of young offenders, rather than its potentially punitive aspects.

In breach cases before the court, the YOT case manager's breach report may be particularly important in guiding the court in its decision-making. There should be a clear indication of the actions that might be appropriate and whether or not the young person could or should be returned to the ISS scheme to continue the order or made subject to a new or amended order with ISS. The YJB Operational Guidance notes that:

- "breach should not be considered as an obstacle to running ISS, but rather as an integral part of it;

- breach can be a positive tool to make clear to young people that the programme will be robustly enforced. If a scheme is using 'therapeutic breach' in this way, they should make clear to the court that they want to see the young person returned to the programme and make the case for why this should be done (citing other attendance, behaviour and engagement wherever possible)."

(Youth Justice Board, 2009d: 23)

II. ISS bail

The legislative basis for an ISS programme on bail is s.3 of the Bail Act 1976 which allows the court to add conditions to bail in order to ensure that the young person:

- surrenders to custody at the due date and time;

- does not commit an offence whilst on bail; and

- does not interfere with witnesses or otherwise obstruct the course of justice.

An ISS condition can be used where it is felt to be necessary to achieve these objectives and also to reduce the use of remands to custody or local authority accommodation. The young person must be at risk of a remand in custody or local authority accommodation. If placed on bail as an alternative, he or she will be subject to a 25 hours per week ISS package (Band 1).

An ISS programme will include an electronically monitored curfew by virtue of s.3(6ZAA). This is available for any young person over the age of 12 but only where the YOT has assessed the young person and his or her circumstances and has indicated that electronic monitoring would be suitable. If the curfew element of the bail package is breached, the electronic monitoring contractor will inform the police directly.

During the period of bail, the young person must comply with a programme established by the YOT. This should cover the ISS core elements, although the fact that the young person is on bail rather than being convicted, means that reparation would not be appropriate. Direct work on the alleged offences would also be inappropriate but ISS practitioners may set up more general work around offending behaviours, perhaps relating to previous convictions.

Any failures to comply with the programme must be followed up within 24 hours (not one working day) by telephone or home visit to establish whether the failure was acceptable or otherwise. The outcome should be clearly recorded. If the decision is that a particular failure is unacceptable, a written warning must be issued. Breach proceedings must be started after a second unacceptable failure to comply, but can be started after the first failure if the breach is sufficiently serious or if there is an indication that the level of risk of serious harm to others has increased.

Breach will be initiated by contacting the police, working in line with any local protocols allowing the fast tracking of cases involving serious offences or persistent young offenders. This will mean preparation of a s.9 witness statement by the responsible YOT case manager (see Appendix B for an example).

When a young person is brought before the court, the YOT should present a report outlining the circumstances of the breach and other relevant information. It should make a clear recommendation for action and, specifically, indicate whether it is appropriate for the young person to be returned to the ISS scheme.

Where the young person denies the allegation of breach, the court does not have the power to adjourn for a hearing but must make a decision on the day the young person is produced in court. However, the young person and his or her representatives must have opportunity to comment on the prosecution materials before the court and present evidence to support his or her case.

III. ISS as a requirement of a youth rehabilitation order (YRO)

Section 1(3)(b) of the CJ&IA 2008 makes provision for ISS be added to a YRO as an "extended activity requirement". This allows the court to direct a young person to engage in activities for periods longer than those allowed under a simple activity requirement, i.e. from 91 to 180 days.

By virtue of s.4, an extended activity requirement can normally only be made for imprisonable offences where the court's opinion is that the offence or offences before it meet the *so serious* custody threshold. If under the age of 15, the court must also be of the opinion that the young person is also a *persistent offender* (see Chapter 3 for a discussion of *persistence*).

There are additional restricted circumstances in which this requirement may be used for non-imprisonable offences by a Crown Court in breach proceeding but only where a young person has wilfully and persistently failed to comply with a YRO (Sch.2 para.8(12)). For further details see Chapter 10.

If a requirement of this kind is imposed, the court must also impose a supervision requirement and a curfew requirement (which will be electronically monitored unless exceptional circumstances exist). Other YRO requirements may be added to the order but the court is not permitted to use a fostering requirement in combination with an extended activity requirement.

Breach, revocation and amendments to YROs are dealt with under Sch.2 of the CJ&IA 2008. In the event of breach, the information laid before the court must be clear about which requirement or requirements the allegation of breach refers to as this is the legal basis for the breach action. Court appearances may be fast tracked in line with local protocols dealing with persistent young offenders or PPO cases as appropriate. The total time from the breach event to court appearance should be no more than 10 days.

Because of the risk of custody associated with breach action, YOT case managers should be proactive in giving guidance to the court about available options to deal with the breach. If it is felt that the order and ISS should be allowed to continue the YOT case manager should advise the court of any amendments needed in order to ensure future compliance and should indicate any actions that the ISS scheme itself might take to prevent another instance of breach.

IV. ISS as a requirement of post-custody licence

Participation in ISS may be stipulated as an additional condition on a detention and training order (DTO) notice of supervision or a licence after release from a longer determinate or indeterminate sentence. The notice or licence should also contain a separate condition relating to electronic monitoring allowing that aspect of the surveillance to be effected. Custodial sentences and arrangements for additional conditions to be added to notices/licences are discussed fully in Chapter 10.

ISS as a post-custody measure should be reserved for those young people who represent a high risk of serious harm or of re-offending. The appropriateness of ISS might be indicated by eligibility for MAPPA (at levels 1, 2 or 3) or an Asset score of more than 33, but these are not stipulated as requirements. Decisions about whether to impose an ISS condition should be made on the basis of careful risk assessment, with regard to proportionality and effective management of risk. If such a condition is imposed, it would be managed at the Band 1 level, but with some adjustments to the length of the intensive part of the requirement may be needed depending on the period of the young person's notice or licence.

Breach action relating to a notice of supervision will be dealt with through the youth court (or magistrates' court if the young person has reached the age of 18 when the allegation is made). An information will be laid in the same way as for a YRO.

Breach of other post-custody licences are subject to executive recall procedures, either standard recall or emergency recall depending on the urgency of the situation and assessment of risk. These procedures are detailed in Chapter 7.

V. Absence or absconding

The ISSP Management Guidance (YJB 2008) indicates that absence from the programme for 48 hours, including curfew periods, should be treated as absconding, if there has been no contact and no valid explanation received. Breach action should be initiated immediately through the courts or executive recall procedures.

VI. Periods on remand whilst subject to ISS

Because of the nature of young people subject to ISS, remand episodes are not infrequent, particularly following alleged breaches of electronic curfew. These raise issues for continuity of programmes and viability if the remand periods are lengthy.

Youth Justice Board guidance (2008) suggests that, if a young person is released and is able to return to the programme within a month, the programme can be continued and a number of days can be added to the programme to make up for the missed days. This particularly ensures that the required number of days on the intensive phase is still achieved.

Where a young person on a YRO is returned to the ISS scheme after a period of more than one month, the scheme should apply to the court for the order to be revoked and replaced with another YRO with a new extended activity requirement so that the programme can be implemented in full.

Chapter 12
PARENTING ORDERS

The focus on parenting has become a central feature of the current youth justice system, with poor and inconsistent parenting clearly highlighted as a risk factor in relation to anti-social behaviour and criminality. The first court orders became available under the Crime and Disorder Act 1998 (C&DA 1998) and these were further expanded by the Anti-social Behaviour Act 2003 (ASBA 2003). This later legislation also introduced parenting contracts, which are voluntary agreements with parents. While these are not legally binding, non-compliance or non-co-operation may be cited in an application for a full parenting order, in much the same way that failure to comply with an acceptable behaviour contract can be cited in an application for an anti-social behaviour order (ASBO).

As with ASBOs and other measures relating to dangerous offenders (covered in Chapter 13), parenting orders are a hybrid order. They are civil orders in the first instance but have a backing in criminal law in that breach of the order is a criminal offence.

Parenting orders may be made against named parents, guardians or any other individual with parental responsibility for a young person. Reference to "parent" within this chapter will encompass the full range of individuals who may be subject to such orders.

On occasions parenting orders may be made in respect of looked after children, after negotiation with children's social care. This would occur usually in situations where a young person is placed with one or more parents or where a care plan aims to reunite the family. Parenting orders should not be made against a local authority in its capacity as corporate parent (Youth Justice Board, 2007).

Legal basis of parenting orders

Parenting orders are established by s.8 of the C&DA 1998 and are available in youth, magistrates' and Crown Courts as well as family proceedings court and a magistrates' court acting in a civil capacity. Following amendments to the original legislation, they can now be made:

- as free standing orders in the magistrates' court; or
- in proceedings where:
  - a young person is convicted of an offence;
  - a young person is made subject to an ASBO or sexual offences prevention order (SOPO);
  - a parental compensation order has been made in respect of a young person's behaviour (s.144, of the Serious Organised Crime and Police Act 2005);
  - a parent or carer is convicted of failure to comply with an order under s.20 of the CJA 2003, requiring attendance at a young offender panel (see Chapter 8);
  - a child safety order is made in respect of a young person (s.11 C&DA 1998) or the court is dealing with a failure to comply with a child safety order; or

- a parent is convicted of an offence under ss.443 or 444 of the Education Act 1996, both these sections referring to school attendance.

In the above cases where parenting orders are attached to other court orders, the court must be satisfied that making the parenting order is desirable in the interests of preventing the commission of further offences or repetition of the behaviour that led to an order being made (s.8(6) of the C&DA 1998). However, where a young person under the age of 16 has been convicted of an offence, the presumption is in favour of a parenting order being made (s.9(1) of the C&DA 1998).

Free-standing orders are available on application by a youth offending team (YOT) or by local authorities and registered social landlords (ss.26 and 26A of the, ASBA 2003). In order to make a free-standing parenting order the court must be satisfied that:

(a) the young person has been involved in anti-social behaviour (and/or criminal conduct in respect of YOT applications); AND

(b) that making the order would be desirable in preventing the young person engaging in further anti-social behaviour and/or criminal conduct.

In all these instances, where the young person involved in the case is under the age of 16, the court must obtain and consider information about the young person's family circumstances and the likely effect of a parenting order, before it can make such an order.

A parenting order may be made against a parent, guardian or any individual with parental responsibility for a young person. Consent is not required. An order can last up to 12 months and is overseen by a responsible officer who may be:

- an officer of a local probation trust;

- a social worker of a local authority social services department;

- a person nominated by a director of children's services or chief education officer; or

- a member of a YOT.

In most cases the responsible officer will be determined according to local protocol.

I. When a parenting order is appropriate

Parenting orders are by their nature intrusive and have implications for private and family life. Their use should therefore be carefully considered and a ruling by the Divisional Court in R. (on the application of M) v Inner London Crown Court [2003] 1 F.L.R. 994 may be instructive. The Divisional Court found that parenting orders were not incompatible with the ECHR but gave guidance on the making of such orders in criminal proceedings where the YOT has prepared a pre-sentence report:

(a) Prominence should normally be given to the views of the author of the pre-sentence report as he or she has had the advantage of interviewing the parent and child.

(b) The seriousness of the offence is likely to be one of the factors taken into account in deciding whether a parenting order is desirable in the interests of preventing future misconduct.

(c) If a parent has acted so reasonably that that their parenting skills would not be improved by a parenting order, then a court would be entitled to say that it is not desirable to make such an order.

II. Obligations under a parenting order

A parenting order requires the parent:

(a) to comply, for a period not exceeding 12 months, with requirements specified in the order; and

(b) to attend, for a concurrent period not exceeding three months, any counselling or guidance programme specified in directions given by the responsible officer.

The requirements that may be specified in an order are those which the court considers desirable in the interests of preventing repetition of anti-social behaviour, commission of further offences or other behaviours that led to the parenting order being made. Such requirements should avoid any conflict with the parent's religious beliefs and interference with the time when he or she works or attends an educational establishment (s.9(4)).

All orders must include an additional core requirement to attend a counselling or guidance programme except where a parent has been made subject to a parenting order on a previous occasion. The court will determine the length of the programme, based on advice from the YOT or local authority. The counselling or guidance programme may include a residential course but only where the court is satisfied that:

(a) parental attendance at a residential course is likely to be more effective than attendance at a non-residential course in preventing commission of further offences or repetition of behaviours; AND

(b) that any interference with family life which is likely to result from the parent attending a residential course is proportionate in the circumstances.

III. Enforcement of parenting orders

The responsible officer is required to enforce the order and promote compliance. In the first instance, he or she should ensure that the parent is given appropriate information and that he or she understands what is expected under the terms of the order. Establishing an open and transparent relationship is important in engaging the parent, particularly where he or she is unhappy about being subject to a parenting order as is often the case.

Where a parent fails to comply with an element of the order, the responsible officer should contact the parent within one working day to seek an explanation. The explanation should be recorded and, if it is not acceptable, the responsible officer should issue a written warning.

If there is more than one unacceptable failure to comply within three months, the responsible officer should call a meeting with the parent and any other agency involved in the delivery of interventions, to review the order and determine how it could be made to work. This meeting may consider amending the order to make it more workable or revocation, if this is appropriate in the circumstances. Following this meeting, if there is a further failure to comply without reasonable excuse, breach action should be initiated.

Although a parenting order is a civil measure, failure to comply with the requirements is a criminal offence which will be heard in the magistrates' court. The responsible officer should refer the matter to the police, in line with local protocols, for the alleged breach to be investigated. The police have discretion to caution the parent if this seems reasonable, given the level of compliance to date. Otherwise the case will be passed to the Crown Prosecution Service who will decide whether there is a realistic prospect of securing a conviction and whether or not prosecution would be in the public interest. If the matter is brought to court, the prosecution will be conducted by the Crown Prosecution Service, not the YOT itself or the local authority.

On conviction, the court may impose a fine not exceeding Level 3 (currently £1,000) or an absolute or conditional discharge. Because breach of a parenting order is a non-imprisonable (summary) offence, a community order is not available as a penalty.

The court is not able to make a new parenting order during breach proceedings, but it may discharge the order. If the order is still allowed to run its course, the responsible officer may direct the parent to attend a new groupwork programme or to attend a number of sessions to make up for missed sessions, as long as there is sufficient time left on the order.

IV. Variation or discharge of a parenting order

Under s.9(5) of the C&DA 1998, at any point whilst the order is in force, an application may be made to the magistrates' court by either the responsible officer or the parent requesting the order to be discharged or amended. In this latter case, the court may, if it feels it is appropriate:

- cancel any provision in the order; OR
- insert any provision into the order that could have been included in the order when it was first made. Such provisions may be in addition to or as a substitute for the original provisions or requirements.

If an application for discharge has been dismissed by a court, no further applications can be made by any party unless the court that made the order has given its consent.

121

Chapter 13

PROVISIONS FOR VIOLENT AND SEXUAL OFFENDERS

Since New Labour came into office in 1997, there have been a range of new provisions aimed at prevention of violent and sexual offences. These fall outside the standard sentencing framework and in many cases are examples of the type of hybrid order first introduced in the C&DA 1998, which created Asbos and sex offender orders. These are imposed as civil orders in the first instance, but with a backing in criminal law in that any breach of the requirements of the orders is a criminal offence. Risk of sexual harm orders (RSHOs). sexual offences prevention orders (SOPOs) and violent offender orders (VOOs), covered in this chapter, are more recent examples of such hybrid orders. While the probation service is not responsible for oversight and enforcement of these orders, offender managers (OMs) should have some basic understanding of what the orders entail and how they work, particularly in the areas where they impinge upon offender case management.

Before outlining these orders, the chapter will begin with an account of the sex offender notification requirements.

I. Sex offender notification

Originally introduced by the Sex Offenders Act 1997, the powers relating to the notification scheme or "sex offender register" are now contained in ss.80–103 of the Sexual Offences Act 2003 (SOA 2003).

(i) The scope of the scheme

Section 80 establishes that notification requirements apply to any individual who:

- is convicted of an offence listed in Sch.3 of the Act—the "qualifying offences";
- has been found not guilty of a qualifying offence by reason of insanity;
- is found to be under a disability and to have done the act charged against him in respect of a qualifying offence (effectively this means being unfit to stand trial for the offence); or
- is cautioned for a qualifying offence.

Under s.97, a chief officer of police can also apply for a notification order where the conviction, caution or finding has taken place outside the United Kingdom.

Schedule 3 lists the qualifying offences which include a range of offences from the Sexual Offences Act 1956 as amended (for instance, rape, incest, intercourse with a girl under 13 and buggery, where the offender is 20 or over and the other party is under 18). It also includes more recent offences, such as being in possession of indecent photographs of a child and further covers a broad range of offences specified in the SOA 2003 itself, including those relating to grooming of children and abuse of a position of trust in relation to children or vulnerable adults.

Section 81 ensures that individuals previously subject to the original notification requirements under the Sex Offenders Act 1997 are covered by the new notification powers contained in Pt II of the SOA 2003 until the end of their notification period.

(ii) Notification periods

Notification periods for over 18s are dependent upon the disposal received and are summarised below:

Sentence	Notification period
Imprisonment for life, IPP sentence or custody for life (ss.93 or 94 of the PCC(S)A 2000)	Indefinite
Imprisonment 30 months or more	Indefinite
Admission to hospital under restriction order (s.41, of the Mental Health Act 1983)	Indefinite
Imprisonment 6 months—up to 30 months	10 years
Imprisonment less than 6 months	7 years
Admission to hospital without restriction order	7 years
Caution	2 years
Conditional discharge	Period of discharge
Any other	5 years

(iii) Provisions for young people

Where the young person is under the age of 18 on the relevant date (the date of conviction, caution or finding) the determinate notification periods outlined above are halved. The periods are defined with reference to the youth justice rather than the adult sentencing provisions (for instance, term of detention and training order instead of length of prison sentence). A young person serving an indeterminate sentence under ss.90/91 of the PCC(S)A 2003 or s.226 of the CJA 2003 will be subject to notification requirements for an indefinite period (although this has faced legal challenge on the basis of human rights).

This halving of the notification period also applies to applications made by a chief officer of police for a notification order under s.97 for offences committed abroad. In such cases, the relevant date will be the date of the hearing where the notification order is made.

Section 89 allows a court dealing with a young person under 18 to make a parental direction so that the obligations on the young person are to be treated instead as obligations on the parent (or individual with parental responsibility). A parental direction also means that the parent must ensure that the young person attends the police station with him or her when the notification is being given.

123

Section 90 permits variation, renewal or discharge of a parental direction on application of the young person, parent or chief officer of police for the area where the young person is living or is intending to live.

(iv) Initial notification requirements (section 83)

Within three days of the notification requirements coming into effect the offender must supply the following information:

- date of birth;
- national insurance number;
- name or names used on the relevant date;
- home address on the relevant date;
- name or names used on the date that notification is given;
- home address on the date that notification is given; and
- the address of any other premises in the United Kingdom at which, at the time the notification is given, he or she regularly resides or stays.

The three-day requirement disregards any period spent in custody, serving a sentence of imprisonment or a term of service detention or where the offender is detained in hospital. It also disregards any period where the offender is abroad.

The offender will normally attend at the police station in his or her local area to complete the notification. Alternatively, he or she may give oral notification to any police officer or to any person authorised for the purpose by the officer in charge of the station.

(v) Subsequent notifications (sections 84 and 85)

Following the initial notification, the offender must also notify the police within three days of:

- any change of name used if this has not been previously notified;
- any change of home address;
- the address of any premises in the United Kingdom not previously notified where he or she has stayed for a "qualifying period" of seven days or two or more periods within a 12-month period which together amount to seven days; or
- his or her release from custody, a prison sentence, term of service detention or detention in a hospital, giving the details listed above.

Changes of name and address may be notified in advance of the change as well as in retrospect. If the change notified in advance does not then occur, the offender is required to inform the police of that fact (s.84(4)).

Notifications should be renewed annually, unless the offender has been in contact with the police to advise of changes during that period.

Under s.86(1), offenders subject to notification must inform the police of details of any proposed foreign travel.

(vi) Breach of notification requirements (section 91)

An offender (or parent subject to parental direction under s.89) may be in breach of notification requirements by failing without reasonable excuse to:

- make an initial notification within three days;

- notify within three days changes of name, address or details of premises where he or she has stayed for a qualifying period;

- make a notification within three days of release from custody, prison sentence, term of service detention or detention in hospital;

- notify the police within six days that a change previously notified has not occurred

- make a periodic (annual) notification; or

- comply with a request from the police or authorised person to take fingerprints and/or photographs for the purpose of verifying his or her identity.

In addition, a parent subject to a parental direction will be in breach if he or she fails without reasonable excuse to ensure that the young offender accompanies him or her to the police station when a notification is given.

An offender (or parent subject to parental direction) will also be in breach if he or she notifies to the police any information which he or she knows to be false.

Breach cases will be dealt with in the local justice area where the offender resides or is found, which will not necessarily be the same area where the failure to comply or giving of false information took place.

On conviction in the magistrates' court, the penalties are imprisonment for a period of up to six months and/or a fine not exceeding the statutory maximum. On indictment, the Crown Court may sentence to imprisonment for up to five years.

II. Foreign travel orders

Sections 114–119 and 122 of the Sexual Offences Act 2003 contain the provisions relating to foreign travel orders in England and Wales. The intention of these orders is spelt out in s.115(2) as being to protect children generally or any particular child from serious physical or psychological harm caused by the defendant doing, outside the United Kingdom, anything that would constitute an offence listed in Sch.3 (of the SOA 2003) if done within any part of the United Kingdom.

(i) "Qualifying offenders"

A person is a qualifying offender if he or she has been:

- convicted of an offence within subs.116(2);

- found not guilty of such an offence by reason of insanity;

- found to be under a disability and to have done the act charged against him in respect of such an offence (effectively this means being unfit to stand trial for the offence); or

- in England and Wales and Northern Ireland, cautioned in respect of such an offence.

125

Section 116(2) lists a range of sexual offences against both adults and children under UK law. Section 116(3) also specifies that relevant offences under the law in force in other jurisdictions may be cited in applications for foreign travel orders. Offences are relevant if they would have constituted an offence under s.116(2) if committed within the United Kingdom.

A chief officer of police may apply to a magistrates' court for a foreign travel order in respect of a qualifying offender who resides or intends to reside in his or her police area. In making such an order, the court must be satisfied that the individual is a qualifying offender and that his or her behaviour since *the appropriate date* (the date of conviction, finding or caution) makes it necessary to make such an order for the purpose of protecting children generally or any child from serious sexual harm from the offender outside the United Kingdom.

(ii) Requirements of a foreign travel order

Under the original legislation, a foreign travel order could last for up to six months but was renewable. From April 1, 2010, this has now been extended to five years (Police and Crime Act 2009 s.24). The order may contain specific prohibitions which may prevent the offender from:

- travelling to any country outside the United Kingdom named or described in the order;
- travelling to any country outside the United Kingdom other than a country named or described in the order; or
- travelling to any country outside the United Kingdom.

These prohibitions must be necessary for the purpose of protecting children generally or any child from serious sexual harm from the offender outside the United Kingdom.

In most cases any offender subject to a foreign travel order will also be subject to the notification orders covered earlier in this chapter. However, if this is not the case, then the offender is required, by virtue of the foreign travel order, to inform the police of any proposed foreign travel.

(iii) Variations, renewals and discharges

Applications for variation, renewal or discharge of foreign travel orders can be made by the offender and also by the chief officer of police either from the force which applied for the order or the force for the area where the offender lives or is intending to live.

The magistrates' court dealing with the application will be:

- the court that made the foreign travel order; OR
- a magistrates' court for the area where the offender resides; OR
- where the application was made by a chief officer of police, any magistrates' court within his or her police area.

Under s.118(4) an order may be renewed or varied so as to impose additional prohibitions only if it necessary for the purpose of protecting children generally or any child from serious sexual harm from the offender outside the United Kingdom.

(iv) Breach of foreign travel orders

An offender is in breach of the order if he or she does anything specifically prohibited in the order without reasonable excuse.

On conviction in the magistrates' court, the penalties are imprisonment for a period of up to six months and/or a fine not exceeding the statutory maximum. On indictment, the Crown Court may sentence to imprisonment for up to five years.

III. Sexual offences prevention orders (SOPOs)

The provisions relating to SOPOs are contained in ss.104–113 of the SOA 2003.

(i) "Qualifying offenders"

The court may make a SOPO in proceedings where an offender is:

- convicted of an offence listed in Sch.3 or Sch.5 of the Act;
- found not guilty of a Sch.3 or a Sch.5 offence by reason of insanity; or
- found to be under a disability and to have done the act charged against him in respect of a Sche.3 or Sch.5 offence (effectively this means being unfit to stand trial for the offence).

In doing so, it must be satisfied that the order is necessary in order to protect the public from serious sexual harm from the offender. The offences in Sch.3 are all sexual offences while Sch.5 contains a range of other violent offences, including murder as well as all the offences listed in Sch.15 of the CJA 2003 relating to the "dangerous offender" provisions.

In addition, under subss.104(5) and (6), a chief officer of police may make an application for a SOPO to any court in his or her police area where it appears to him or her that:

- a person living or intending to live in the police area is a qualifying offender; AND
- the person has since *the appropriate date* acted in such a way as to give reasonable cause to believe that it is necessary for such an order to be made.

In this case, before making an order, the court must be satisfied that the offender is a qualifying offender and that the offender's behaviour since *the appropriate date* makes it necessary to make such an order, for the purposes of protecting the public from serious sexual harm from the offender. A qualifying offender is defined in subss.106(6) and (7) as a person who has been cautioned, convicted or subject to a finding in relation to a Sch.3 or Sch.5 offence. *Appropriate date* refers to the date of caution, conviction or finding.

SOPOs can be made in cases where the caution, conviction or finding has been made under the law in another country outside the United Kingdom (s.106(7)).

Interim SOPOs can be made by virtue of s.109 whilst a determination in relation to an application by a chief officer of police for a full SOPO is pending. This will have effect for a fixed period only specified in the order and will cease to have effect when a determination on a full SOPO is made.

127

(ii) Requirements of a SOPO

The SOPO will be for a fixed period of at least five years and will contain specific prohibitions. The prohibitions can only be included if necessary for the purpose of protecting the public or any particular members of the public from serious sexual harm from the offender. It is important that these are realistic, proportionate and understandable to the offender. Although applications for SOPOs are not initiated by the probation service, OMs may be able to influence the nature of conditions to be suggested to the court where these are discussed at MAPP panels or other multi-agency meetings.

If a SOPO is made on an offender already subject to a SOPO, the earlier order will cease to have effect.

(iii) Variations, renewals and discharges

Applications for variation, renewal or discharge of full or interim SOPOs can be made by the offender and also by the chief officer of police either from the force which applied for the order or the force for the area where the offender lives or is intending to live.

The court dealing with the application will be:

- the Crown Court where the SOPO was made in Crown Court or the Court of Appeal;
- the youth court where the order was made in youth court. this will usually be the youth court for the LJA where the young person lives, but where the SOPO was initiated by an application from the chief officer of police, this could be any youth court within the police area; or
- the magistrates' court where the order was made in magistrates' court. again, this will usually be the court for the LJA where the offender lives, but where the SOPO was initiated by an application from the chief officer of police, this could be any magistrates' court within the police area.

Under s.108(3) an order may be renewed or varied so as to impose additional prohibitions only if it necessary for the purpose of protecting the public or particular members of the public from serious sexual harm from the offender. Conversely, prohibitions should be deleted if they are no longer justified for public protection.

A court cannot discharge a SOPO which has run for less than five years without the consent of the offender and:

- the chief officer of police where the application for the SOPO was generated by the police; OR
- the chief officer of police for the area where the offender resides.

(iv) Breach of SOPOs or interim SOPOs

Section 113 contains powers in relation to breach of SOPOs, full and interim, and also restraining orders and sex offender orders. These latter orders are no longer available to the court but there are still small numbers of offenders subject to them.

On conviction in the magistrates' court, the penalties are imprisonment for a period of up to six months and/or a fine not exceeding the statutory maximum. On indictment, the Crown Court may sentence to imprisonment for up to five years.

IV. Risk of sexual harm orders (RSHOs)

(i) Availability of RSHOs

Section 123 of the SOA 2003 establishes the RSHO, another addition to the range of civil preventative orders introduced over the past decade. They apply to individuals who are believed to have engaged in specific acts spelt out in subs.(3). These are:

- engaging in sexual activity involving a child or in the presence of a child;
- causing or inciting a child to watch a person engaging in sexual activity or to look at a moving or still image that is sexual;
- giving a child anything that relates to sexual activity or contains a reference to such activity; and
- communicating with a child, where any part of the communication is sexual.

A chief officer of police may apply for a RHSO in respect of a person over the age of 18 living or intending to live in his or her police area, if it appears to that chief officer that:

- the person has done an act in subs.(3) on at least two occasions; and
- as a result of these acts, there is reasonable cause to believe that it is necessary for such an order to be made.

The application will be made to any magistrates' court within the chief officer's police area or in the area where it is alleged that the person committed the acts in subs.(3). Before making an order the court must be satisfied that:

- the person has done an act in subs.(3) on at least two occasions; AND
- it is necessary to make such an order for the purpose of protecting children generally or any child from harm from the person.

Section 128 permits the court to make an interim RSHO whilst a determination is pending on a full RSHO.

(ii) Requirements of a RSHO

The RSHO will be for a fixed period of at least two years and will contain specific prohibitions. The prohibitions can only be included if necessary for the purpose of protecting children generally or any child from harm from the person.

If an RSHO is made on an offender already subject to an RSHO, the earlier order will cease to have effect.

(iii) Variations, renewals and discharges

Applications for variation, renewal or discharge of full or interim RSHOs can be made by the offender and also by the chief officer of police either from the force which applied for the order or the force for the area where the offender lives or is intending to live.

The court dealing with the application will be:

- the court which made the risk of sexual harm order;
- a magistrates' court for the area in which the defendant resides; or

- where the application is made by a chief officer of police, any magistrates' court within the police area.

Under s.125(4) an order may be renewed or varied so as to impose additional prohibitions only if it necessary for the purpose of protecting children generally or any child from harm from the subject of the order. Conversely, prohibitions should be deleted if they are no longer justified for this purpose.

A court cannot discharge a RSHO which has run for less than two years without the consent of the offender and:

- the chief officer of police where the application for the SOPO was generated by the police; OR

- the chief officer of police for the area where the offender resides.

(iv) Breach of RSHOs or interim RSHOs

Section 128 contains powers in relation to breach of RSHOs, full and interim. On conviction in the magistrates' court, the penalties are imprisonment for a period of up to six months and/or a fine not exceeding the statutory maximum. On indictment, the Crown Court may sentence to imprisonment for up to five years.

V. Violent offender orders (VOOs)

Introduced by the CJ&IA 2008, violent offender orders have been available since August 3, 2009. As with SOPOs and RHSOs, a VOO is a civil preventative order but with criminal sanctions available for any breach of requirements.

A VOO cannot be made whilst an offender is in prison or subject to a post-custody licence. There is no specific prohibition in the legislation preventing a VOO being made on an offender subject to a community order who meets the eligibility criteria. However, the intention is clearly to target these orders at violent offenders at a point where they are not under statutory supervision from the probation service nor subject to other statutory restrictions. OMs may find themselves involved in decision-making in relation to a VOO for an offender coming to the end of a licence period and/or subject to MAPPA supervision at Level 3. Whereas the police are the responsible agency for VOOs, clearly OMs can constructively contribute to the discussions around VOOs in relevant multi-agency meetings, helping to ensure that prohibitions are proportionate to risk, realistic and enforceable.

(i) "Qualifying offenders"

Section 99 establishes that a VOO may only be made on an offender who:

- is aged 18 years or over; AND

- has been convicted of a specified offence and sentenced to at least 12 months imprisonment; OR

- has been convicted of a specified offence and made subject to a hospital order, with or without restrictions; OR

- has been found not guilty of a specified offence by reason of insanity and made subject to either a hospital order, with or without restrictions, or a supervision order under the Criminal Procedure (Insanity) Act 1964; OR

- has been found to be under a disability and to have done the act charged against him in respect of a specified offence and has been made subject to either a hospital order, with or without restrictions, or a supervision order under the Criminal Procedure (Insanity) Act 1964.

The specified offences for a VOO are:

- manslaughter;
- soliciting murder (s.4, of the Offences Against the Persons Act 1861);
- wounding with intent to cause grievous bodily harm or malicious wounding (ss.18 and 20, of the Offences Against the Person Act 1861);
- attempting to commit murder or conspiracy to commit murder;
- offences under s.70 of the Army Act 1955, s.70 of the Air Force Act 1955 or s.42 of the Naval Discipline Act 1957;
- any offence under s.42 of the Armed Forces Act 2006.

Section 99(4) ensures that convictions or findings in relation to relevant offences abroad may be considered for the purposes of a VOO.

Under s.100, a chief officer of police may make an application for a VOO where it appears to him or her that:

- a person living or intending to live in the police area is a qualifying offender; AND
- the person has since *the appropriate date* has acted in such a way as to give reasonable cause to believe that it is necessary for such an order to be made.

The application can be made to any magistrates' court within the chief officer's police area or alternatively in any place where the behaviours giving cause for concern have taken place. *Appropriate date* refers to the date of conviction or finding, whether in the United Kingdom or abroad.

Before making an order, the court must be satisfied that the offender is a qualifying offender and that the offender has, since *the appropriate date*, acted in such a way as to make it necessary to make such an order, for the purposes of protecting the public from serious violent harm from the offender (s.101(3)). By virtue of s.101(4), the court must have regard to any other measures to which the offender may be subject in order to protect the public from serious harm from him or her. The requirements of a community order may be of relevance here and there may be situations where the probation service is required to provide details of court orders for which it is responsible and risk management plans, although in most instances relevant communication should take place between probation and the police before any court hearing.

A VOO cannot come into force whilst the offender is:

- subject to a custodial sentence;
- on licence as part of a custodial sentence; or
- subject to a hospital order or supervision order.

However, an application can be made whilst an offender is in prison or subject to a hospital order with a view to its coming into force on release or discharge. A VOO can be made whilst an offender is in hospital under the civil provisions of the Mental Health Act 1983 (i.e. whilst the offender is "sectioned").

Section 104 allows interim VOOs to be made pending determination on a full VOO.

(ii) Requirements of a VOO

The VOO will be for a fixed period between two and five years and will contain specific prohibitions, restrictions or conditions. Under section 102, these may prevent the offender from:

- going to any specified premises or other specified place (at any time or at or between any specified time or times);

- attending any specific event; or

- having any, or any specified description of, contact with any specified individual.

It is important that these are realistic, proportionate and understandable to the offender. Although applications for VOOs are not initiated by the probation service, OMs may be able to influence the nature of conditions to be suggested to the court where these are discussed at MAPP panels or other multi-agency meetings.

(iii) Notification requirements (sections 108–112)

When a VOO or an interim VOO is made, the offender becomes subject to notification requirements similar to those for sex offenders on the "sex offender register" for the duration of the order.

Within three days of the VOO/interim VOO coming into force, the offender must supply the following information:

- date of birth;

- national insurance number;

- name or names used on the relevant date;

- home address on the relevant date;

- name or names used on the date that notification is given;

- home address on the date that notification is given;

- the address of any other premises in the United Kingdom at which, at the time the notification is given, he or she regularly resides or stays; and

- any prescribed information (as specified in regulations made by the Secretary of State).

The three-day requirement disregards any period spent in custody, serving a sentence of imprisonment or a term of service detention or where the offender is detained in hospital. It also disregards any period where the offender is abroad.

The offender will normally attend at the police station in his or her local area to complete the notification. Alternatively, he or she may give oral notification to any police officer or to any person authorised for the purpose by the officer in charge of the station.

Following the initial notification, the offender must also notify the police within three days of:

- any change of name used if this has not been previously notified;
- any change of home address;
- the address of any premises in the United Kingdom not previously notified where he or she has stayed for a "qualifying period" of seven days or two or more periods within a 12-month period which together amount to seven days;
- any prescribed change in circumstances; or
- his or her release from custody, a prison sentence, term of service detention or detention in a hospital, giving the details listed above.

Changes of name and address may be notified in advance of the change as well as in retrospect. If the change notified in advance does not then occur, the offender is required to inform the police of that fact (s.109(6)).

Notifications should be renewed annually, unless the offender has been in contact with the police to advise of changes during that period.

(iv) Variations, renewals and discharges

An application for variation, renewal or discharge of VOO can be made by the offender and also by the chief officer of police either from the force which applied for the order or the force for the area where the offender lives or is intending to live. The application should normally go to the magistrates' court that made the order, unless the offender lives in a different area, in which case it will go to the magistrates' court for that area. Where the application was made by the chief officer of police, it can be heard in any court within the force area.

Under s.103(5), a VOO may only be renewed or varied so as to impose additional prohibitions, restrictions or conditions on the offender where the court considers it is necessary to do so for the purpose of protecting the public from the risk of serious violent harm caused by the offender. Conversely, prohibitions, restrictions or conditions should be deleted if they are no longer justified for public protection.

A court cannot discharge a VOO which has run for less than two years without the consent of the offender and:

- the chief officer of police where the application for the VOO was generated by the police; OR
- the chief officer of police for the area where the offender resides.

(v) Breach of VOOs (section 113)

An offender will be in breach of a full or an interim VOO if he or she fails without reasonable excuse to comply with any prohibition, restriction or condition specified in his or her order.

An offender may also be in breach of notification requirements by failing without reasonable excuse to:

- make an initial notification within three days;

- notify within three days changes of name, address or details of premises where he or she has stayed for a qualifying period;

- make a notification within three days of release from custody, prison sentence, term of service detention or detention in hospital;

- notify the police within six days that a change previously notified has not occurred;

- make a periodic (annual) notification; or

- comply with a request from the police or authorised person to take fingerprints and/or photographs for the purpose of verifying his or her identity.

Compliance with VOOs is monitored and enforced by the police, who will notify the court of any alleged breach. Breach proceedings may be commenced in any court having jurisdiction in any place where the offender charged with the alleged breach resides or is found (s.113(8)).

On conviction in the magistrates' court, the penalties are imprisonment for a period of up to 12 months and/or a fine not exceeding the statutory maximum. On indictment, the Crown Court may sentence to imprisonment for up to five years and/or impose a fine.

Chapter 14
APPROVED PREMISES

Hostels may be under the direct management of probation trusts or may be run by voluntary or private sector organisations, if approved by the Secretary of State under s.9 of the Criminal Justice and Court Services Act 2000. Approved premises may be used for bailees and offenders subject to community orders or post-custody licences. Currently offenders representing a high risk of serious harm and in need of an enhanced level of supervision are given priority for such accommodation. This has resulted in a significant shift in the population in approved premises away from bailees and in favour of offenders on release from prison (National Probation Service, 2005c).

I. Hostel rules

On entering approved premises, residents will be required to agree to a set of house rules as one of the conditions of residence. PC 19/2007 established a consistent set of rules to be applied nationally but allows freedom for individual premises to add their own rules to meet local needs and circumstances (National Probation Service, 2007e). The set of national rules is set out below.

As a resident of ....Approved Premises you must:

1. Be in the building during the standard hours of curfew, which are 11pm to 6am; comply with any additional curfew and other conditions imposed by the Court or contained in your Licence; and comply with any additional curfew hours, imposed by the Approved Premises manager and/or your Offender Manager, which they consider to be necessary in your case.

2. Pay rent and other maintenance charges as instructed by staff and notified to you in writing.

3. Undergo drug and/or alcohol testing if required to do so by staff.

4. Give all prescribed medication to staff, and take medication as prescribed by your doctor.

5. See a medical practitioner, health professional or psychiatric worker if reasonably required to do so by staff.

6. Participate in the hostel programme as instructed, including meetings, key working sessions, group work and any other activities specified in your sentence/supervision plan.

7. Allow staff to search your room and personal belongings at any time without interference.

8. Pay attention to your personal hygiene and keep your room clean and tidy for health and safety reasons.

9. Not smoke on the premises, except in designated smoking rooms as notified to you by staff.

10. Not bring onto the premises (including the grounds), or have in your possession any weapons, dangerous items, alcohol, solvents, illegal drugs or drugs paraphernalia.

11. Not steal, attempt to steal or damage anything that belongs to the Approved Premises, staff, contractors, visitors or other residents.

12. Not behave in a violent, threatening, disruptive, racist, sexist or other discriminatory way which could cause offence to staff, other residents, the local community or members of the general public.

13. Not bring anyone under the age of 18 onto the premises (including the grounds) at any time.

14. Not bring visitors aged 18 or over onto the premises (including the grounds) without the permission of staff, ensure that your visitors remain in the communal areas of the hostel at all times and that they leave by the time standard curfew begins, or earlier if required by staff.

15. Not bring onto the premises, without the prior written permission of staff, DVD or video recorders/players, combined TV with DVD/video player, personal computers or laptops, cameras or other photographic equipment, games consoles with DVD readability or mobile phones with cameras or Internet access.

16. Not act in a manner that is inconsistent with the aims and objectives of the Approved Premises; that may bring the Approved Premises, its staff or residents into disrepute; that may reasonably be regarded as a nuisance to the local neighbourhood; or that may jeopardise the health and safety of staff, other residents or members of the general public.

17. Comply with any reasonable instruction given to you by staff, which may include the requirement to undertake routine domestic chores. I have read (or had read to me) these rules. I understand and agree to abide by them. I am aware that if I fail to comply with any of the rules consideration will be given to immediate enforcement action, which might result in recall to prison, return to Court or withdrawal of my place at the Approved Premises.

I understand that my residence in the Approved Premises is temporary, and that I will not acquire any rights of tenancy.

I understand that staff will report to the police any offences committed by, or suspected of being committed by, residents of the hostel, regardless of whether they were committed on the premises.

PC 19/2007 goes on to say that:

> "Enforcement action in response to any breach of the rules, whether major or minor, needs to be reasonable and proportionate. Where possible, residents should be afforded the opportunity to explain their actions before a decision is made, although in cases of more serious breach, this may be neither possible nor appropriate. Close liaison with offender managers and the involvement of senior managers, where necessary, should ensure that enforcement decisions are defensible and able to withstand subsequent challenge."

(National Probation Service, 2007d: Annex B: 3)

Breach of rules will be dealt with by the courts where the resident is on bail or subject to a community order and by means of executive recall in post-custody licence cases. However, circumstances may be such that action short of breach proceedings may be appropriate, for instance, a warning letter. Such decisions will be dependent upon the nature of the breach and whether it suggests that the offender poses an increased risk of serious harm.

II. Residents on bail

A defendant may be made subject to bail with a condition to reside in approved premises by virtue of s.3 of the Bail Act 1976, which also requires compliance with hostel rules. Breaking a bail condition is not in itself an offence, although it renders the defendant liable to arrest and to be brought before the relevant court. Absconding from a hostel premises or failing to surrender to bail, however, are offences.

Approved premises should contact the police immediately if a defendant fails to arrive at the premises having been bailed there by the court, fails to observe the curfew or commits a further offence. There is more discretion in relation to breaking other hostel rules, but where breach action is considered necessary and appropriate, the police should be informed.

Where a defendant has failed to surrender to court, the court will issue an arrest warrant. The powers of arrest for absconding or breaking conditions of bail are contained in s.7 of the Bail Act 1976. S.7(3) states that:

> A person who has been released on bail in criminal proceedings and is under a duty to surrender into the custody of a court may be arrested without warrant by a constable—
>
> (a) "if the constable has reasonable grounds for believing that the person is not likely to surrender to custody;
>
> (b) if the constable has reasonable grounds for believing that the person is likely to break any of the conditions of his bail or has reasonable grounds for suspecting that that person has broken any of those conditions ... ."

When arrested, the defendant should be brought before a court within 24 hours (excluding Christmas Day, Good Friday and any Sunday). In most instances, this will be the court for the LJA where the defendant has been arrested. However, if the arrest takes place within 24 hours of the date he or she is due to appear in court, then he or she should be taken to the court to which he or she is due to surrender.

If a defendant denies the allegation of breach, the court does not have the power to adjourn and must deal with the matter within 24 hours of arrest as established by *R.(on the application of Culley) v Dorchester Crown Court* [2007] EWHC 109.

The court does not hold a full hearing, but will consider evidence put forward by the Crown Prosecution Service regarding the allegation. Critically, as a breach of bail conditions does not constitute an offence, there does not have to be of a criminal standard of proof (*R. (on the application of Hussain) v Derby Magistrates' Court* [2001] EWHC Admin 507). Hearsay evidence is therefore admissible and this might include, for instance, a police officer relaying an account of an incident that took place in an approved premises before he or she arrived there. The defendant will be given an opportunity to respond but neither side will be able to call witnesses. This means that hostel staff will not be called to give evidence, under oath or otherwise, but will need to give full details of the allegation to the police which can then be presented to the court. This will usually be in the form of a s.9 statement (see Appendix B).

Where the defendant admits or is found guilty of a breach of bail conditions, the court may remand or commit the defendant to custody under s.7(5), if of the opinion that he or she is not likely to surrender to custody or has broken or is likely to break any condition of bail. Alternatively the court may grant bail again subject to the same or different conditions, although the general presumption in favour of bail will no longer apply (Sch.1 para.6).

Where the court is not of that opinion, however, then it must grant bail subject to the same conditions as were originally imposed. This may mean that the court asks an approved premises to readmit the defendant, although this would be at the discretion of the approved premises. If the approved premises then refuses, it would be open to the court to make a similar condition of residence at an alternative premises.

III. Residents on statutory supervision

Unlike bailees, residents on community orders or post-custody licences will have an OM responsible for overseeing their order. OMs should be informed of any infringements of the hostel rules and the action the approved premises intends to take. Where possible, OMs should be involved in meetings to discuss problems and to encourage future compliance.

If a place in an approved premises is withdrawn, the OM should be informed. Withdrawal of a place will normally result in immediate breach action, whether referral to the court or recall to prison. On occasions, circumstances may require prompt action to evict a resident but this should only be done with the approval of a senior manager.

IV. Testing for drug and alcohol use

PC 05/2006 sets out expectations in terms of drug testing of residents in approved premises. Hostel rules must allow for drug testing of every resident should this be required, on the basis of reasonable suspicion. However, in practice testing should be targeted at known drug users or used to deal with situations where, for instance, drug paraphernalia is found on the premises but cannot be traced to any individual(s). Testing will usually be for heroin and cocaine/crack cocaine but may include other substances.

The guidance states that approved premises may randomly test known drug users, but not those without a known history of drug use due to concerns about undue intrusion into privacy. A positive test result should not automatically lead to eviction if the resident is motivated to accept treatment, and decisions about managing the situation will be based on:

- assessment of risk;
- the perceived effectiveness of treatment;
- the number of positive tests;
- the extent to which repeated breaches undermine respect for the rules and/or encourage drug use in others; and

- the order or licence to which the resident is subject.

(National Probation Service, 2006)

The guidance goes on to say that:

"Balancing these issues is a matter best determined on a case by case basis ..... the primary criterion in coming to a decision should always be the risk of harm caused by the resident. This is more important than continuing drug treatment in the community."

(National Probation Service, 2006: 3)

Hostels may also test residents for alcohol use. Again, this should not be done on a random basis, except in relation to residents with a history of alcohol-related offending. More usually tests will be conducted on the basis of reasonable suspicion and where there is a concern about possible behaviour within the hostel and its impact on others, or where alcohol is a known factor in previous offending.

Appendix A
SAMPLE FORMS

...................PROBATION SERVICE

.................Magistrates Court

Information for breach of Community Sentence

Date:

Accused:

Date of birth:

Address:

Type of Community Sentence: Community Order with the following Requirement/s

Made on: **Expiry date:**

By:

Offence details:

Local Justice Area concerned:

Alleged failure to comply: *that the Defendant on (date) and (date) failed without reasonable excuse to report in accordance with his/her instructions.*

The information of:

Address:

Tel No.

Taken (and sworn) before me………………..

Justice of the Peace

Date of hearing: **Time:**

REF

DATE

OFFENDER NAME

ADDRESS

Dear (Offender name)

BREACH NOTIFICATION—COURT APPEARANCE

It is alleged that you are in breach of your (Type of Order) made by

(Name & Type of Court) Court on (Sentence Date), for offence/s of

…………………in that you failed without reasonable excuse to report

in accordance with your instructions on (Breach dates)

As you have failed to provide acceptable evidence for the

failure/s to comply, the failures are deemed **UNACCEPTABLE**

and you are in breach of your order/s and

your case has been listed for a breach hearing as detailed below:

At:

On:

Location: Court

YOU ARE INSTRUCTED TO ATTEND THIS HEARING. SHOULD

YOU FAIL TO

ATTEND COURT AT THE TIME AND PLACE STATED IN THIS

LETTER, AN APPLICATION FOR A WARRANT FOR YOUR

ARREST WILL BE MADE.

**I would advise you to see a solicitor before the day of the court
hearing, particularly if you intend to apply for legal aid. You should
take this letter with you.**

Yours sincerely

Offender Manager

Date

For Office Use Only:

This is a copy of the letter served by 1st class post on the ...... of ....

Signed .... Name (Block capitals) ....

In the Crown Court at

Crown Court Case Number:
Crown Court Location Code:
PTI URN:

Summons after failing to comply with a suspended sentence order

To   (date of birth:)

On [redacted]
you were sentenced to a suspended sentence order

☐ **On** [redacted]
you were convicted at   of an offence, punishable with imprisonment, committed by you during the period of suspension.

☐ **On** [redacted]
you failed, without reasonable excuse, to comply with the requirement(s) of your order, in that

You are therefore summoned to appear
at the Crown Court at

on   at

when the court will consider whether you should serve the suspended sentence and/or reconsider the requirements of your community supervision.

[redacted]

An Officer of the Crown Court

145

Appendix B
EXAMPLE OF A SECTION 9 STATEMENT

STATEMENT OF WITNESS

(C.J.ACT 1967 s9; M.C.A. 1980 s102;

M.C.RULES 1981 r70)

STATEMENT OF   Arthur Moment

AGE OF WITNESS   Over 18

OCCUPATION OF WITNESS   Probation Service
                                     Officer

ADDRESS AND TELEPHONE NUMBER   Probation Office,
                                     15 Railway Street,
                                     Shefton,S38 9PS

This statement, consisting of 2 pages each signed by me, is true to the best of my knowledge and belief and I make it knowing that if it is tendered in evidence, I shall be liable to prosecution if I have wilfully stated in it anything which I know to be false or do not believe to be true.
Dated the 1st day of March 2009

Signed *A Moment*
Signature witnessed by *Ann Day*

Joe Fisher appeared before the Shefton Magistrates' Court on 6th November 2008 when for 3 offences of theft he was made the subject of a Community Order consisting of a 120 hour Unpaid Work Requirement. Later that same day I saw him at the Community Payback office in Shefton and gave him written instructions for work. I explained these to him and he signed to indicate that he understood. The instructions were that he was to work on Thursday of each week starting on Thursday 13th November 2008. I attach a copy of his work instructions to this statement.

I was Duty Officer on Thursday 20th November 2008. Part of my duty that day was to check who attended for Community Payback and who failed to attend. I was expecting Joe Fisher to attend but he failed to do so.

On Thursday 27th November I was once again the duty officer. At about 9.10 a.m. I saw Joe Fisher talking to somebody who was in a Community Payback van which was ready to leave. I asked Mr Fisher to move away as the group needed to go to work. Mr Fisher was not part of that group so I asked him to join his group who were loading tools into another vehicle. Mr Fisher reacted angrily, saying that he was talking to his friend. I asked him two or three times to move out of the way but he did not do so.

I put my hand under his elbow and on his arm in an attempt to encourage him to move towards his group. He told me to get off him and said that, although he should have been attending that day to do his Community Payback, he "Fucking wasn't now". He continued to be aggressive, shouting that he was not going to work that day. I told him that if he did not work he would get into trouble. He put his face close to mine and said "Touch me again and I'll smash your fucking face in". I told him that I would be writing to him and sent him off the work site, at which point he left.

Later that day following a conversation with my Senior Probation Officer, I wrote a letter to Mr Fisher informing him that I was returning him to court by way of breach proceedings and I attach a copy of that letter.

Signed *A Moment*
Witnessed *Ann Day*

SCHEDULE 8 CRIMINAL JUSTICE ACT 2003 (AS AMENDED)

BREACH, REVOCATION OR AMENDMENT OF COMMUNITY ORDER

PART 1
PRELIMINARY

Interpretation

1   In this Schedule—

"the offender", in relation to a community order, means the person in respect of whom the order is made;

"the local justice area concerned", area in relation to a community order, means the local justice area for the time being specified in the order;

"the responsible officer" has the meaning given by section 197.

2   In this Schedule—

(a) references to a drug rehabilitation requirement of a community order being subject to review are references to that requirement being subject to review in accordance with section 210(1)(b);

(b) references to the court responsible for a community order imposing a drug rehabilitation requirement which is subject to review are to be construed in accordance with section 210(2).

3   For the purposes of this Schedule—

(a) a requirement falling within any paragraph of section 177(1) is of the same kind as any other requirement falling within that paragraph, and

(b) an electronic monitoring requirement is a requirement of the same kind as any requirement falling within section 177(1) to which it relates.

Orders made on appeal

4   Where a community order has been made on appeal, it is to be taken for the purposes of this Schedule to have been made by the Crown Court.

PART 2

BREACH OF REQUIREMENT OF ORDER

Duty to give warning

5 (1) If the responsible officer is of the opinion that the offender has failed without reasonable excuse to comply with any of the requirements of a community order, the officer must give him a warning under this paragraph unless—

(a) the offender has within the previous twelve months been given a warning under this paragraph in relation to a failure to comply with any of the requirements of the order, or

(b) the officer causes an information to be laid before a justice of the peace in respect of the failure.

(2) A warning under this paragraph must—

(a) describe the circumstances of the failure,

(b) state that the failure is unacceptable, and

(c) inform the offender that, if within the next twelve months he again fails to comply with any requirement of the order, he will be liable to be brought before a court.

(3) The responsible officer must, as soon as practicable after the warning has been given, record that fact.

(4) In relation to any community order which was made by the Crown Court and does not include a direction that any failure to comply with the requirements of the order is to be dealt with by a magistrates' court, the reference in sub-paragraph (1)(b) to a justice of the peace is to be read as a reference to the Crown Court.

Breach of order after warning

6 (1) If—

(a) the responsible officer has given a warning under paragraph 5 to the offender in respect of a community order, and

(b) at any time within the twelve months beginning with the date on which the warning was given, the responsible officer is of the opinion that the offender has since that date failed without reasonable excuse to comply with any of the requirements of the order, the officer must cause an information to be laid before a justice of the peace in respect of the failure in question.

(2) In relation to any community order which was made by the Crown Court and does not include a direction that any failure to comply with the requirements of the order is to be dealt with by a magistrates' court, the reference in sub-paragraph (1) to a justice of the peace is to be read as a reference to the Crown Court.

Issue of summons or warrant by justice of the peace

7 (1) This paragraph applies to—

(a) a community order made by a magistrates' court, or

(b) any community order which was made by the Crown Court and includes a direction that any failure to comply with the requirements of the order is to be dealt with by a magistrates' court.

(2) If at any time while a community order to which this paragraph applies is in force it appears on information to a justice of the peace that the offender has failed to comply with any of the requirements of the order, the justice may—

(a) issue a summons requiring the offender to appear at the place and time specified in it, or

(b) if the information is in writing and on oath, issue a warrant for his arrest.

(3) Any summons or warrant issued under this paragraph must direct the offender to appear or be brought—

(a) in the case of a community order imposing a drug rehabilitation requirement which is subject to review, before the magistrates' court responsible for the order, or

(b) in any other case, before a magistrates' court acting in the local justice area] in which the offender resides or, if it is not known where he resides, before a magistrates' court acting for the petty sessions area concerned.

(4) Where a summons issued under sub-paragraph (2)(a) requires the offender to appear before a magistrates' court and the offender does not appear in answer to the summons, the magistrates' court may issue a warrant for the arrest of the offender.

Issue of summons or warrant by Crown Court

8   (1) This paragraph applies to a community order made by the Crown Court which does not include a direction that any failure to comply with the requirements of the order is to be dealt with by a magistrates' court.

(2) If at any time while a community order to which this paragraph applies is in force it appears on information to the Crown Court that the offender has failed to comply with any of the requirements of the order, the Crown Court may—

(a) issue a summons requiring the offender to appear at the place and time specified in it, or

(b) if the information is in writing and on oath, issue a warrant for his arrest.

(3) Any summons or warrant issued under this paragraph must direct the offender to appear or be brought before the Crown Court.

(4) Where a summons issued under sub-paragraph (2)(a) requires the offender to appear before the Crown Court and the offender does not appear in answer to the summons, the Crown Court may issue a warrant for the arrest of the offender.

Powers of magistrates' court

9   (1) If it is proved to the satisfaction of a magistrates' court before which an offender appears or is brought under paragraph 7 that he has failed without reasonable excuse to comply with any of the requirements of the community order, the court must deal with him in respect of the failure in any one of the following ways—

(a) by amending the terms of the community order so as to impose more onerous requirements which the court could include if it were then making the order;

(b) where the community order was made by a magistrates' court, by dealing with him, for the offence in respect of which the order was made, in any way in which the court could deal with him if he had just been convicted by it of the offence;

(c) where—

(i) the community order was made by a magistrates' court,

(ii) the offence in respect of which the order was made was not an offence punishable by imprisonment,

(iii) the offender is aged 18 or over, and

(iv) the offender has wilfully and persistently failed to comply with the requirements of the order, by dealing with him, in respect of that offence, by imposing a sentence of imprisonment for a term not exceeding 51 weeks.

(2) In dealing with an offender under sub-paragraph (1), a magistrates' court must take into account the extent to which the offender has complied with the requirements of the community order.

(3) In dealing with an offender under sub-paragraph (1)(a), the court may extend the duration of particular requirements (subject to any limit imposed by Chapter 4 of Part 12 of this Act) but may not extend the period specified under section 177(5).

(4) In dealing with an offender under sub-paragraph (1)(b), the court may, in the case of an offender who has wilfully and persistently failed to comply with the requirements of the community order, impose a custodial sentence (where the order was made in respect of an offence punishable with such a sentence) notwithstanding anything in section 152(2).

(5) Where a magistrates' court deals with an offender under sub-paragraph (1)(b) or (c), it must revoke the community order if it is still in force.

(5A) Where a magistrates' court dealing with an offender under sub-paragraph (1)(a) would not otherwise have the power to amend the community order under paragraph 16 (amendment by reason of change of residence), that paragraph has effect as if the references to the appropriate court were references to the court dealing with the offender.

(6) Where a community order was made by the Crown Court and a magistrates' court would (apart from this sub-paragraph) be required to deal with the offender under sub-paragraph (1)(a), (b) or (c), it may instead commit him to custody or release him on bail until he can be brought or appear before the Crown Court.

(7) A magistrates' court which deals with an offender's case under sub-paragraph (6) must send to the Crown Court—

(a) a certificate signed by a justice of the peace certifying that the offender has failed to comply with the requirements of the community order in the respect specified in the certificate, and

(b) such other particulars of the case as may be desirable; and a certificate purporting to be so signed is admissible as evidence of the failure before the Crown Court.

(8) A person sentenced under sub-paragraph (1)(b) or (c) for an offence may appeal to the Crown Court against the sentence.

Powers of Crown Court

10 (1) Where under paragraph 8 or by virtue of paragraph 9(6) an offender appears or is brought before the Crown Court and it is proved to the satisfaction of that court that he has failed without reasonable excuse to comply with any of the requirements of the community order, the Crown Court must deal with him in respect of the failure in any one of the following ways—

(a) by amending the terms of the community order so as to impose more onerous requirements which the Crown Court could impose if it were then making the order;

(b) by dealing with him, for the offence in respect of which the order was made, in any way in which he could have been dealt with for that offence by the court which made the order if the order had not been made;

(c) where—

(i) the offence in respect of which the order was made was not an offence punishable by imprisonment,

(ii) the offender is aged 18 or over,

(iii) the offender has wilfully and persistently failed to comply with the requirements of the order, by dealing with him, in respect of that offence, by imposing a sentence of imprisonment for a term not exceeding 51 weeks.

(2) In dealing with an offender under sub-paragraph (1), the Crown Court must take into account the extent to which the offender has complied with the requirements of the community order.

(3) In dealing with an offender under sub-paragraph (1)(a), the court may extend the duration of particular requirements (subject to any limit imposed by Chapter 4 of Part 12 of this Act) but may not extend the period specified under section 177(5).

(4) In dealing with an offender under sub-paragraph (1)(b), the Crown Court may, in the case of an offender who has wilfully and persistently failed to comply with the requirements of the community order, impose a custodial sentence (where the order was made in respect of an offence punishable with such a sentence) notwithstanding anything in section 152(2).

(5) Where the Crown Court deals with an offender under sub-paragraph (1)(b) or (c), it must revoke the community order if it is still in force.

(6) In proceedings before the Crown Court under this paragraph any question whether the offender has failed to comply with the requirements of the community order is to be determined by the court and not by the verdict of a jury.

Restriction of powers in paragraphs 9 and 10 where treatment required

11 (1) An offender who is required by any of the following requirements of a community order—

(a) a mental health treatment requirement,

(b) a drug rehabilitation requirement, or

(c) an alcohol treatment requirement, to submit to treatment for his mental condition, or his dependency on or propensity to misuse drugs or alcohol, is not to be treated for the purposes of paragraph 9 or 10 as having failed to comply with that requirement on the ground only that he had refused to undergo any surgical, electrical or other treatment if, in the opinion of the court, his refusal was reasonable having regard to all the circumstances.

(2) A court may not under paragraph 9(1)(a) or 10(1)(a) amend a mental health treatment requirement, a drug rehabilitation requirement or an alcohol treatment requirement unless the offender expresses his willingness to comply with the requirement as amended.

Supplementary

12 Where a community order was made by a magistrates' court in the case of an offender under 18 years of age in respect of an offence triable only on indictment in the case of an adult, any powers exercisable under paragraph 9(1)(b) in respect of the offender after he attains the age of 18 are powers to do either or both of the following—

(a) to impose a fine not exceeding £5,000 for the offence in respect of which the order was made;

(b) to deal with the offender for that offence in any way in which a magistrates' court could deal with him if it had just convicted him of an offence punishable with imprisonment for a term not exceeding 51 weeks.

PART 3

REVOCATION OF ORDER

Revocation of order with or without re-sentencing: powers of magistrates' court

13 (1) This paragraph applies where a community order, other than an order made by the Crown Court and falling within paragraph 14(1)(a), is in force and on the application of the offender or the responsible officer it appears to the appropriate magistrates' court that, having regard to circumstances which have arisen since the order was made, it would be in the interests of justice—

(a) for the order to be revoked, or

(b) for the offender to be dealt with in some other way for the offence in respect of which the order was made.

(2) The appropriate magistrates' court may—

(a) revoke the order, or

(b) both—

    (i)   revoke the order, and

    (ii) deal with the offender, for the offence in respect of which the order was made, in any way in which it could deal with him if he had just been convicted by the court of the offence.

(3) The circumstances in which a community order may be revoked under sub-paragraph (2) include the offender's making good progress or his responding satisfactorily to supervision or treatment (as the case requires).

(4) In dealing with an offender under sub-paragraph (2)(b), a magistrates' court must take into account the extent to which the offender has complied with the requirements of the community order.

(5) A person sentenced under sub-paragraph (2)(b) for an offence may appeal to the Crown Court against the sentence.

(6) Where a magistrates' court proposes to exercise its powers under this paragraph otherwise than on the application of the offender, it must summon him to appear before the court and, if he does not appear in answer to the summons, may issue a warrant for his arrest.

(7) In this paragraph "the appropriate magistrates' court" means—

(a) in the case of an order imposing a drug rehabilitation requirement which is subject to review, the magistrates' court responsible for the order, and

(b) in the case of any other community order, a magistrates' court acting in the local justice area concerned.

Revocation of order with or without re-sentencing: powers of Crown Court

14 (1) This paragraph applies where—

(a) there is in force a community order made by the Crown Court which does not include a direction that any failure to comply with the requirements of the order is to be dealt with by a magistrates' court, and

(b) the offender or the responsible officer applies to the Crown Court for the order to be revoked or for the offender to be dealt with in some other way for the offence in respect of which the order was made.

(2) If it appears to the Crown Court to be in the interests of justice to do so, having regard to circumstances which have arisen since the order was made, the Crown Court may—

(a) revoke the order, or

(b) both—

    (i)   revoke the order, and

    (ii) deal with the offender, for the offence in respect of which the order was made, in any way in which he could have been dealt with for that offence by the court which made the order if the order had not been made.

(3) The circumstances in which a community order may be revoked under sub-paragraph (2) include the offender's making good progress or his responding satisfactorily to supervision or treatment (as the case requires).

(4) In dealing with an offender under sub-paragraph (2)(b), the Crown Court must take into account the extent to which the offender has complied with the requirements of the order.

(5) Where the Crown Court proposes to exercise its powers under this paragraph otherwise than on the application of the offender, it must summon him to appear before the court and, if he does not appear in answer to the summons, may issue a warrant for his arrest.

Supplementary

15 Paragraph 12 applies for the purposes of paragraphs 13 and 14 as it applies for the purposes of paragraph 9 above, but as if for the words "paragraph 9(1)(b)" there were substituted "paragraph 13(2)(b)(ii) or 14(2)(b)(ii)".

Part 4

Amendment of order

Amendment by reason of change of residence

16 (1) This paragraph applies where, at any time while a community order is in force in respect of an offender, the appropriate court is satisfied that the offender proposes to change, or has changed, his residence from the local justice area concerned to another local justice area.

(2) Subject to sub-paragraphs (3) and (4), the appropriate court may, and on the application of the responsible officer must, amend the community order by substituting the other local justice area for the area specified in the order.

(3) The court may not under this paragraph amend a community order which contains requirements which, in the opinion of the court, cannot be complied with unless the offender continues to reside in the local justice area concerned unless, in accordance with paragraph 17, it either—

(a) cancels those requirements, or

(b) substitutes for those requirements other requirements which can be complied with if the offender ceases to reside in that area.

(4) The court may not amend under this paragraph a community order imposing a programme requirement unless it appears to the court that the accredited programme specified in the requirement is available in the other local justice area.

(5) In this paragraph "the appropriate court" means—

(a) in relation to any community order imposing a drug rehabilitation requirement which is subject to review, the court responsible for the order,

(b) in relation to any community order which was made by the Crown Court and does not include any direction that any failure to comply with the requirements of the order is to be dealt with by a magistrates' court, the Crown Court, and

(c) in relation to any other community order, a magistrates' court [acting in the local justice area] concerned.

Amendment of requirements of community order

17 (1) The appropriate court may, on the application of the offender or the responsible officer, by order amend a community order—

(a) by cancelling any of the requirements of the order, or

(b) by replacing any of those requirements with a requirement of the same kind, which the court could include if it were then making the order.

(2) The court may not under this paragraph amend a mental health treatment requirement, a drug rehabilitation requirement or an alcohol treatment requirement unless the offender expresses his willingness to comply with the requirement as amended.

(3) If the offender fails to express his willingness to comply with a mental health treatment requirement, drug rehabilitation requirement or alcohol treatment requirement as proposed to be amended by the court under this paragraph, the court may—

(a) revoke the community order, and

(b) deal with him, for the offence in respect of which the order was made, in any way in which he could have been dealt with for that offence by the court which made the order if the order had not been made.

(4) In dealing with the offender under sub-paragraph (3)(b), the court—

(a) must take into account the extent to which the offender has complied with the requirements of the order, and

(b) may impose a custodial sentence (where the order was made in respect of an offence punishable with such a sentence) notwithstanding anything in section 152(2).

(5) Paragraph 12 applies for the purposes of this paragraph as it applies for the purposes of paragraph 9, but as if for the words "paragraph 9(1)(b)" there were substituted "paragraph 17(3)(b)".

(6) In this paragraph "the appropriate court" has the same meaning as in paragraph 16.

Amendment of treatment requirements of community order on report of practitioner

18 (1) Where the medical practitioner or other person by whom or under whose direction an offender is, in pursuance of any requirement to which this sub-paragraph applies, being treated for his mental condition or his dependency on or propensity to misuse drugs or alcohol—

(a) is of the opinion mentioned in sub-paragraph (3), or

(b) is for any reason unwilling to continue to treat or direct the treatment of the offender, he must make a report in writing to that effect to the responsible officer and that officer must apply under paragraph 17 to the appropriate court for the variation or cancellation of the requirement.

(2) The requirements to which sub-paragraph (1) applies are—

(a) a mental health treatment requirement,

(b) a drug rehabilitation requirement, and

(c) an alcohol treatment requirement.

(3) The opinion referred to in sub-paragraph (1) is—

(a) that the treatment of the offender should be continued beyond the period specified in that behalf in the order,

(b) that the offender needs different treatment,

(c) that the offender is not susceptible to treatment, or

(d) that the offender does not require further treatment.

(4) In this paragraph "the appropriate court" has the same meaning as in paragraph 16.

Amendment in relation to review of drug rehabilitation requirement

19 Where the responsible officer is of the opinion that a community order imposing a drug rehabilitation requirement which is subject to review should be so amended as to provide for each subsequent periodic review (required by section 211) to be made without a hearing instead of at a review hearing, or vice versa, he must apply under paragraph 17 to the court responsible for the order for the variation of the order.

Extension of unpaid work requirement

20 (1) Where—

(a) a community order imposing an unpaid work requirement is in force in respect of any offender, and

(b) on the application of the offender or the responsible officer, it appears to the appropriate court that it would be in the interests of justice to do so having regard to circumstances which have arisen since the order was made, the court may, in relation to the order, extend the period of twelve months specified in section 200(2).

(2) In this paragraph "the appropriate court" has the same meaning as in paragraph 16.

PART 5

POWERS OF COURT IN RELATION TO ORDER FOLLOWING SUBSEQUENT CONVICTION

Powers of magistrates' court following subsequent conviction

21 (1) This paragraph applies where—

(a) an offender in respect of whom a community order made by a magistrates' court is in force is convicted of an offence by a magistrates' court, and

(b) it appears to the court that it would be in the interests of justice to exercise its powers under this paragraph, having regard to circumstances which have arisen since the community order was made.

(2) The magistrates' court may—

(a) revoke the order, or

(b) both—

(i) revoke the order, and

(ii) deal with the offender, for the offence in respect of which the order was made, in any way in which he could have been dealt with for that offence by the court which made the order if the order had not been made.

(3) In dealing with an offender under sub-paragraph (2)(b), a magistrates' court must take into account the extent to which the offender has complied with the requirements of the community order.

(4) A person sentenced under sub-paragraph (2)(b) for an offence may appeal to the Crown Court against the sentence.

22 (1) Where an offender in respect of whom a community order made by the Crown Court is in force is convicted of an offence by a magistrates' court, the magistrates' court may commit the offender in custody or release him on bail until he can be brought before the Crown Court.

(2) Where the magistrates' court deals with an offender's case under sub-paragraph (1), it must send to the Crown Court such particulars of the case as may be desirable.

Powers of Crown Court following subsequent conviction

23 (1) This paragraph applies where—

(a) an offender in respect of whom a community order is in force—

(i) is convicted of an offence by the Crown Court, or

(ii) is brought or appears before the Crown Court by virtue of paragraph 22 or having been committed by the magistrates' court to the Crown Court for sentence, and

(b) it appears to the Crown Court that it would be in the interests of justice to exercise its powers under this paragraph, having regard to circumstances which have arisen since the community order was made.

(2) The Crown Court may—

(a) revoke the order, or

(b) both—

(i) revoke the order, and

(ii) deal with the offender, for the offence in respect of which the order was made, in any way in which he could have been dealt with for that offence by the court which made the order if the order had not been made.

(3) In dealing with an offender under sub-paragraph (2)(b), the Crown Court must take into account the extent to which the offender has complied with the requirements of the community order.

PART 6

SUPPLEMENTARY

24 (1) No order may be made under paragraph 16, and no application may be made under paragraph 13, 17 or 20, while an appeal against the community order is pending.

(2) Sub-paragraph (1) does not apply to an application under paragraph 17 which—

(a) relates to a mental health treatment requirement, a drug rehabilitation requirement or an alcohol treatment requirement, and

(b) is made by the responsible officer with the consent of the offender.

25 (1) Subject to sub-paragraph (2), where a court proposes to exercise its powers under Part 4 or 5 of this Schedule, otherwise than on the application of the offender, the court—

(a) must summon him to appear before the court, and

(b) if he does not appear in answer to the summons, may issue a warrant for his arrest.

(2) This paragraph does not apply to an order cancelling a requirement of a community order or reducing the period of any requirement, or substituting a new [local justice area] or a new place for the one specified in the order.

26 Paragraphs 9(1)(a), 10(1)(a) and 17(1)(b) have effect subject to the provisions mentioned in subsection (2) of section 177, and to subsections (3) and (6) of that section.

27 (1) On the making under this Schedule of an order revoking or amending a community order, the proper officer of the court must—

(a) provide copies of the revoking or amending order to the offender and the responsible officer,

(b) in the case of an amending order which substitutes a new local justice area, provide a copy of the amending order to—

(i) the local probation board acting for that area, and

(ii) the magistrates' court acting [in that area], and

(c) in the case of an amending order which imposes or amends a requirement specified in the first column of Schedule 14, provide a copy of so much of the amending order as relates to that requirement to the person specified in relation to that requirement in the second column of that Schedule[, and

(d)   where the court acts for a petty sessions area other than the one specified in the order prior to the revocation or amendment, provide a copy of the revoking or amending order to a magistrates' court acting for the area so specified.]]

(2) Where under sub-paragraph (1)(b) the proper officer of the court provides a copy of an amending order to a magistrates' court acting in a different area, the officer must also provide to that court such documents and information relating to the case as it considers likely to be of assistance to a court acting in that area]in the exercise of its functions in relation to the order.

(3) In this paragraph "proper officer" means—

(a) in relation to a magistrates' court, the designated officer for the court; and

(b) in relation to the Crown Court, the appropriate officer.

SCHEDULE 12 CRIMINAL JUSTICE ACT 2003 (AS AMENDED)

BREACH OR AMENDMENT OF SUSPENDED SENTENCE ORDER, AND EFFECT OF
FURTHER CONVICTION

PART 1

PRELIMINARY

Interpretation

1   In this Schedule—

"the offender", in relation to a suspended sentence order, means the person in
respect of whom the order is made;

"the local justice area concerned", in relation to a suspended sentence order,
means the local justice area for the time being specified in the order;

"the responsible officer" has the meaning given by section 197.

2   In this Schedule—

(a) any reference to a suspended sentence order being subject to review is a
reference to such an order being subject to review in accordance with section
191(1)(b) or to a drug rehabilitation requirement of such an order being subject
to review in accordance with section 210(1)(b);

(b) any reference to the court responsible for a suspended sentence order which is
subject to review is to be construed in accordance with section 191(3) or, as the
case may be, 210(2).

Orders made on appeal

3   Where a suspended sentence order is made on appeal it is to be taken for the purposes
of this Schedule to have been made by the Crown Court.

PART 2

BREACH OF COMMUNITY REQUIREMENT OR CONVICTION OF FURTHER OFFENCE

Duty to give warning in relation to community requirement

4   (1) If the responsible officer is of the opinion that the offender has failed without
reasonable excuse to comply with any of the community requirements of a suspended
sentence order, the officer must give him a warning under this paragraph unless—

(a) the offender has within the previous twelve months been given a warning under this paragraph in relation to a failure to comply with any of the community requirements of the order, or

(b) the officer causes an information to be laid before a justice of the peace in respect of the failure.

(2) A warning under this paragraph must—

(a) describe the circumstances of the failure,

(b) state that the failure is unacceptable, and

(c) inform the offender that if within the next twelve months he again fails to comply with any requirement of the order, he will be liable to be brought before a court.

(3) The responsible officer must, as soon as practicable after the warning has been given, record that fact.

(4) In relation to any suspended sentence order which is made by the Crown Court and does not include a direction that any failure to comply with the community requirements of the order is to be dealt with by a magistrates' court, the reference in sub-paragraph (1)(b) to a justice of the peace is to be read as a reference to the Crown Court.

Breach of order after warning

5   (1) If—

(a) the responsible officer has given a warning under paragraph 4 to the offender in respect of a suspended sentence order, and

(b) at any time within the twelve months beginning with the date on which the warning was given, the responsible officer is of the opinion that the offender has since that date failed without reasonable excuse to comply with any of the community requirements of the order, the officer must cause an information to be laid before a justice of the peace in respect of the failure in question.

(2) In relation to any suspended sentence order which is made by the Crown Court and does not include a direction that any failure to comply with the community requirements of the order is to be dealt with by a magistrates' court, the reference in sub-paragraph (1) to a justice of the peace is to be read as a reference to the Crown Court.

Issue of summons or warrant by justice of the peace

6   (1) This paragraph applies to—

(a) a suspended sentence order made by a magistrates' court, or

(b) any suspended sentence order which was made by the Crown Court and includes a direction that any failure to comply with the community requirements of the order is to be dealt with by a magistrates' court.

(2) If at any time while a suspended sentence order to which this paragraph applies is in force it appears on information to a justice of the peace . . . that the offender

has failed to comply with any of the community requirements of the order, the justice may—

(a) issue a summons requiring the offender to appear at the place and time specified in it, or

(b) if the information is in writing and on oath, issue a warrant for his arrest.

(3) Any summons or warrant issued under this paragraph must direct the offender to appear or be brought—

(a) in the case of a suspended sentence order which is subject to review, before the court responsible for the order,

(b) in any other case, before a magistrates' court acting for the petty sessions area in which the offender resides or, if it is not known where he resides, before a magistrates' court [acting in the local justice area] concerned.

(4) Where a summons issued under sub-paragraph (2)(a) requires the offender to appear before a magistrates' court and the offender does not appear in answer to the summons, the magistrates' court may issue a warrant for the arrest of the offender.

Issue of summons or warrant by Crown Court

7   (1) This paragraph applies to a suspended sentence order made by the Crown Court which does not include a direction that any failure to comply with the community requirements of the order is to be dealt with by a magistrates' court.

(2) If at any time while a suspended sentence order to which this paragraph applies is in force it appears on information to the Crown Court that the offender has failed to comply with any of the community requirements of the order, the Crown Court may—

(a) issue a summons requiring the offender to appear at the place and time specified in it, or

(b) if the information is in writing and on oath, issue a warrant for his arrest.

(3) Any summons or warrant issued under this paragraph must direct the offender to appear or be brought before the Crown Court.

(4) Where a summons issued under sub-paragraph (1)(a) requires the offender to appear before the Crown Court and the offender does not appear in answer to the summons, the Crown Court may issue a warrant for the arrest of the offender.

Powers of court on breach of community requirement or conviction of further offence

8   (1) This paragraph applies where—

(a) it is proved to the satisfaction of a court before which an offender appears or is brought under paragraph 6 or 7 or by virtue of section 192(6) that he has failed without reasonable excuse to comply with any of the community requirements of the suspended sentence order, or

(b) an offender is convicted of an offence committed during the operational period of a suspended sentence (other than one which has already taken effect) and either—

(i)   he is so convicted by or before a court having power under paragraph 11 to deal with him in respect of the suspended sentence, or

(ii) he subsequently appears or is brought before such a court.

(2) The court must consider his case and deal with him in one of the following ways—

(a) the court may order that the suspended sentence is to take effect with its original term and custodial period unaltered,

(b) the court may order that the sentence is to take effect with either or both of the following modifications—

(i)   the substitution for the original term of a lesser term complying with section 181(2), and

(ii) the substitution for the original custodial period of a lesser custodial period complying with section 181(5) and (6),

(c) the court may amend the order by doing any one or more of the following—

(i)   imposing more onerous community requirements which the court could include if it were then making the order,

(ii) subject to subsections (3) and (4) of section 189, extending the supervision period, or

(iii) subject to subsection (3) of that section, extending the operational period.

(3) The court must make an order under sub-paragraph (2)(a) or (b) unless it is of the opinion that it would be unjust to do so in view of all the circumstances, including the matters mentioned in sub-paragraph (4); and where it is of that opinion the court must state its reasons.

(4) The matters referred to in sub-paragraph (3) are—

(a) the extent to which the offender has complied with the community requirements of the suspended sentence order, and

(b) in a case falling within sub-paragraph (1)(b), the facts of the subsequent offence.

(4A) Where a magistrates' court dealing with an offender under sub-paragraph (2)(c) would not otherwise have the power to amend the suspended sentence order under paragraph 14 (amendment by reason of change of residence), that paragraph has effect as if the references to the appropriate court were references to the court dealing with the offender.

(5) Where a court deals with an offender under sub-paragraph (2) in respect of a suspended sentence, the appropriate officer of the court must notify the appropriate officer of the court which passed the sentence of the method adopted.

(6) Where a suspended sentence order was made by the Crown Court and a magistrates' court would (apart from this sub-paragraph) be required to deal with the offender under sub-paragraph (2)(a), (b) or (c) it may instead commit him to custody or release him on bail until he can be brought or appear before the Crown Court.

(7) A magistrates' court which deals with an offender's case under sub-paragraph (6) must send to the Crown Court—

(a) a certificate signed by a justice of the peace certifying that the offender has failed to comply with the community requirements of the suspended sentence order in the respect specified in the certificate, and

(b) such other particulars of the case as may be desirable; and a certificate purporting to be so signed is admissible as evidence of the failure before the Crown Court.

(8) In proceedings before the Crown Court under this paragraph any question whether the offender has failed to comply with the community requirements of the suspended sentence order and any question whether the offender has been convicted of an offence committed during the operational period of the suspended sentence is to be determined by the court and not by the verdict of a jury.

Further provisions as to order that suspended sentence is to take effect

9   (1) When making an order under paragraph 8(2)(a) or (b) that a sentence is to take effect (with or without any variation of the original term and custodial period), the court—

(a) must also make a custody plus order, and

(b) may order that the sentence is to take effect immediately or that the term of that sentence is to commence on the expiry of another term of imprisonment passed on the offender by that or another court.

(2) The power to make an order under sub-paragraph (1)(b) has effect subject to section 265 (restriction on consecutive sentences for released prisoners).

(3) For the purpose of any enactment conferring rights of appeal in criminal cases, any order made by the court under paragraph 8(2)(a) or (b) is to be treated as a sentence passed on the offender by that court for the offence for which the suspended sentence was passed.

Restriction of powers in paragraph 8 where treatment required

10   (1) An offender who is required by any of the following community requirements of a suspended sentence order—

(a) a mental health treatment requirement,

(b) a drug rehabilitation requirement, or

(c) an alcohol treatment requirement, to submit to treatment for his mental condition, or his dependency on or propensity to misuse drugs or alcohol, is not to be treated for the purposes of paragraph 8(1)(a) as having failed to comply with that requirement on the ground only that he had refused to undergo any surgical, electrical or other treatment if, in the opinion of the court, his refusal was reasonable having regard to all the circumstances.

(2) A court may not under paragraph 8(2)(c)(i) amend a mental health treatment requirement, a drug rehabilitation requirement or an alcohol treatment requirement unless the offender expresses his willingness to comply with the requirement as amended.

Court by which suspended sentence may be dealt with under paragraph 8(1)(b)

11 (1) An offender may be dealt with under paragraph 8(1)(b) in respect of a suspended sentence by the Crown Court or, where the sentence was passed by a magistrates' court, by any magistrates' court before which he appears or is brought.

(2) Where an offender is convicted by a magistrates' court of any offence and the court is satisfied that the offence was committed during the operational period of a suspended sentence passed by the Crown Court—

(a) the court may, if it thinks fit, commit him in custody or on bail to the Crown Court, and

(b) if it does not, must give written notice of the conviction to the appropriate officer of the Crown Court.

Procedure where court convicting of further offence does not deal with suspended sentence

12 (1) If it appears to the Crown Court, where that court has jurisdiction in accordance with sub-paragraph (2), or to a justice of the peace having jurisdiction in accordance with that sub-paragraph—

(a) that an offender has been convicted in the United Kingdom of an offence committed during the operational period of a suspended sentence, and

(b) that he has not been dealt with in respect of the suspended sentence, that court or justice may, subject to the following provisions of this paragraph, issue a summons requiring the offender to appear at the place and time specified in it, or a warrant for his arrest.

(2) Jurisdiction for the purposes of sub-paragraph (1) may be exercised—

(a) if the suspended sentence was passed by the Crown Court, by that court;

(b) if it was passed by a magistrates' court, by a justice acting in the local justice area in which the court acted

(3) Where—

(a) an offender is convicted in Scotland or Northern Ireland of an offence, and

(b) the court is informed that the offence was committed during the operational period of a suspended sentence passed in England or Wales, the court must give written notice of the conviction to the appropriate officer of the court by which he suspended sentence was passed.

(4) Unless he is acting in consequence of a notice under sub-paragraph (3), a justice of the peace may not issue a summons under this paragraph except on information and may not issue a warrant under this paragraph except on information in writing and on oath.

(5) A summons or warrant issued under this paragraph must direct the offender to appear or be brought before the court by which the suspended sentence was passed.

PART 3

AMENDMENT OF SUSPENDED SENTENCE ORDER

Cancellation of community requirements of suspended sentence order

13 (1) Where at any time while a suspended sentence order is in force, it appears to the appropriate court on the application of the offender or the responsible officer that, having regard to the circumstances which have arisen since the order was made, it would be in the interests of justice to do so, the court may cancel the community requirements of the suspended sentence order.

(2) The circumstances in which the appropriate court may exercise its power under sub-paragraph (1) include the offender's making good progress or his responding satisfactorily to supervision.

(3) In this paragraph "the appropriate court" means—

(a) in the case of a suspended sentence order which is subject to review, the court responsible for the order,

(b) in the case of a suspended sentence order which was made by the Crown Court and does not include any direction that any failure to comply with the community requirements of the order is to be dealt with by a magistrates' court, the Crown Court, and

(c) in any other case, a magistrates' court acting in the local justice area concerned.

Amendment by reason of change of residence

14 (1) This paragraph applies where, at any time while a suspended sentence order is in force, the appropriate court is satisfied that the offender proposes to change, or has changed, his residence from the local justice area concerned to another local justice area.

(2) Subject to sub-paragraphs (3) and (4), the appropriate court may, and on the application of the responsible officer must, amend the suspended sentence order by substituting the other local justice area for the area specified in the order.

(3) The court may not amend under this paragraph a suspended sentence order which contains requirements which, in the opinion of the court, cannot be complied with unless the offender resides in the local justice area concerned unless, in accordance with paragraph 15 it either—

(a) cancels those requirements, or

(b) substitutes for those requirements other requirements which can be complied with if the offender does not reside in that area.

(4) The court may not amend under this paragraph any suspended sentence order imposing a programme requirement unless it appears to the court that the accredited programme specified in the requirement is available in the other local justice area.

(5) In this paragraph "the appropriate court" has the same meaning as in paragraph 13.

Amendment of community requirements of suspended sentence order

15 (1) At any time during the supervision period, the appropriate court may, on the application of the offender or the responsible officer, by order amend any community requirement of a suspended sentence order—

(a) by cancelling the requirement, or

(b) by replacing it with a requirement of the same kind, which the court could include if it were then making the order.

(2) For the purposes of sub-paragraph (1)—

(a) a requirement falling within any paragraph of section 190(1) is of the same kind as any other requirement falling within that paragraph, and

(b) an electronic monitoring requirement is a requirement of the same kind as any requirement falling within section 190(1) to which it relates.

(3) The court may not under this paragraph amend a mental health treatment requirement, a drug rehabilitation requirement or an alcohol treatment requirement unless the offender expresses his willingness to comply with the requirement as amended.

(4) If the offender fails to express his willingness to comply with a mental health treatment requirement, drug rehabilitation requirement or alcohol treatment requirement as proposed to be amended by the court under this paragraph, the court may—

(a) revoke the suspended sentence order and the suspended sentence to which it relates, and

(b) deal with him, for the offence in respect of which the suspended sentence was imposed, in any way in which it could deal with him if he had just been convicted by or before the court of the offence.

(5) In dealing with the offender under sub-paragraph (4)(b), the court must take into account the extent to which the offender has complied with the requirements of the order.

(6) In this paragraph "the appropriate court" has the same meaning as in paragraph 13.

Amendment of treatment requirements on report of practitioner

16 (1) Where the medical practitioner or other person by whom or under whose direction an offender is, in pursuance of any requirement to which this sub-paragraph applies, being treated for his mental condition or his dependency on or propensity to misuse drugs or alcohol—

(a) is of the opinion mentioned in sub-paragraph (3), or

(b) is for any reason unwilling to continue to treat or direct the treatment of the offender, he must make a report in writing to that effect to the responsible officer and that officer must apply under paragraph 15 to the appropriate court for the variation or cancellation of the requirement.

(2) The requirements to which sub-paragraph (1) applies are—

(a) a mental health treatment requirement,

(b) a drug rehabilitation requirement, and

(c) an alcohol treatment requirement.

(3) The opinion referred to in sub-paragraph (1) is—

(a) that the treatment of the offender should be continued beyond the period specified in that behalf in the order,

(b) that the offender needs different treatment,

(c) that the offender is not susceptible to treatment, or

(d) that the offender does not require further treatment.

(4) In this paragraph "the appropriate court" has the same meaning as in paragraph 13.

Amendment in relation to review of drug rehabilitation requirement

17 Where the responsible officer is of the opinion that a suspended sentence order imposing a drug rehabilitation requirement which is subject to review should be so amended as to provide for each periodic review (required by section 211) to be made without a hearing instead of at a review hearing, or vice versa, he must apply under paragraph 15 to the court responsible for the order for the variation of the order.

Extension of unpaid work requirement

18 (1) Where—

(a) a suspended sentence order imposing an unpaid work requirement is in force in respect of the offender, and

(b) on the application of the offender or the responsible officer, it appears to the appropriate court that it would be in the interests of justice to do so having regard to circumstances which have arisen since the order was made, the court may, in relation to the order, extend the period of twelve months specified in section 200(2).

(2) In this paragraph "the appropriate court" has the same meaning as in paragraph 13.

Supplementary

19 (1) No application may be made under paragraph 13, 15 or 18, and no order may be made under paragraph 14, while an appeal against the suspended sentence is pending.

(2) Sub-paragraph (1) does not apply to an application under paragraph 15 which—

(a) relates to a mental health treatment requirement, a drug rehabilitation requirement or an alcohol treatment requirement, and

(b) is made by the responsible officer with the consent of the offender.

20 (1) Subject to sub-paragraph (2), where a court proposes to exercise its powers under paragraph 15, otherwise than on the application of the offender, the court—

(a) must summon him to appear before the court, and

(b) if he does not appear in answer to the summons, may issue a warrant for his arrest.

(2) This paragraph does not apply to an order cancelling any community requirement of a suspended sentence order.

21 Paragraphs 8(2)(c) and 15(1)(b) have effect subject to the provisions mentioned in subsection (2) of section 190, and to subsections (3) and (5) of that section.

22 (1) On the making under this Schedule of an order amending a suspended sentence order, the proper officer of the court must—

(a) provide copies of the amending order to the offender and the responsible officer,

(b) in the case of an amending order which substitutes a new [local justice area], provide a copy of the amending order to—

(i) the local probation board acting for that area, and

(ii) the magistrates' court [acting in that area], and

(c) in the case of an amending order which imposes or amends a requirement specified in the first column of Schedule 14, provide a copy of so much of the amending order as relates to that requirement to the person specified in relation to that requirement in the second column of that Schedule, and

(d) where the court acts for a petty sessions area other than the one specified in the order prior to the revocation or amendment, provide a copy of the revoking or amending order to a magistrates' court acting for the area so specified.

(2) Where under sub-paragraph (1)(b) the proper officer of the court provides a copy of an amending order to a magistrates' court acting in a different area, the officer must also provide to that court such documents and information relating to the case as it considers likely to be of assistance to a court acting in that area in the exercise of its functions in relation to the order.

(3) In this paragraph "proper officer" means—

(a) in relation to a magistrates' court, the designated officer for the court; and

(b) in relation to the Crown Court, the appropriate officer.

SCHEDULE 2 CRIMINAL JUSTICE AND IMMIGRATION ACT 2008

BREACH, REVOCATION OR AMENDMENT OF YOUTH REHABILITATION ORDERS

PART 1

PRELIMINARY

Interpretation

1   (1) In this Schedule, "the offender", in relation to a youth rehabilitation order, means the person in respect of whom the order is made.

(2) In this Schedule—

(a) any reference (however expressed) to an offender's compliance with a youth rehabilitation order is a reference to the offender's compliance with—

(i)   the requirement or requirements imposed by the order, and

(ii) if the order imposes an attendance centre requirement, rules made under section 222(1)(d) or (e) of the Criminal Justice Act 2003 (c. 44) ("attendance centre rules"), and

(b) any reference (however expressed) to the offender's failure to comply with the order is a reference to any failure of the offender to comply—

(i)   with a requirement imposed by the order, or

(ii) if the order imposes an attendance centre requirement, with attendance centre rules.

(3) For the purposes of this Schedule—

(a) a requirement falling within any paragraph of Part 2 of Schedule 1 is of the same kind as any other requirement falling within that paragraph, and

(b) an electronic monitoring requirement is a requirement of the same kind as any requirement falling within Part 2 of Schedule 1 to which it relates.

Orders made on appeal

2   Where a youth rehabilitation order has been made on appeal, for the purposes of this Schedule it is to be treated—

(a) if it was made on an appeal from a magistrates' court, as having been made by a magistrates' court;

(b) if it was made on an appeal brought from the Crown Court or from the criminal division of the Court of Appeal, as having been made by the Crown Court.

Part 2

Breach of requirement of order

Duty to give warning

3 (1) If the responsible officer is of the opinion that the offender has failed without reasonable excuse to comply with a youth rehabilitation order, the responsible officer must give the offender a warning under this paragraph unless under paragraph 4(1) or (3) the responsible officer causes an information to be laid before a justice of the peace in respect of the failure.

(2) A warning under this paragraph must—

(a) describe the circumstances of the failure,

(b) state that the failure is unacceptable, and

(c) state that the offender will be liable to be brought before a court—

(i) in a case where the warning is given during the warned period relating to a previous warning under this paragraph, if during that period the offender again fails to comply with the order, or

(ii) in any other case, if during the warned period relating to the warning, the offender fails on more than one occasion to comply with the order.

(3) The responsible officer must, as soon as practicable after the warning has been given, record that fact.

(4) In this paragraph, "warned period", in relation to a warning under this paragraph, means the period of 12 months beginning with the date on which the warning was given.

Breach of order

4 (1) If the responsible officer—

(a) has given a warning ("the first warning") under paragraph 3 to the offender in respect of a youth rehabilitation order,

(b) during the warned period relating to the first warning, has given another warning under that paragraph to the offender in respect of a failure to comply with the order, and

(c) is of the opinion that, during the warned period relating to the first warning, the offender has again failed without reasonable excuse to comply with the order, the responsible officer must cause an information to be laid before a justice of the peace in respect of the failure mentioned in paragraph (c).

(2) But sub-paragraph (1) does not apply if the responsible officer is of the opinion that there are exceptional circumstances which justify not causing an information to be so laid.

(3) If—

(a) the responsible officer is of the opinion that the offender has failed without reasonable excuse to comply with a youth rehabilitation order, and

(b) sub-paragraph (1) does not apply (in a case not within sub-paragraph (2)), the responsible officer may cause an information to be laid before a justice of the peace in respect of that failure.

(4) In this paragraph, "warned period" has the same meaning as in paragraph 3.

Issue of summons or warrant by justice of the peace

5   (1) If at any time while a youth rehabilitation order is in force it appears on information to a justice of the peace that an offender has failed to comply with a youth rehabilitation order, the justice may—

(a) issue a summons requiring the offender to appear at the place and time specified in it, or

(b) if the information is in writing and on oath, issue a warrant for the offender's arrest.

(2) Any summons or warrant issued under this paragraph must direct the offender to appear or be brought—

(a) if the youth rehabilitation order was made by the Crown Court and does not include a direction under paragraph 36 of Schedule 1, before the Crown Court, and

(b) in any other case, before the appropriate court.

(3) In sub-paragraph (2), "appropriate court" means—

(a) if the offender is aged under 18, a youth court acting in the relevant local justice area, and

(b) if the offender is aged 18 or over, a magistrates' court (other than a youth court) acting in that local justice area.

(4) In sub-paragraph (3), "relevant local justice area" means—

(a) the local justice area in which the offender resides, or

(b) if it is not known where the offender resides, the local justice area specified in the youth rehabilitation order.

(5) Sub-paragraphs (6) and (7) apply where the offender does not appear in answer to a summons issued under this paragraph.

(6) If the summons required the offender to appear before the Crown Court, the Crown Court may—

(a) unless the summons was issued under this sub-paragraph, issue a further summons requiring the offender to appear at the place and time specified in it, or

(b) in any case, issue a warrant for the arrest of the offender.

(7) If the summons required the offender to appear before a magistrates' court, the magistrates' court may issue a warrant for the arrest of the offender.

Powers of magistrates' court

6   (1) This paragraph applies where—

(a) an offender appears or is brought before a youth court or other magistrates' court under paragraph 5, and

(b) it is proved to the satisfaction of the court that the offender has failed without reasonable excuse to comply with the youth rehabilitation order.

(2) The court may deal with the offender in respect of that failure in any one of the following ways—

(a) by ordering the offender to pay a fine of an amount not exceeding—

(i)   £250, if the offender is aged under 14, or

(ii) £1,000, in any other case;

(b) by amending the terms of the youth rehabilitation order so as to impose any requirement which could have been included in the order when it was made—

(i)   in addition to, or

(ii) in substitution for, any requirement or requirements already imposed by the order;

(c) by dealing with the offender, for the offence in respect of which the order was made, in any way in which the court could have dealt with the offender for that offence (had the offender been before that court to be dealt with for it).

(3) Sub-paragraph (2)(b) is subject to sub-paragraphs (6) to (9).

(4) In dealing with the offender under sub-paragraph (2), the court must take into account the extent to which the offender has complied with the youth rehabilitation order.

(5) A fine imposed under sub-paragraph (2)(a) is to be treated, for the purposes of any enactment, as being a sum adjudged to be paid by a conviction.

(6) Any requirement imposed under sub-paragraph (2)(b) must be capable of being complied with before the date specified under paragraph 32(1) of Schedule 1.

(7) Where—

(a) the court is dealing with the offender under sub-paragraph (2)(b), and

(b) the youth rehabilitation order does not contain an unpaid work requirement, paragraph 10(2) of Schedule 1 applies in relation to the inclusion of such a requirement as if for "40" there were substituted "20".

(8) The court may not under sub-paragraph (2)(b) impose—

(a) an extended activity requirement, or

(b) a fostering requirement, if the order does not already impose such a requirement.

(9) Where—

(a) the order imposes a fostering requirement (the "original requirement"), and

(b) under sub-paragraph (2)(b) the court proposes to substitute a new fostering requirement ("the substitute requirement") for the original requirement, paragraph 18(2) of Schedule 1 applies in relation to the substitute requirement as if the reference to the period of 12 months beginning with the date on which the original requirement first had effect were a reference to the period of 18 months beginning with that date.

(10) Where—

(a) the court deals with the offender under sub-paragraph (2)(b), and

(b) it would not otherwise have the power to amend the youth rehabilitation order under paragraph 13 (amendment by reason of change of residence), that paragraph has effect as if references in it to the appropriate court were references to the court which is dealing with the offender.

(11) Where the court deals with the offender under sub-paragraph (2)(c), it must revoke the youth rehabilitation order if it is still in force.

(12) Sub-paragraphs (13) to (15) apply where—

(a) the court is dealing with the offender under sub-paragraph (2)(c), and

(b) the offender has wilfully and persistently failed to comply with a youth rehabilitation order.

(13) The court may impose a youth rehabilitation order with intensive supervision and surveillance notwithstanding anything in section 1(4)(a) or (b).

(14) If—

(a) the order is a youth rehabilitation order with intensive supervision and surveillance, and

(b) the offence mentioned in sub-paragraph (2)(c) was punishable with imprisonment, the court may impose a custodial sentence notwithstanding anything in section 152(2) of the Criminal Justice Act 2003 (c. 44) (general restrictions on imposing discretionary custodial sentences).

(15) If—

(a) the order is a youth rehabilitation order with intensive supervision and surveillance which was imposed by virtue of sub-paragraph (13) or paragraph 8(12), and

(b) the offence mentioned in sub-paragraph (2)(c) was not punishable with imprisonment, for the purposes of dealing with the offender under sub-paragraph (2)(c), the court is to be taken to have had power to deal with the offender for that offence by making a detention and training order for a term not exceeding 4 months.

(16) An offender may appeal to the Crown Court against a sentence imposed under sub-paragraph (2)(c).

Power of magistrates' court to refer offender to Crown Court

7   (1) Sub-paragraph (2) applies if—

(a) the youth rehabilitation order was made by the Crown Court and contains a direction under paragraph 36 of Schedule 1, and

(b) a youth court or other magistrates' court would (apart from that sub-paragraph) be required, or has the power, to deal with the offender in one of the ways mentioned in paragraph 6(2).

(2) The court may instead—

(a) commit the offender in custody, or

(b) release the offender on bail, until the offender can be brought or appear before the Crown Court.

(3) Where a court deals with the offender's case under sub-paragraph (2) it must send to the Crown Court—

(a) a certificate signed by a justice of the peace certifying that the offender has failed to comply with the youth rehabilitation order in the respect specified in the certificate, and

(b) such other particulars of the case as may be desirable; and a certificate purporting to be so signed is admissible as evidence of the failure before the Crown Court.

Powers of Crown Court

8   (1) This paragraph applies where—

(a) an offender appears or is brought before the Crown Court under paragraph 5 or by virtue of paragraph 7(2), and

(b) it is proved to the satisfaction of that court that the offender has failed without reasonable excuse to comply with the youth rehabilitation order.

(2) The Crown Court may deal with the offender in respect of that failure in any one of the following ways—

(a) by ordering the offender to pay a fine of an amount not exceeding—

(i)   £250, if the offender is aged under 14, or

(ii)   £1,000, in any other case;

(b) by amending the terms of the youth rehabilitation order so as to impose any requirement which could have been included in the order when it was made—

(i)   in addition to, or

(ii) in substitution for, any requirement or requirements already imposed by the order;

(c) by dealing with the offender, for the offence in respect of which the order was made, in any way in which the Crown Court could have dealt with the offender for that offence.

(3) Sub-paragraph (2)(b) is subject to sub-paragraphs (6) to (9).

(4) In dealing with the offender under sub-paragraph (2), the Crown Court must take into account the extent to which the offender has complied with the youth rehabilitation order.

(5) A fine imposed under sub-paragraph (2)(a) is to be treated, for the purposes of any enactment, as being a sum adjudged to be paid by a conviction.

(6) Any requirement imposed under sub-paragraph (2)(b) must be capable of being complied with before the date specified under paragraph 32(1) of Schedule 1.

(7) Where—

(a) the court is dealing with the offender under sub-paragraph (2)(b), and

(b) the youth rehabilitation order does not contain an unpaid work requirement, paragraph 10(2) of Schedule 1 applies in relation to the inclusion of such a requirement as if for "40" there were substituted "20".

(8) The court may not under sub-paragraph (2)(b) impose—

(a) an extended activity requirement, or

(b) a fostering requirement, if the order does not already impose such a requirement.

(9) Where—

(a) the order imposes a fostering requirement (the "original requirement"), and

(b) under sub-paragraph (2)(b) the court proposes to substitute a new fostering requirement ("the substitute requirement") for the original requirement, paragraph 18(2) of Schedule 1 applies in relation to the substitute requirement as if the reference to the period of 12 months beginning with the date on which the original requirement first had effect were a reference to the period of 18 months beginning with that date.

(10) Where the Crown Court deals with an offender under sub-paragraph (2)(c), it must revoke the youth rehabilitation order if it is still in force.

(11) Sub-paragraphs (12) to (14) apply where—

(a) an offender has wilfully and persistently failed to comply with a youth rehabilitation order; and

(b) the Crown Court is dealing with the offender under sub-paragraph (2)(c).

(12) The court may impose a youth rehabilitation order with intensive supervision and surveillance notwithstanding anything in section 1(4)(a) or (b).

(13) If—

(a) the order is a youth rehabilitation order with intensive supervision and surveillance, and

(b) the offence mentioned in sub-paragraph (2)(c) was punishable with imprisonment, the court may impose a custodial sentence notwithstanding anything in section 152(2) of the Criminal Justice Act 2003 (c. 44) (general restrictions on imposing discretionary custodial sentences).

(14) If—

(a) the order is a youth rehabilitation order with intensive supervision and surveillance which was imposed by virtue of paragraph 6(13) or sub-paragraph (12), and

(b)the offence mentioned in sub-paragraph (2)(c) was not punishable with imprisonment, for the purposes of dealing with the offender under sub-paragraph

(2)(c), the Crown Court is to be taken to have had power to deal with the offender for that offence by making a detention and training order for a term not exceeding 4 months.

(15) In proceedings before the Crown Court under this paragraph any question whether the offender has failed to comply with the youth rehabilitation order is to be determined by the court and not by the verdict of a jury.

Restriction of powers in paragraphs 6 and 8 where treatment required

9 (1) Sub-paragraph (2) applies where a youth rehabilitation order imposes any of the following requirements in respect of an offender—

(a) a mental health treatment requirement;

(b) a drug treatment requirement;

(c) an intoxicating substance treatment requirement.

(2) The offender is not to be treated for the purposes of paragraph 6 or 8 as having failed to comply with the order on the ground only that the offender had refused to undergo any surgical, electrical or other treatment required by that requirement if, in the opinion of the court, the refusal was reasonable having regard to all the circumstances.

Power to amend amounts of fines

10 (1) The Secretary of State may by order amend any sum for the time being specified in paragraph 6(2)(a)(i) or (ii) or 8(2)(a)(i) or (ii).

(2) The power conferred by sub-paragraph (1) may be exercised only if it appears to the Secretary of State that there has been a change in the value of money since the relevant date which justifies the change.

(3) In sub-paragraph (2), "the relevant date" means—

(a) if the sum specified in paragraph 6(2)(a)(i) or (ii) or 8(2)(a)(i) or (ii) (as the case may be) has been substituted by an order under sub-paragraph (1), the date on which the sum was last so substituted;

(b) otherwise, the date on which this Act was passed.

(4) An order under sub-paragraph (1) (a "fine amendment order") must not have effect in relation to any youth rehabilitation order made in respect of an offence committed before the fine amendment order comes into force.

PART 3

REVOCATION OF ORDER

Revocation of order with or without re-sentencing: powers of appropriate court

11 (1) This paragraph applies where—

(a) a youth rehabilitation order is in force in respect of any offender,

(b) the order—

(i) was made by a youth court or other magistrates' court, or

(ii) was made by the Crown Court and contains a direction under paragraph 36 of Schedule 1, and

(c) the offender or the responsible officer makes an application to the appropriate court under this sub-paragraph.

(2) If it appears to the appropriate court to be in the interests of justice to do so, having regard to circumstances which have arisen since the order was made, the appropriate court may—

(a) revoke the order, or

(b) both—

(i) revoke the order, and

(ii) deal with the offender, for the offence in respect of which the order was made, in any way in which the appropriate court could have dealt with the offender for that offence (had the offender been before that court to be dealt with for it).

(3) The circumstances in which a youth rehabilitation order may be revoked under sub-paragraph (2) include the offender's making good progress or responding satisfactorily to supervision or treatment (as the case requires).

(4) In dealing with an offender under sub-paragraph (2)(b), the appropriate court must take into account the extent to which the offender has complied with the requirements of the youth rehabilitation order.

(5) A person sentenced under sub-paragraph (2)(b) for an offence may appeal to the Crown Court against the sentence.

(6) No application may be made by the offender under sub-paragraph (1) while an appeal against the youth rehabilitation order is pending.

(7) If an application under sub-paragraph (1) relating to a youth rehabilitation order is dismissed, then during the period of three months beginning with the date on which it was dismissed no further such application may be made in relation to the order by any person except with the consent of the appropriate court.

(8) In this paragraph, "the appropriate court" means—

(a) if the offender is aged under 18 when the application under sub-paragraph (1) was made, a youth court acting in the local justice area specified in the youth rehabilitation order, and

(b) if the offender is aged 18 or over at that time, a magistrates' court (other than a youth court) acting in that local justice area.

Revocation of order with or without re-sentencing: powers of Crown Court

12 (1) This paragraph applies where—

(a) a youth rehabilitation order is in force in respect of an offender,

(b) the order—

(i)   was made by the Crown Court, and

(ii) does not contain a direction under paragraph 36 of Schedule 1, and

(c) the offender or the responsible officer makes an application to the Crown Court under this sub-paragraph.

(2) If it appears to the Crown Court to be in the interests of justice to do so, having regard to circumstances which have arisen since the youth rehabilitation order was made, the Crown Court may—

(a) revoke the order, or

(b) both—

(i)   revoke the order, and

(ii) deal with the offender, for the offence in respect of which the order was made, in any way in which the Crown Court could have dealt with the offender for that offence.

(3) The circumstances in which a youth rehabilitation order may be revoked under sub-paragraph (2) include the offender's making good progress or responding satisfactorily to supervision or treatment (as the case requires).

(4) In dealing with an offender under sub-paragraph (2)(b), the Crown Court must take into account the extent to which the offender has complied with the youth rehabilitation order.

(5) No application may be made by the offender under sub-paragraph (1) while an appeal against the youth rehabilitation order is pending.

(6) If an application under sub-paragraph (1) relating to a youth rehabilitation order is dismissed, then during the period of three months beginning with the date on which it was dismissed no further such application may be made in relation to the order by any person except with the consent of the Crown Court.

Part 4
Amendment of order

Amendment by appropriate court

13   (1) This paragraph applies where—

(a) a youth rehabilitation order is in force in respect of an offender,

(b) the order—

(i)   was made by a youth court or other magistrates' court, or

(ii) was made by the Crown Court and contains a direction under paragraph 36 of Schedule 1, and

(c) an application for the amendment of the order is made to the appropriate court by the offender or the responsible officer.

(2) If the appropriate court is satisfied that the offender proposes to reside, or is residing, in a local justice area ("the new local justice area") other than the local justice area for the time being specified in the order, the court—

(a) must, if the application under sub-paragraph (1)(c) was made by the responsible officer, or

(b) may, in any other case, amend the youth rehabilitation order by substituting the new local justice area for the area specified in the order.

(3) Sub-paragraph (2) is subject to paragraph 15.

(4) The appropriate court may by order amend the youth rehabilitation order—

(a) by cancelling any of the requirements of the order, or

(b) by replacing any of those requirements with a requirement of the same kind which could have been included in the order when it was made.

(5) Sub-paragraph (4) is subject to paragraph 16.

(6) In this paragraph, "the appropriate court" means—

(a) if the offender is aged under 18 when the application under sub-paragraph (1) was made, a youth court acting in the local justice area specified in the youth rehabilitation order, and

(b) if the offender is aged 18 or over at that time, a magistrates' court (other than a youth court) acting in that local justice area.

Amendment by Crown Court

14 (1) This paragraph applies where—

(a) a youth rehabilitation order is in force in respect of an offender,

(b) the order—

(i)   was made by the Crown Court, and

(ii) does not contain a direction under paragraph 36 of Schedule 1, and

(c) an application for the amendment of the order is made to the Crown Court by the offender or the responsible officer.

(2) If the Crown Court is satisfied that the offender proposes to reside, or is residing, in a local justice area ("the new local justice area") other than the local justice area for the time being specified in the order, the court—

(a) must, if the application under sub-paragraph (1)(c) was made by the responsible officer, or

(b) may, in any other case, amend the youth rehabilitation order by substituting the new local justice area for the area specified in the order.

(3) Sub-paragraph (2) is subject to paragraph 15.

(4) The Crown Court may by order amend the youth rehabilitation order—

(a) by cancelling any of the requirements of the order, or

(b) by replacing any of those requirements with a requirement of the same kind which could have been included in the order when it was made.

(5) Sub-paragraph (4) is subject to paragraph 16.

Exercise of powers under paragraph 13(2) or 14(2): further provisions

15 (1) In sub-paragraphs (2) and (3), "specific area requirement", in relation to a youth rehabilitation order, means a requirement contained in the order which, in the opinion of the court, cannot be complied with unless the offender continues to reside in the local justice area specified in the youth rehabilitation order.

(2) A court may not under paragraph 13(2) or 14(2) amend a youth rehabilitation order which contains specific area requirements unless, in accordance with paragraph 13(4) or, as the case may be, 14(4), it either—

(a) cancels those requirements, or

(b) substitutes for those requirements other requirements which can be complied with if the offender resides in the new local justice area mentioned in paragraph 13(2) or (as the case may be) 14(2).

(3) If—

(a) the application under paragraph 13(1)(c) or 14(1)(c) was made by the responsible officer, and

(b) the youth rehabilitation order contains specific area requirements, the court must, unless it considers it inappropriate to do so, so exercise its powers under paragraph 13(4) or, as the case may be, 14(4) that it is not prevented by sub-paragraph (2) from amending the order under paragraph 13(2) or, as the case may be, 14(2).

(4) The court may not under paragraph 13(2) or, as the case may be, 14(2) amend a youth rehabilitation order imposing a programme requirement unless the court is satisfied that a programme which—

(a) corresponds as nearly as practicable to the programme specified in the order for the purposes of that requirement, and

(b) is suitable for the offender, is available in the new local justice area.

Exercise of powers under paragraph 13(4) or 14(4): further provisions

16 (1) Any requirement imposed under paragraph 13(4)(b) or 14(4)(b) must be capable of being complied with before the date specified under paragraph 32(1) of Schedule 1.

(2) Where—

(a) a youth rehabilitation order imposes a fostering requirement (the "original requirement"), and

(b) under paragraph 13(4)(b) or 14(4)(b) a court proposes to substitute a new fostering requirement ("the substitute requirement") for the original requirement, paragraph 18(2) of Schedule 1 applies in relation to the substitute requirement as if the reference to the period of 12 months beginning with the date on which the original requirement first had effect were a reference to the period of 18 months beginning with that date.

(3) The court may not under paragraph 13(4) or 14(4) impose—

(a) a mental health treatment requirement,

(b) a drug treatment requirement, or

(c) a drug testing requirement, unless the offender has expressed willingness to comply with the requirement.

(4) If an offender fails to express willingness to comply with a mental health treatment requirement, a drug treatment requirement or a drug testing requirement which the court proposes to impose under paragraph 13(4) or 14(4), the court may—

(a) revoke the youth rehabilitation order, and

(b) deal with the offender, for the offence in respect of which the order was made, in any way in which that court could have dealt with the offender for that offence (had the offender been before that court to be dealt with for it).

(5) In dealing with the offender under sub-paragraph (4)(b), the court must take into account the extent to which the offender has complied with the order.

Extension of unpaid work requirement

17 Where—

(a) a youth rehabilitation order imposing an unpaid work requirement is in force in respect of an offender, and

(b) on the application of the offender or the responsible officer, it appears to the appropriate court that it would be in the interests of justice to do so having regard to circumstances which have arisen since the order was made, the court may, in relation to the order, extend the period of 12 months specified in paragraph 10(6) of Schedule 1.

PART 5

POWERS OF COURT IN RELATION TO ORDER FOLLOWING SUBSEQUENT CONVICTION

Powers of magistrates' court following subsequent conviction

18 (1) This paragraph applies where—

(a) a youth rehabilitation order is in force in respect of an offender, and

(b) the offender is convicted of an offence (the "further offence") by a youth court or other magistrates' court ("the convicting court").

(2) Sub-paragraphs (3) and (4) apply where—

(a) the youth rehabilitation order—

(i) was made by a youth court or other magistrates' court, or

(ii) was made by the Crown Court and contains a direction under paragraph 36 of Schedule 1, and

(b) the convicting court is dealing with the offender for the further offence.

(3) The convicting court may revoke the order.

(4) Where the convicting court revokes the order under sub-paragraph (3), it may deal with the offender, for the offence in respect of which the order was made, in any way in which it could have dealt with the offender for that offence (had the offender been before that court to be dealt with for the offence).

(5) The convicting court may not exercise its powers under sub-paragraph (3) or (4) unless it considers that it would be in the interests of justice to do so, having regard to circumstances which have arisen since the youth rehabilitation order was made.

(6) In dealing with an offender under sub-paragraph (4), the sentencing court must take into account the extent to which the offender has complied with the order.

(7) A person sentenced under sub-paragraph (4) for an offence may appeal to the Crown Court against the sentence.

(8) Sub-paragraph (9) applies where—

(a) the youth rehabilitation order was made by the Crown Court and contains a direction under paragraph 36 of Schedule 1, and

(b) the convicting court would, but for that sub-paragraph, deal with the offender for the further offence.

(9) The convicting court may, instead of proceeding under sub-paragraph (3)—

(a) commit the offender in custody, or

(b) release the offender on bail, until the offender can be brought before the Crown Court.

(10) Sub-paragraph (11) applies if the youth rehabilitation order was made by the Crown court and does not contain a direction under paragraph 36 of Schedule 1.

(11) The convicting court may—

(a) commit the offender in custody, or

(b) release the offender on bail, until the offender can be brought or appear before the Crown Court.

(12) Where the convicting court deals with an offender's case under sub-paragraph (9) or (11), it must send to the Crown Court such particulars of the case as may be desirable.

Powers of Crown Court following subsequent conviction

19 (1) This paragraph applies where—

(a) a youth rehabilitation order is in force in respect of an offender, and

(b) the offender—

(i)   is convicted by the Crown Court of an offence, or

(ii) is brought or appears before the Crown Court by virtue of paragraph 18(9) or (11) or having been committed by the magistrates' court to the Crown Court for sentence.

(2) The Crown Court may revoke the order.

(3) Where the Crown Court revokes the order under sub-paragraph (2), the Crown Court may deal with the offender, for the offence in respect of which the order was made, in any way in which the court which made the order could have dealt with the offender for that offence.

(4) The Crown Court must not exercise its powers under sub-paragraph (2) or (3) unless it considers that it would be in the interests of justice to do so, having regard to circumstances which have arisen since the youth rehabilitation order was made.

(5) In dealing with an offender under sub-paragraph (3), the Crown Court must take into account the extent to which the offender has complied with the order.

(6) If the offender is brought or appears before the Crown Court by virtue of paragraph 18(9) or (11), the Crown Court may deal with the offender for the further offence in any way which the convicting court could have dealt with the offender for that offence.

(7) In sub-paragraph (6), "further offence" and "the convicting court" have the same meanings as in paragraph 18.

PART 6

SUPPLEMENTARY

Appearance of offender before court

20 (1) Subject to sub-paragraph (2), where, otherwise than on the application of the offender, a court proposes to exercise its powers under Part 3, 4 or 5 of this Schedule, the court—

(a) must summon the offender to appear before the court, and

(b) if the offender does not appear in answer to the summons, may issue a warrant for the offender's arrest.

(2) Sub-paragraph (1) does not apply where a court proposes to make an order—

(a) revoking a youth rehabilitation order,

(b) cancelling, or reducing the duration of, a requirement of a youth rehabilitation order, or

(c) substituting a new local justice area or place for one specified in a youth rehabilitation order.

Warrants

21 (1) Sub-paragraph (2) applies where an offender is arrested in pursuance of a warrant issued by virtue of this Schedule and cannot be brought immediately before the court before which the warrant directs the offender to be brought ("the relevant court").

(2) The person in whose custody the offender is—

(a) may make arrangements for the offender's detention in a place of safety for a period of not more than 72 hours from the time of the arrest, and

(b) must within that period bring the offender before a magistrates' court.

(3) In the case of a warrant issued by the Crown Court, section 81(5) of the Supreme Court Act 1981 (c. 54) (duty to bring person before magistrates' court) does not apply.

(4) A person who is detained under arrangements made under sub-paragraph (2)(a) is deemed to be in legal custody.

(5) In sub-paragraph (2)(a) "place of safety" has the same meaning as in the Children and Young Persons Act 1933.

(6) Sub-paragraphs (7) to (10) apply where, under sub-paragraph (2), the offender is brought before a court ("the alternative court") which is not the relevant court.

(7) If the relevant court is a magistrates' court—

(a) the alternative court may—

(i) direct that the offender be released forthwith, or

(ii) remand the offender, and

(b) for the purposes of paragraph (a), section 128 of the Magistrates' Courts Act 1980 (c. 43) (remand in custody or on bail) has effect as if the court referred to in subsections (1)(a), (3), (4)(a) and (5) were the relevant court.

(8) If the relevant court is the Crown Court, section 43A of that Act (functions of magistrates' court where a person in custody is brought before it with a view to appearance before the Crown Court) applies as if, in subsection (1)—

(a) the words "issued by the Crown Court" were omitted, and

(b) the reference to section 81(5) of the Supreme Court Act 1981 were a reference to sub-paragraph (2)(b).

(9) Any power to remand the offender in custody which is conferred by section 43A or 128 of the Magistrates' Courts Act 1980 is to be taken to be a power—

(a) if the offender is aged under 18, to remand the offender to accommodation provided by or on behalf of a local authority, and

(b) in any other case, to remand the offender to a prison.

(10) Where the court remands the offender to accommodation provided by or on behalf of a local authority, the court must designate, as the authority which is to receive the offender, the local authority for the area in which it appears to the court that the offender resides.

Adjournment of proceedings

22 (1) This paragraph applies to any hearing relating to an offender held by a youth court or other magistrates' court in any proceedings under this Schedule.

(2) The court may adjourn the hearing, and, where it does so, may—

(a) direct that the offender be released forthwith, or

(b) remand the offender.

(3) Where the court remands the offender under sub-paragraph (2)—

(a) it must fix the time and place at which the hearing is to be resumed, and

(b) that time and place must be the time and place at which the offender is required to appear or be brought before the court by virtue of the remand.

(4) Where the court adjourns the hearing under sub-paragraph (2) but does not remand the offender—

(a) it may fix the time and place at which the hearing is to be resumed, but

(b) if it does not do so, must not resume the hearing unless it is satisfied that the offender, the responsible officer and, if the offender is aged under 14, a parent or guardian of the offender have had adequate notice of the time and place of the resumed hearing.

(5) The powers of a magistrates' court under this paragraph may be exercised by a single justice of the peace, notwithstanding anything in the Magistrates' Courts Act 1980 (c. 43).

(6) This paragraph—

(a) applies to any hearing in any proceedings under this Schedule in place of section 10 of the Magistrates' Courts Act 1980 (adjournment of trial) where that section would otherwise apply, but

(b) is not to be taken to affect the application of that section to hearings of any other description.

Restrictions on imposition of intensive supervision and surveillance or fostering

23 Subsection (4), and the provisions mentioned in subsection (6), of section 1 apply in relation to a power conferred by paragraph 6(2)(b), 8(2)(b), 13(4)(b) or 14(4)(b) to impose a requirement as they apply in relation to any power conferred by section 1 or Part 1 of Schedule 1 to make a youth rehabilitation order which includes such a requirement.

Provision of copies of orders etc

24 (1) Where a court makes an order under this Schedule revoking or amending a youth rehabilitation order, the proper officer of the court must forthwith—

(a) provide copies of the revoking or amending order to the offender and, if the offender is aged under 14, to the offender's parent or guardian,

(b) provide a copy of the revoking or amending order to the responsible officer,

(c) in the case of an amending order which substitutes a new local justice area, provide copies of the amending order to—

(i) the local probation board acting for that area or (as the case may be) a provider of probation services operating in that area, and

(ii) the magistrates' court acting in that area,

(d) in the case of an amending order which imposes or cancels a requirement specified in the first column of the Table in paragraph 34(4) of Schedule 1, provide a copy of so much of the amending order as relates to that requirement to the person specified in relation to that requirement in the second column of that Table,

(e) in the case of an order which revokes a requirement specified in the first column of that Table, provide a copy of the revoking order to the person specified in relation to that requirement in the second column of that Table, and

(f) if the court is a magistrates' court acting in a local justice area other than the area specified in the youth rehabilitation order, provide a copy of the revoking or amending order to a magistrates' court acting in the local justice area specified in the order.

(2) Where under sub-paragraph (1)(c) the proper officer of the court provides a copy of an amending order to a magistrates' court acting in a different area, the officer must also provide to that court such documents and information relating to the case as appear likely to be of assistance to a court acting in that area in the exercise of its functions in relation to the order.

(3) In this paragraph "proper officer" means—

(a) in relation to a magistrates' court, the designated officer for the court, and

(b) in relation to the Crown Court, the appropriate officer.

Power to amend maximum period of fostering requirement

25 The Secretary of State may by order amend paragraph 6(9), 8(9) or 16(2) by substituting, for—

(a) the period of 18 months specified in the provision, or

(b) any other period which may be so specified by virtue of a previous order under this paragraph, such other period as may be specified in the order.

INDEX

introduction of, 1–2
sentence planning
  participation in, 5
Sentencing Guidelines Council
  breach of community orders, 35
  measure of last resort, 24
  persistent offenders, 23
  suspended sentence orders, 40, 41
  young people
    custody and, 24, 100
    welfare of, 21
  youth rehabilitation orders, 96, 100
Serious harm
  concerns about, 2
Sexual offences
  See Violent and sexual offences
Summons
  sample of, Appendix A
Supervision
  release, on, 46
Suspended sentence order
  amendment of, 44–45, Appendix D
  breach of
    further convictions and, 42–43, Appendix D
    handling of, 41–42, Appendix D
  community requirements
    compliance with, 43
  general observations, 40
  legal basis for, 39–40
  powers of the court when order has expired, 42
  requirements on, 40–41
  review of, 44

Violent and sexual offenders
  foreign travel orders, 125–127
  human rights, 123
  notification
    breach of, 125
    initial, 124
    period, 123
    subsequent, 124
  provisions for, 122
  risk of sexual harm orders, 129–130
  sex offender notification, 122–125
  sexual offences prevention orders, 127–128
  violent offender orders, 130–134
  young people, 123

Witness
  statement of, Appendix B

Young people
  See also Detention and training orders; Referral orders; Suspended sentence

orders; Youth rehabilitation orders;
  contact levels and, 24–25
  custody and, 24, 99–100
  discretionary life sentences, 52–53
  explaining proceedings to, 22
  first tier penalties, 71
  looked after, 23, 77, 118
  recall procedures, 108–109
  rights of, 21
  welfare of, 21
Youth Court
  breaches prosecuted in, 21
  referrals back to court, 81–83
Youth Justice Board
  establishment of, 7
  guidance from, 11
  intensive supervision and surveillance orders, 114, 117
  parenting orders, 118
  public protection, 108
  risk management, 108
  scaled approach, 78
Youth offender panels
  attendance at panel meetings, 77
  progress meetings, 79–80
  referrals back to court, 81–83
  reports of, 78
  roles and responsibilities, 76
Youth offending team
  compliance, 81, 96, 102
Youth rehabilitation order
  amendment of, 98, Appendix E
  attendance centre, 88
  breach of
    persistent and willful refusal to comply, 96
    powers of court, 95–96
    process, 94–95, Appendix E
  curfew, 89
  drug testing, 93
  drug treatment, 92
  education, 94
  exclusion, 89–90
  further convictions and, 98, Appendix E
  intoxicating substance treatment, 93–94
  legal basis for, 84–85
  mental health treatment, 91–92
  powers of court, 95–97
  prohibited activity, 88–89
  programme, 87–88
  requirements on the, 85–86
  residence, 90–91
  residential exercises, 86
  responsible officer
    instructions of, 86